OPERANT LEARNING

Procedures for Changing Behavior

OPERANT LEARNING

Procedures for Changing Behavior

Jon L. Williams

KENYON COLLEGE

BROOKS/COLE PUBLISHING COMPANY
MONTEREY, CALIFORNIA
A Division of Wadsworth Publishing Company, Inc.

To My Mother and Father

ISBN: 0-8185-0058-1
L.C. Catalog Card No: 72-91088
Printed in the United States of America
1 2 3 4 5 6 7 8 9 10—77 76 75 74 73

This book was edited by Dorothy Conway, with production supervised by Micky Lawler. It was designed by Jane Mitchell. Technical art was drawn by John Foster. The book was typeset by Continental Data Graphics, Culver City, California, and printed and bound by Kingsport Press, Kingsport, Tennessee.

PREFACE

This book gives a concise but detailed account of the theory, experimental research, and recent applications of operant learning. It is intended to be used by students who have had an introductory course in psychology and are currently taking a course in learning or in behavior modification.

The concepts of operant learning are presented in a logical order. Numerous everyday examples are given of behavioral phenomena (such as stimulus generalization) and control procedures (such as avoidance learning) before their theoretical significance is discussed. In Chapter 1, the experimental analysis of behavior is contrasted with other approaches to the psychology of learning. Much of this chapter is concerned with defining and clarifying the terminology used in operant conditioning. In Chapters 2 and 3, the major reinforcement variables (number, amount, delay, and schedules) are systematically examined. Chapter 4 is concerned with the acquisition of conditioned reinforcers and their function in maintaining long sequences or chains of responses. The processes of stimulus generalization, discrimination, and attention are discussed in Chapter 5. Chapter 6 evaluates the aversive procedures (escape, avoidance, and punishment) frequently used to control behavior. In the last two chapters, a critical review is presented of the recent applications of operant procedures to the fields of mental health (behavior therapy) and education (programmed instruction). The final chapter also contains a discussion of moral and ethical considerations involved in controlling human behavior by operant techniques.

In writing a textbook, one is indebted to innumerable individuals. As a teacher one acquires useful information and ideas from interacting with his colleagues and students. I am particularly grateful to the editor of the Brooks/Cole Psychology Series, Edward L. Walker of the University of Michigan, who encouraged me to write this book. For his complete and critical review of the manuscript, I extend my appreciation to Charles E. Rice of Kenyon College. Thanks are also due to Marcella Halderman, Sally Marcus, and Frances Kline for their secretarial assistance and to Herb Agnew of the Kenyon College Printing Office for making prepublication copies of the manuscript.

Jon L. Williams

CONTENTS

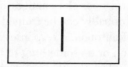

INTRODUCTION TO
OPERANT LEARNING

A great many human activities—reading, writing, solving mathematical problems; playing a guitar or adjusting a carburetor; even an individual's beliefs or attitudes—are learned. In fact, it would be impossible to understand the behavior of human beings, or even of animals, without some knowledge of the basic principles involved in learning. Therefore, a thorough knowledge of these principles should provide us with better explanations of the causes of behavior and should also enable us to develop more effective methods for teaching children in school, training people in various occupations, and providing therapy for the mentally ill.

Before describing the two major types of learning (respondent learning and operant learning), we should distinguish between two classes of *responses* (specific acts that can be clearly identified and objectively measured): *respondent,* or *reflexive*, responses; and *operant,* or *voluntary,* responses. Respondent responses are elicited by specific stimuli in the environment: tears from the slicing of onions, the mouth watering at the sight of a steak, a cold breeze raising goose pimples, hands perspiring just before one is scheduled to give a speech. Respondents are generally regulated by the autonomic nervous system, and organisms usually do not have voluntary control over the changes in this system (although, as we shall see, a person probably can be trained to exercise considerable control over a number of autonomic responses). Operant, or voluntary, responses have an effect on or do something to the individual's environment; either directly or indirectly, these responses—for instance, turning on a stereo, picking up a ringing telephone, throwing a ball—*operate* on the world.

RESPONDENT (CLASSICAL) CONDITIONING

The acquisition or learning of respondent behavior is frequently referred to as *classical conditioning*. Many psychologists consider classical conditioning the basic form of learning; they believe that it serves as a foundation for more complex behavior. Consequently, a large number of classical conditioning experiments are conducted in psychological laboratories. Let us look at two very simple examples of such experiments.

Example 1. With an apparatus that records eye blinks, and with a friend who agrees to serve as subject, you attempt to condition your subject's eye-blink response. First of all, by directing a puff of air at the cornea of his eye, you find that you can reliably elicit the eye-blink reflex. You then present the subject with the sound of a buzzer just before every puff of air. After you have presented the buzzer and puff of air five times or so, you probably notice that your friend is making an eye-blink response to the buzzer even *before* the puff of air is released. Such a response is considered to be a learned, or *conditioned*, response.

Example 2. With a device that monitors heart rate, and with the same friend serving as subject, you now attempt to condition his heart rate. While his heart rate is being monitored, you deliver several brief, low-intensity shocks to his leg. If he is still willing to participate in the experiment, you then turn on a warning light just before you administer the shocks. After a number of pairings of the light and the shock, you probably discover that your friend's heart rate increases considerably when the light is presented—even *before* the occurrence of the shock. Since this is not a typical response to the presentation of a light, you can assume that respondent conditioning has taken place.

Probably the best-known laboratory experiments in classical conditioning were performed by the Russian physiologist and Nobel Prize winner Ivan Pavlov, who accidentally discovered that innate reflexes can be conditioned. Pavlov (1902) was studying the processes of digestion in dogs, using an apparatus that collected and measured the secretions of gastric juices and saliva by means of tubes implanted in the stomach and cheek. In these experiments, meat powder was placed in the dog's mouth, and his salivary response to the food was observed. After a number of trials, the dog began to salivate when he saw the food, *before* it was actually placed in his mouth. With more trials, the dog salivated at the sight of the food dish and finally even at the sound of the experimenter's approaching footsteps. Pavlov, realizing the importance of this phenomenon, changed the course of his investigations and began to study the conditioning process.

In a series of later experiments, Pavlov (1927) established the terminology that is still used to describe this type of learning. He applied the term *unconditioned stimulus* (US) to the food in the mouth, which elicited an inborn *unconditioned response* (UR) of salivation. A bell was then sounded immediately before the presentation of food, and eventually the sound of the bell alone produced an increase in the flow of saliva. Pavlov called this change in the animal's behavior a *conditioned response* (CR). Finally, the bell (which originally had had no effect on salivation) became a *conditioned stimulus* (CS) when it elicited a definite salivary response.

Now let us examine in more detail the principles pertinent to this type of learning. Figure 1-1 shows a diagram of the stimulus events

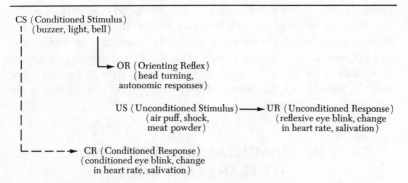

FIGURE 1-1. Diagram of the paradigm of stimulus and response events that occur during a single classical conditioning trial.

and responses that occur during a single trial of a classical conditioning experiment. The first stimulus that the organism experiences is the conditioned stimulus. In the two previously described examples of classical conditioning and in Pavlov's study, the CSs were the buzzer, the light, and the bell, respectively. Any stimulus can be used as a CS in a respondent conditioning experiment, provided it can be perceived by the subject and does not produce the conditioned response before the conditioning procedure has begun. The CS usually at first elicits responses other than the CR; these other responses are collectively referred to as the *orienting reflex* (OR). A dog, for example, may prick up his ears, turn his head, or show changes in autonomic responses upon presentation of the CS. During the course of conditioning, the orienting reflex gradually disappears and is replaced by the conditioned response. According to the paradigm of classical conditioning, the unconditioned stimulus (US) is usually presented within seconds after the CS. The unconditioned stimuli employed in the previously described experiments were a puff of air, an electric shock, and meat powder. Any stimulus that reliably elicits an inborn or previously conditioned response may be used as an unconditioned stimulus in classical conditioning. When the US is presented after the CS a number of times, the conditioned stimulus will come to elicit a conditioned response.

The process of respondent conditioning may occur very quickly. Only a few pairings of the CS and US may be required if the experiment is properly arranged. If, however, the eliciting stimulus (US) is presented a few minutes rather than a few seconds after the neutral stimulus (CS), conditioning will require a considerably greater number of trials. Or if the CS follows rather than precedes the US on each trial, there probably will be no conditioning at all. Moreover, the rate at which conditioning takes place is influenced by the time interval between trials. Most efficient conditioning usually is obtained with intervals of at least one minute between trials. The number of distracting stimuli present at the time of the trials, the motivated state of the organism, and the intensity of the neutral stimulus also affect the success of the conditioning procedure.

INSTRUMENTAL CONDITIONING
(OPERANT LEARNING)

In classical conditioning, the presentation of two stimuli, CS and US, is determined by the experimenter and is completely independent of the subject's behavior. In the second type of learning, termed *instrumental conditioning* or, in the case of some experiments, *operant learning*, the organism's behavior is instrumental in bringing about the occurrence of the US. If, for instance, one of Pavlov's dogs had been given the US (meat powder) immediately after something he himself had done (after responding correctly to the command "Sit up" or "Speak," for instance), his conditioning would have been instrumental rather than respondent.

In operant learning, a stimulus is called a *reinforcer* if it increases the frequency of occurrence of the operant (if, for example, the giving of meat powder to the dog after he sits up or speaks results in increasing the occurrence of such responses). When a particular stimulus (for instance, a shock) leads to a *reduction* in the frequency of the operant, it is termed an *aversive* or *punishing stimulus* (if, for example, scolding the dog results in his learning not to jump up on people). Reinforcers in operant learning illustrate a powerful principle of behavior, Thorndike's (1913, 1932) "Law of Effect." In essence, this law states that an act (the dog's sitting up) may be altered in its strength (increased or decreased) by its consequences (presentation of food or a shock).

Figure 1-2 shows the paradigm that applies when a subject undergoes operant conditioning. In the presence of an environmental stimulus (such as the command "Sit up"), a particular operant response (the dog's sitting up) will produce stimulus event S^x (food or a shock). If S^x is a positive reinforcer (such as food), then it increases the frequency of occurrence of the operant response. If S^x is an aversive or a punishing stimulus (a shock), it will decrease the frequency of the operant. However, under certain conditions, organisms may learn to make escape or avoidance responses, which result in terminating or preventing the presentation of an aversive stimulus. In this case, the aversive stimulus is termed a *negative reinforcer*. For example, when a dog goes to the door and barks so that he will be let outside, he is avoiding the possibility of being punished for misbehaving.

All reinforcers of operant behavior must be *trans-situational*—that is, capable of strengthening all or most responses that an organism

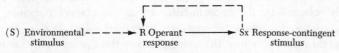

(S) Environmental - - - - -→ R Operant ——————→ S^x Response-contingent
     stimulus   response   stimulus

FIGURE 1-2.   Diagram of the sequence of events in operant conditioning.

can learn. In other words, if a particular stimulus is considered a rein-forcer in training a dog to sit up, it should also be an effective reinforcer in teaching the dog to shake hands. Similarly, if a particular stimulus is not an effective reinforcer for conditioning one particular response, it should not be an adequate reinforcer in conditioning any other re-sponse for that particular organism. Thus, whether a given stimulus is likely to function as a reinforcer depends on the particular organism being trained and not on the specific response to be learned.

EXPERIMENTAL METHODS IN OPERANT CONDITIONING

Basic Operant Equipment. B. F. Skinner (Figure 1-3), the psychologist who has made the most important contributions to the field of operant learning, developed the *Skinner box*, the standard apparatus used in operant conditioning studies. A typical Skinner box used to condition a rat to press a lever is shown in Figure 1-4, and a similar box for training a pecking response in a pigeon is shown in Figure 1-5. As can be seen from the figures, a box designed for training an operant has a number of different components. First, it has some type of operan-dum, such as a lever or key, which can be manipulated by the subject. Second, there is a device for storing and dispensing a reward, such as a pellet of food or a dipper of water. This device is usually located in the vicinity of the operandum for the response. Third, most operant chambers have some kind of *discriminative stimulus* (such as a tone from a small speaker or a colored light projected from outside the box onto the translucent response key), used as a warning signal or as a signal for the possible presentation of a reward. Finally, the box is enclosed within an insulated chest equipped with an exhaust fan, so that virtually all extraneous and distracting stimuli are eliminated.

The experimental procedure used in operant conditioning is simple. The experimenter places the subject (a food- or water-deprived rat or pigeon, for example) in the Skinner box. Every time the animal presses the lever or pecks at the key, a reward (food or water) is deliv-ered. In more general terms, when the subject makes a response pre-viously selected by the experimenter to be the correct response, the subject is usually given the reward. During the first session, it may be several minutes before the animal makes the first response. During subsequent sessions, however, he may respond almost immediately and may maintain a fairly high rate of responding throughout the entire

FIGURE 1-3. B. F. Skinner, the contemporary psychologist who has made most of the major contributions to the experimental analysis of behavior. His teachings have concerned complex learning processes, animal psychophysics, social interaction, child development, language acquisition, behavioral modification, and programmed instruction. (Courtesy of B. F. Skinner.)

FIGURE 1-4. Interior view of experimental chamber used with a rat or small mammals. (Courtesy of the Grason-Stadler Company, Inc., a GR company.)

FIGURE 1-5. Interior view of experimental chamber used with a pigeon. (Courtesy of the Grason-Stadler Company, Inc., a GR company.)

session. Again, it is important to remember that the responses made in the operant chamber are not *elicited* by a particular stimulus, as they are in classical conditioning, but rather are *emitted* voluntarily by the subject.

Some Skinner boxes are designed to study the effects of aversive stimulation on operant behavior. Such boxes are very much like those previously described, except that an electric shock can be delivered to an animal through the metal-grid floor of the box.

In addition to the Skinner box and its components, two other types of equipment are employed in most operant conditioning studies. The first, an electronic control panel, programs the presentation of the discriminative stimuli and reinforcement contingencies. The second instrument, a recorder, automatically plots the cumulative record of operant responses. Figure 1-6 shows a graph of a typical cumulative recorder in operation; Figure 1-7 illustrates the way in which this recorder plots the progress of the experiment. The recording pen normally draws a horizontal line across the paper, which continuously passes under the pen at a constant speed. Whenever the animal makes an operant response, the pen moves one unit upward and then continues drawing a horizontal line. In this way, a slope is generated with successive responses, as shown in the first four tracings of Figure 1-7. After

FIGURE 1-6.   Cumulative response recorder. (Courtesy of the Ralph Gerbrands Company, Inc.)

FIGURE 1-7. Illustrations of tracings made by a cumulative recorder. Tracings 1 through 4 show the way in which the slope is generated by successive responses. Tracing 5 depicts the cumulative record of a subject responding at a high rate. Notice that the pen returns to the bottom edge of the paper once it reaches the top edge. Tracing 6 shows the cumulative record of a subject for whom every third response results in reinforcement. Slash marks indicate the presentation of reinforcement.

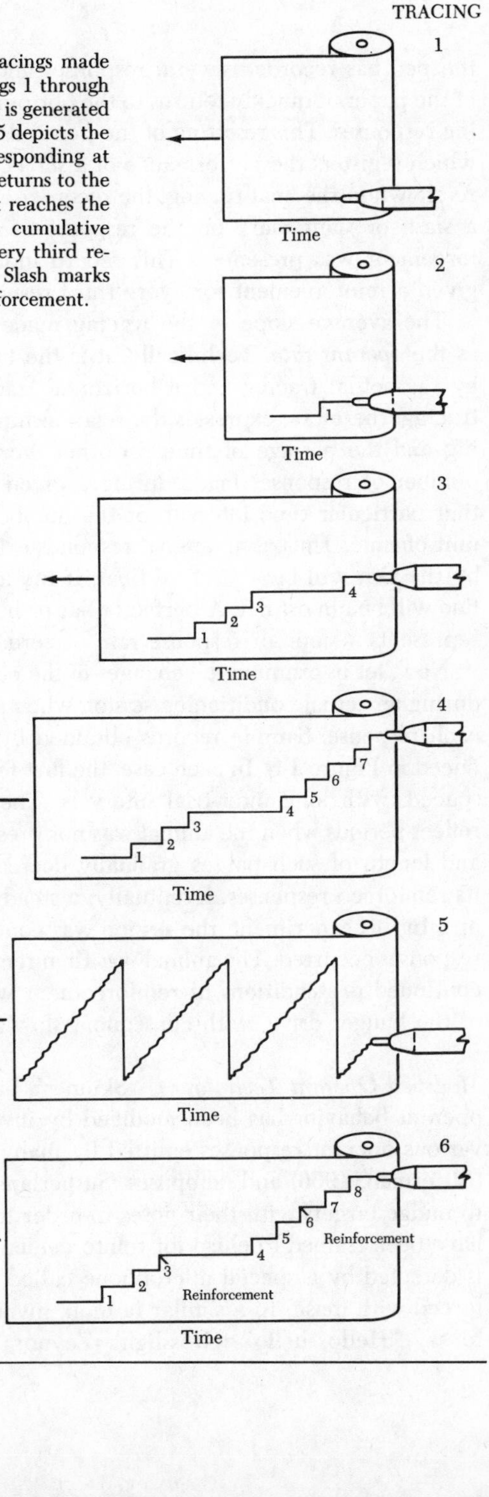

the pen has recorded several responses and has reached the top edge of the paper, it quickly returns to the bottom edge and continues recording responses. This resetting of the pen is illustrated in the fifth tracing, which registers the performance of a subject responding at a high rate. As shown in the final tracing, the recorder also can indicate, by making a slash or slant mark on the response record, the times when reinforcement was presented. This record indicates that the subject was given a reinforcement for every third response.

The average slope of the tracing made by the pen is referred to as the *operant rate*. Technically, it is the tangent of the angle formed by the actual tracing and a horizontal tracing. The slope of the pen tracing, therefore, expresses the relationship between operant responding and the passage of time. In other words, the operant rate is the number of responses made during a given period of time divided by that particular time interval, or the number of operant responses per unit of time. Thus, if an animal responds extremely fast, the line traced by the pen will be almost vertical; if the animal responds slowly, the line will be almost flat. A perfectly flat or horizontal cumulative record represents a slope or response rate of zero.

Now, let us examine the changes in the cumulative record that occur during an actual conditioning session when reinforcement is given after each response. Sample records obtained by Skinner (1938) are reproduced in Figure 1-8. In each case, the first few responses are irregularly spaced, with long inter-trial intervals. The flat places in the records reflect periods when the animal was not pressing the lever. The number and length of such pauses gradually decrease as the animal increases its reinforced responses. Eventually, a steady rate of responding develops. In this experiment, the session was continued until fifty reinforced responses occurred. The animal was then removed from the box because continued presentations of reinforcement would have led to satiation of the hunger drive, with consequent slowing of the response rate

Modified Operant Techniques.   Skinner's basic apparatus for studying operant behavior has been modified by investigators seeking to study various operant responses emitted by many different species. Goldfish (Bitterman, 1966) and octopuses (Sutherland, 1957) have been trained to nudge targets with their noses in order to gain food. Baby chickens have been trained to chirp for reinforcements (Lane, 1960); each chirp is detected by a special microphone called a "voice key" and is reinforced with mash. In a similar fashion, mynah birds have been trained to say "Hello, hello" (Grosslight, Zaynor, & Lively, 1964). Finally,

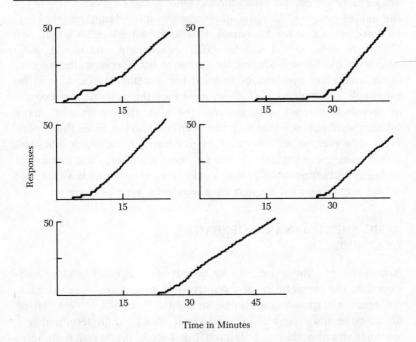

FIGURE 1-8. Cumulative records of five subjects during the acquisition of a lever-pressing response. (Adapted from: *The Behavior of Organisms: An Experimental Analysis*, by B. F. Skinner. Copyright 1938 by D. Appleton-Century Company, Inc. Paperback 1966. Reprinted by permission of Appleton-Century-Crofts, Educational Division, Meredith Corporation.)

monkeys have been trained to flip toggle switches, displace objects, and perform many kinds of operant responses to gain a reward.

Some of the most ingenious types of operant devices have been developed to condition operant responses in children (see, for instance, Bijuo & Baer, 1966). Preschool children have been conditioned to press the nose on the face of a toy clown to receive marbles as a reward. Children have also learned to perform specific "cooperation" responses with a partner—and even to make relatively complex discriminations between different geometric forms, printed words, and tone patterns— in order to obtain candy as a reward.

Operant techniques and social reinforcements have been used in conditioning experiments with adult subjects. In one such experiment (Greenspoon, 1955), college students were individually asked a series of questions on controversial topics. During the interview, whenever the subject expressed an opinionated statement involving the word "I," he was given social reinforcement; that is, the experimenter would pay closer attention, would nod his head approvingly, and would make comments like "I see." During the course of the interview, the subjects made increasing numbers of opinionated statements—far above the previously determined normal frequency of this response. Moreover, as revealed by questionnaires answered after the experiment, many subjects were unaware that they had been conditioned. Since this experiment, however, other investigators (Spielberger, Levin, & Shepard, 1962), using more extensive postexperiment questionnaires, found that verbal conditioning usually occurs only when the subject is aware that he is being reinforced for making a particular type of response.

BASIC PHENOMENA OF OPERANT LEARNING

Acquisition of a Response.   As we have seen, an operant can be conditioned by the presentation of a positive reinforcer after its occurrence. An operant response can also be learned if it results in terminating an aversive stimulus, such as an electric shock, or in terminating a warning stimulus that is presented just before the aversive stimulus is scheduled to occur. Thus, the acquisition of an operant can be established by either positive or negative reinforcement, operating according to the Law of Effect.

Extinction of a Response.   When a previously learned operant response is no longer reinforced, the operant rate of that response decreases to the point that the reponse is rarely made. This reduction in response rate, caused by withdrawal of reinforcement, is referred to as *extinction*. Examples of extinction occur every day: when parents restrain from picking up baby, so that he will stop crying for attention; when teachers ignore children who show off in the classroom in order to receive attention; whenever objectionable behavior is no longer rewarded and consequently stops.

Figure 1-9 shows a cumulative record of a rat during extinction. Notice that the general shape of this curve is different from the one usually found during acquisition. As time passes with no reinforcement, the number of operant responses eventually decreases. When reinforcement is first withdrawn, however, the responses not only do not decrease but are made with much more force—perhaps because the

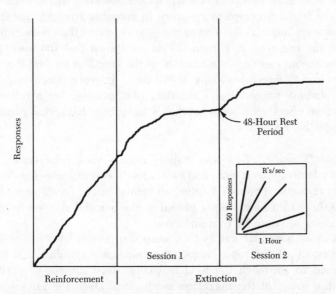

Responses

50 Responses

R's/sec

1 Hour

48-Hour Rest
Period

Session 1

Session 2

Reinforcement

Extinction

FIGURE 1-9.   Cumulative record of a rat during two extinction (nonrein-forcement) sessions following reward training. After the two-day rest period, spontaneous recovery is seen during the initial portion of the second session.

subject experiences frustration when he is confronted with the extinction procedure (Amsel & Roussel, 1952; Brown, 1961). After a period of time in extinction, responses cease for long periods of time. After these pauses exceed some arbitrary criterion, such as three consecutive minutes without a response, it is assumed that the response has been extinguished. The number of responses emitted during the course of extinction varies from subject to subject. This measure, referred to as *resistance to extinction*, is often used to assess response strength, the degree to which a particular response has been learned. Thus, a record showing few responses in extinction would indicate little resistance to extinction and low response strength; a record showing many responses would indicate considerable resistance to extinction and very high response strength.

After a rest period, an extinguished operant response may occur spontaneously when the animal is again placed in the Skinner box. This phenomenon is referred to as *spontaneous recovery*. Figure 1-9 shows the occurrence of spontaneous recovery during the second extinction session, after two days of rest. Notice, however, that spontaneous recovery is not a complete recovery in response strength; fewer responses were made at the start of the second session than were emitted during the first session. Ellison (1938) has shown that the magnitude of spontaneous recovery is a function of the length of the rest interval; but even with intervals as long as five days, recovery is not complete. These findings suggest that extinction, like learning, has a relatively permanent effect upon behavior; that is, the subject has actually learned to inhibit his responses.

Response Shaping.   Response shaping occurs when behavior is reinforced selectively, as it more and more closely approximates the desired type of response. Through shaping, an animal can be conditioned more efficiently than if he is simply placed in the box and allowed to make the correct response by trial and error.

Let us see how a laboratory rat is shaped to press a lever in a Skinner box. First of all, the rat is subjected to *magazine training*; that is, he is trained to approach the food magazine (food dispenser) when he hears the sound of the magazine mechanism. Once the rat responds reliably and quickly to the magazine, the shaping procedure is begun. The rat is first reinforced every time he approaches the side of the box where the lever is located. The rat is then reinforced only if he explores or sniffs at the lever. Next, a reward is given only when the animal begins to exert some effort with his forepaws on the lever. Eventually, the animal's response will become strong and deliberate enough to operate the automatic reinforcement mechanism. Shaping, then, not only extinguishes imprecise responses but strengthens the desired response.

The procedure used in shaping is determined to a great extent by the judgment of the experimenter. Skillful shaping consists of selecting the right responses to be reinforced and knowing how long to reward a particular approximation to the desired operant before requiring a more specific response. Since responses must be reinforced immediately after they have occurred, the experimenter virtually has to anticipate the next response to be made by the subject.

Various characteristics of operant responses have been conditioned through the use of selective reinforcement (shaping). For example, Herrick (1964) attempted to teach rats to depress a lever a specific distance, or amplitude. During the first few sessions, Herrick reinforced thirsty rats with water for every lever response they made. In subsequent training sessions, however, he rewarded only those responses that were within a relatively narrow range of amplitude values. He continued narrowing the acceptable range of responses for nine sessions. In the initial sessions, he found, responses varied considerably in amplitude; but when the reinforcement criterion was made more specific, the subjects learned to match the amplitude of their responses with the amplitude required for reinforcement.

Stimulus Generalization.   An operant response reinforced in the presence of one particular stimulus will probably also be performed in the presence of stimuli that are similar to the first. For example, a pigeon reinforced for pecking at a key illuminated with a blue light will probably also emit some pecking responses to a blue-green light. The spreading of the effects of reinforcement to similar stimuli is called *stimulus generalization.* However, the pigeon probably will emit fewer responses to a green light and still fewer to a yellow light. This gradual decrease in response strength is termed a *stimulus-generalization gradient.*

In a stimulus-generalization experiment by Guttman and Kalish (1956), pigeons were shaped to peck at a disc illuminated by a light with a 550-millimicron (mμ) wavelength. This wavelength of light appears yellow-green to the human eye. When the operant response to this discriminative stimulus was well established, the subjects were only occasionally reinforced for responding. After they had received a number of training sessions, they were tested with a series of different wavelength values, repeatedly presented in a random order but without reinforcements.

Figure 1-10 shows the results of this experiment, with the total number of responses plotted as a function of the wavelength values. The value of 470 mμ appears blue to the human eye; the other end of the spectrum, 610 mμ, is seen as orange. The greatest number of responses was emitted to the previously reinforced value of 550 mμ; however, many responses also generalized to colored values close to 550 mμ, with the fewest responses at each extreme of the spectrum.

Stimulus Discrimination.   When an organism is reinforced for responding to one stimulus and is not reinforced for responding to another, the organism may learn *stimulus discrimination.* Thus, at least two stimulus conditions are necessary to establish discrimination training: (1) a *positive discriminative stimulus* (S^D or S^+), which is always present when the operant is reinforced; (2) a *negative discriminative stimulus* (S^Δ or S^-), which is never associated with reinforcement. The S^Δ may

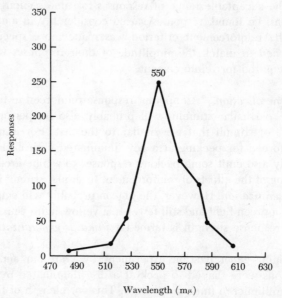

FIGURE 1-10. Number of responses emitted to test values following training with a value of 550 mμ on the response key. The data reflect a bidirectional stimulus-generalization gradient.

simply be the absence of an S^D value. In an experiment on discrimination learning with pigeons, Skinner (1938) used a red stimulus as an S^D and a green stimulus as an S^Δ in an operant chamber. These birds had previously been trained to peck at the red light and receive a reward. Then presentations of the S^D were alternated with presentations of the S^Δ. During the initial training, the birds emitted responses to *both* red and green; that is, there was some stimulus generalization between the two stimuli. During subsequent training sessions, however, responding was gradually extinguished when the S^Δ was presented. Eventually, the cumulative record indicated, the subjects' performances were completely controlled by the stimuli: when the S^D was present, the response rate was high; when the S^Δ was present, the rate was almost zero. In addition, after they had learned to suppress responses during the green light, the subjects responded more frequently in the presence of the red light—almost as if they were thereby compensating for the decrease in responses to green. (This phenomenon, known as *behavior contrast*, is examined in more detail in Chapter 5.)

BASIC PROCEDURES USED IN OPERANT LEARNING

The various procedures used in operant learning probably can be classified according to four main features: (1) whether the procedure uses a *positive* or a *negative reinforcer*; (2) whether the procedure presents a *discriminative stimulus* (a visual or an auditory stimulus serving as a cue for the possible presentation of a positive or negative reinforcer); (3) whether the response results in the *presentation or* the *withdrawal of* the *reinforcing stimulus*; (4) whether the procedure results in the *emission or* the *suppression of* an *operant*. Table 1-1 summarizes these features with regard to the six basic procedures used in operant learning. (In some experiments, certain of these basic procedures are used in combination.) Now let us look at experimental situations illustrating each of these procedures.

TABLE 1-1

Basic Procedures Used in Operant Learning

Type of Procedure	Positive or Negative Reinforcement?	Discriminative Stimulus Present or Absent?	Reinforcer Presented or Withdrawn?	Response Emitted or Suppressed?
Reward Training	positive	absent	presented	emitted
Discrimination Training	positive	S^D and S^Δ present	presented with S^D; not presented with S^Δ	emitted for S^D; suppressed for S^Δ
Omission Training	positive	absent	presented	suppressed
Punishment Training	negative and positive	absent	presented	suppressed
Escape Training	negative	absent	withdrawn	emitted
Avoidance Training	negative	present	withdrawn	emitted

Reward Training. A white rat is placed in a Skinner box that contains a small lever projecting from the wall. Whenever the lever is pressed, it automatically operates a magazine containing food pellets, and one pellet is dispensed to the rat. After a period of magazine training, in which the rat learns to approach the food hopper every time he hears the sound of the dispenser, the experimenter shapes the rat to press the lever by reinforcing successive approximations to the desired response. In this procedure, no specific discriminative stimuli are used to evoke the operant, and reward is usually given after every appropriate response. In this experiment, the effect of the positive reinforcement is to increase the rate at which the response is emitted.

Discrimination Training. In a Skinner box, an animal is trained to press a lever to receive reinforcement. Initial training takes place in the presence of a dim light. Then the subject is periodically presented with a bright light in the box, and responses are not reinforced during such periods. The dim light, therefore, serves as a positive discriminative stimulus (S^D), and the bright light acts as a negative discriminative stimulus (S^Δ). After a session or two in which the S^D and S^Δ values are presented for alternate one-minute periods, the rat begins to discriminate between them. That is, he responds at a fairly high rate during the S^D and shows almost complete response suppression during the S^Δ. At this point, we claim that the discriminative stimuli are exerting control over the organism's behavior.

Omission Training. A subject is first trained to press a lever for food. The procedure is then reversed; that is, the subject is rewarded (with food) for *not* pressing the lever until a certain period of time (for instance, thirty seconds) has elapsed. Omission training does not involve external discriminative stimuli—although, since the subject must wait for a given interval without responding, it might be said that he is learning some type of temporal discrimination. Because the response results in postponing a free reward, the omission procedure produces a suppression of the rate of the operant response.

Punishment Training. An animal again is trained to press a lever for positive reinforcement. After the response rate is well established, the lever pressing is then occasionally followed by an aversive stimulus, such as an electric shock delivered through the floor of the box to the animal's feet. Since the animal does not know which responses will be punished and which will be reinforced, he begins to respond very slowly. If the shock is of a high intensity or is presented for a long duration, he may cease to respond altogether.

Escape Training. The subject is placed in a Skinner box and given relatively long periods of mild shock. Sooner or later, the subject accidentally hits a lever and thus terminates the aversive stimulus. After he encounters the shock a number of times, he gradually learns to press the lever soon after the onset of the shock. It is then assumed that the subject has acquired an escape response.

Avoidance Training.   The operant situation used in avoidance training is exactly the same as that employed for punishment and escape training, except that a discriminative stimulus (for instance, a light or a tone) is used as a warning signal. The subject usually is first given escape training. Then a tone is sounded approximately ten seconds before the shock. If the rat presses the lever at any time during the tone, the tone subsides and the shock is not given. Thus, by making the operant when the discriminative stimulus is present, the subject can completely avoid receiving the aversive stimulus.

COMPARISON BETWEEN CLASSICAL CONDITIONING AND OPERANT LEARNING

PROCEDURAL DIFFERENCES

There are several reasonably clear procedural differences between classical and operant conditioning: (1) Presentation of a reward in operant conditioning is contingent upon performance; a subject receives a reward in a Skinner box only if he presses the lever. In contrast, the unconditioned stimulus in classical conditioning is presented whether or not the subject performs the conditioned response. (2) The subject in an operant learning experiment has substantial control over his environment; in classical conditioning, the experimenter has major control over the occurrence of events. (3) In operant conditioning, the subject can respond at any time during the session; in classical conditioning, the subject's behavior is examined only during periods when discrete trials are conducted. (4) In classical conditioning, the conditioned response (for instance, salivation at the sound of a bell) is usually similar to the unconditioned response (salivation to food); in operant conditioning, the conditioned response (for instance, lever pressing) is usually different from the unconditioned response, made after the reward is given (eating the food).

OPERANT CONDITIONING OF AUTONOMIC RESPONSES

Some investigators (Skinner, 1938; Mowrer, 1947; Kimble, 1961) claim that classical and operant conditioning involve different processes of learning. According to these theorists, classical conditioning is concerned with responses mediated by the autonomic nervous system and elicited involuntarily by certain stimuli. In contrast, operant learning is assumed to involve responses mediated by the central nervous system and voluntarily emitted by the organism. Furthermore, these investigators claim, autonomic responses cannot be influenced by operant learning procedures.

Many recent experiments, however, seem to refute the above position. The galvanic skin response (Kimmel & Kimmel, 1963), heart rate (Shearn, 1962), and salivation (Miller & Carmona, 1967) have all been conditioned by operant procedures; that is, by making the presentation of a reward contingent upon their occurrence. In the salivation experiment, for example, one group of thirsty dogs were given water whenever they showed an increase in salivation; another group received water for decreasing the rate of salivation. The results of this study indicated that the first group did, in fact, learn to increase salivation, whereas the second group showed a decrease in salivation.

But what if these subjects were actually making *voluntary* motor responses during the conditioning procedure? That is, perhaps a subject who is rewarded for increasing an autonomic response, such as heart rate, can learn to do so indirectly, by tensing certain muscles or breathing at a faster rate. In order to eliminate the possibility of voluntary responses, other investigators (Trowill, 1967; Miller & DiCara, 1967) attempted to condition the heart rate of rats who had been given the drug curare. This drug immobilizes the skeletal musculature and thus prevents subjects from using muscles to mediate autonomic changes. Curare, however, also prevents an organism from breathing, so that experimental animals must be given artificial respiration. Furthermore, since the animals have no control over their musculature—and are therefore unable to eat, drink, or even swallow—it is difficult to select a stimulus that will serve as an effective reinforcer. Miller and DiCara (1967) solved this problem by using electrical brain stimulation as a reinforcer. Intracranial stimulation (ICS), first developed by Olds and Milner (1954), involves inserting electrodes into the septal region of the hypothalamus and stimulating this area with an electrical shock. Such stimulation has been found to be positively reinforcing. In the Miller-DiCara experiment, rats were randomly assigned to one of two groups: (1) a group that received ICS as a reward for increasing the heart rate; (2) a group given ICS for decreasing the heart rate. During the training, all the subjects were given curare and were subjected to a shaping procedure. That is, at first reward (ICS) was given for only small changes in heart rate; later, however, subjects were rewarded only for increases or decreases of at least thirty beats per minute.

The results of this experiment appear in Figure 1-11. It is clear that the subjects learned to slow their hearts or to speed them up, depending upon the reinforcement contingency established by the experimenters. Miller and DiCara report that two subjects died during conditioning. Interestingly, both of these subjects were in the group reinforced for decreasing heart rate. This maladaptive outcome illustrates that learning cannot always be considered as "improvement" in performance.

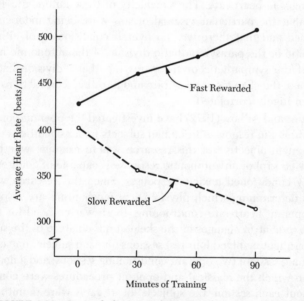

FIGURE 1-11. Learned changes in heart rate for groups rewarded for fast or for slow rates. Each data point represents an average of the number of beats per minute during a period of five minutes. (Adapted from Miller, N. E., and DiCara, L., "Instrumental learning of heart rate changes in curarized rats: Shaping and specificity to discriminative stimuli," *Journal of Comparative and Physiological Psychology*, 1967, 63, 12–19. Copyright 1967 by the American Psychological Association, and reproduced by permission.)

In a subsequent experiment, Miller and Banuazizi (1968) carried the Miller-DiCara procedure a step further. They attempted to condition intestinal contractions and heart rate in curarized rats, using electrical brain stimulation as a positive reinforcer. There were four experimental groups in this study, and each was rewarded for making a specific response: (1) reward for intestinal contractions, (2) reward for intestinal relaxation, (3) reward for fast heart rate, (4) reward for slow heart rate. The results appear in Figure 1-12. The top graph shows the changes in intestinal contractions. In groups 1 and 2 (rewarded for increases and decreases in spontaneous contraction), changes occur in the appropriate direction; in groups 3 and 4 (rewarded for changes in heart rate), intestinal contractions are unaffected. The bottom graph shows changes in heart rate. Now groups 3 and 4 show heart-rate changes in the rewarded direction, and groups 1 and 2 show no significant changes in heart rate. The specificity of these autonomic changes suggests that the particular visceral organs were being independently conditioned and that there was no overall conditioning of either the sympathetic or the parasympathetic division of the autonomic nervous system. If the sympathetic or the parasympathetic division had been conditioned, the changes in heart rate and intestinal contractions would have been highly correlated.

Williams and Adkins (1972) have investigated the operant conditioning of autonomic responses in human subjects under conditions of anxiety. The main objective of this research was to examine whether the voluntary control of an autonomic response is capable of counteracting classically conditioned anxiety responses. Since this research was not aimed at determining which physiological mechanisms are responsible for the operant heart-rate conditioning, there was no need for the use of curare to control changes in the skeletal musculature of the subjects. This experiment involved four test sessions for each subject: one classical conditioning session; two operant conditioning sessions; and a final stress session, in which the classical and operant procedures were combined. Throughout each session, the subjects' heart rates were monitored.

During the classical conditioning session, the subjects were told to watch a display panel of lights—first a series of six white lights and then a series of eighteen red lights. When any one of the red lights was on, subjects were warned, a shock might be given. When the shock did occur, (a .1-second shock to the ankle) it was always given when one of the last six red lights was turned on. In addition, the subjects were presented, alternately, with a high-frequency (2,000-cps) and a low-frequency (200-cps) tone, but they were told that these tones were irrelevant to the procedure.

The top of Figure 1-13 shows the mean number of heart beats per minute (bpm) during the eight conditioning trials for each two-second interval of the trial. During the six-second period before the light sequence (CS) began, the basal heart rate was about 73 bpm. Two seconds

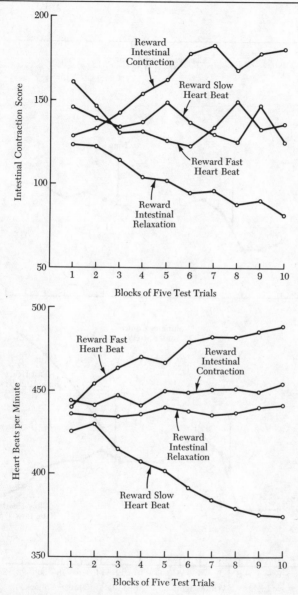

FIGURE 1-12. Results of four groups of rats, each group rewarded for changes of a different autonomic response. The top figure plots the rate of intestinal contractions for each group; the bottom figure plots heart rate. (Adapted from Miller, N. E., and Banuazizi, A., "Instrumental learning by curarized rats of a specific visceral response, intestinal or cardiac," *Journal of Comparative and Physiological Psychology*, 1968, 65, 1–7. Copyright 1968 by the American Psychological Association, and reproduced by permission.)

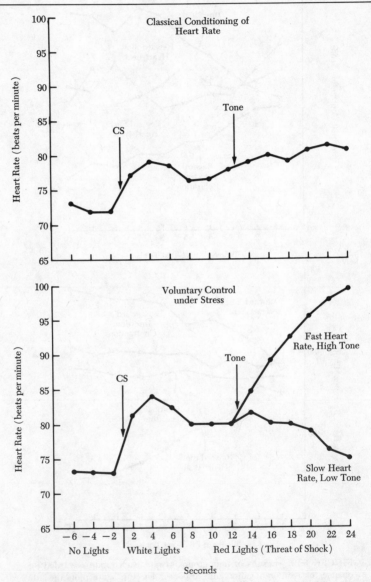

FIGURE 1-13.   Mean changes in heart rate during the course of a trial. Upper portion: classical conditioning of heart rate to presentation of a series of lights, occasionally followed by a shock. Lower portion: voluntary changes in heart rate, in the appropriate direction, during conditions when the subject is threatened by the possible presentation of shock. (From Williams and Adkins, 1972.)

after the onset of the first light, however, a conditioned heart-rate response was observed: at first a significant acceleration in heart rate; then a slight decrease; then as the threat of shock became greater during the red-light sequence, a gradual increase in heart rate up to the time that the shock was scheduled. This response may be interpreted as an anxiety or a stress reaction, which occurs when a subject knows that he might receive an aversive stimulus.

During the next two sessions, the operant conditioning sessions, the subjects were presented alternately with high- and low-frequency tones. Whenever the high tone was on, they were asked to try to increase their heart rate. When they succeeded in doing so, the loudness of the tone was reduced. Likewise, whenever the low tone was heard, they were told to decrease their heart rate in order to reduce the loudness of the tone. In other words, the subjects were always trying to turn off the tone either by speeding up the heart rate during a high tone or slowing it down during a low tone. Shaping was undertaken during the initial training trials; that is, at first the tone was gradually turned off if the subjects succeeded in increasing or decreasing their heart rate only by a few beats, but in later trials more substantial changes were required before the tone was turned off. Twenty tones, ten of high frequency and ten of low frequency, were presented during each of the two training sessions. Each tone was used as a signal for maintaining either a high or a low heart rate for twenty-four seconds.

Figure 1-14 shows the results of this heart-rate training for the first five trials (Trials 1–5) and the last five trials (Trials 16–20) of the second session. The basal heart rate for the subjects during this session was 73 bpm. Even during the first five trials, the subjects had learned to change their heart rates substantially in the appropriate direction. These voluntary changes in heart rate, however, are particularly striking during the last five trials: by the end of each presentation of the high tone, the rate was 90 to 95 bpm; by the end of a low-tone presentation, it was about 65 bpm.

During the final session of this experiment, a "stress session," the classical and operant conditioning methods were combined. First the sequence of lights was shown for twelve seconds, and the conditioned response was observed. Then the subjects were presented with the high- and low-frequency tones, and were told that they could turn off the tones, as they had done before, by increasing or decreasing heart rate. They were also told that if they could maintain their heart rate at either a fast or slow rate (and therefore keep the tone off) throughout the last six seconds of the sequence of lights, they could avoid receiving the shock at the end of the trial. The subjects, in other words, were

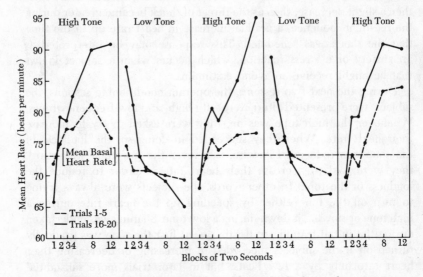

FIGURE 1-14.   Initial and final block of five trials of voluntary heart-rate training. Notice the high degree of stimulus control exerted by the high and low tones and striking changes in heart rate above the baseline value. (From Williams and Adkins, 1972.)

now asked to make voluntary changes in their heart rates under conditions of anxiety. The primary question in this phase of the study was whether a trained subject is capable of voluntarily controlling his heart rate when he is in an emotional or anxiety-inducing situation.

The results of the test session are presented in the lower portion of Figure 1-13. The classically conditioned response of heart-rate acceleration again was observed during the beginning of the light sequence. When the tones were presented, starting with the twelfth second, the operantly trained changes in heart rate occurred, suggesting that trained subjects are capable of voluntarily controlling their heart rates under conditions of anxiety. The increase in heart rate to the high tone, however, was much more striking than the decrease in heart rate to the low tone—probably because an accelerated heart rate is more compatible with the conditioned anxiety response. Even though the attempts made to decrease the heart rate voluntarily were less successful, the subjects were nevertheless able to block the conditioned anxiety response of an increase in heart rate. Presently, Williams and his colleagues are attempting to develop a more effective procedure for enabling subjects to slow down the heart rate voluntarily. Such a procedure might be especially important because of its application to psychosomatic problems and cardiovascular diseases.

The findings reported in the above studies clearly indicate that both skeletal and autonomic responses can be conditioned by operant procedures involving voluntary control over behavior. Thus, Skinner's original notion—that autonomic responses are affected only by classical conditioning and that skeletal responses are affected by operant conditioning—no longer seems valid. Perhaps the only way we can distinguish these types of conditioning is in terms of their experimental paradigms or procedures. The main procedural difference is that in classical conditioning the reinforcement is independent of the subject's behavior whereas in operant conditioning the reinforcement is always contingent upon the subject's response.

EXPERIMENTAL ANALYSIS OF BEHAVIOR

In the last three decades, operant conditioning has become more than just a routine experimental procedure or technique. Skinner (1938, 1948, 1950, 1956, 1957, 1961a, 1971) and many other psychologists have extended the operant procedure into a variety of areas, such as psychotherapy and education (see Chapters 7 and 8). Even with its wide range of applications, however, the operant approach remains unique in its style of experimentation and in its theoretical biases. Ever since 1957, when Skinner published an article with that title, operant psychologists have used the phrase "experimental analysis of behavior" in referring to their theoretical approach. Let us look at some of the main characteristics of this approach.

EMPHASIS ON OBSERVABLE CAUSES OF BEHAVIOR

Investigators who employ operant methods are concerned primarily with determining the effects of observable, and usually external, causes of behavior—such causes as food deprivation or a punishing stimulus. Because of this emphasis on observable causes, and an accompanying avoidance of unobservable constructs and hypothetical mechanisms, this approach to research is sometimes considered "atheoretical" or even "antitheoretical." However, operant methods have been useful in empirical studies of various theoretical problems (see, for example, the discussion of conditioned reinforcement in Chapter 4 or of punishment in Chapter 6). Recently, the emphasis in psychological research has been changing from theory construction to an investigation of the physiological processes underlying certain kinds of behavior. Here, again, operant methodology, with its emphasis on the manipulation of observed variables, has proved useful.

CONTROL OF EXPERIMENTAL ENVIRONMENT

Complete environmental control is crucial to operant experimentation. The experimental chamber is usually light-tight and isolated from laboratory noises. Often, a hissing sound, presented by means of a speaker, masks out irrelevant noises. In addition, a ventilating fan, mounted on the wall of the chamber, keeps the temperature relatively constant inside the unit. By means of electrical connections from the chamber to automatic programming devices, the experimenter has remote control over environmental stimuli such as tones, lights, and food. Thus, the experimenter does not come into direct contact with the subject during the experimental session but is able to observe the subject through a small window and to record responses on a cumulative response recorder. In short, every aspect of the experimental environment is regulated.

INTENSIVE STUDY OF INDIVIDUAL SUBJECTS

Psychologists who conduct operant experiments contend that if sufficient experimental control is exercised over behavior, large groups of subjects are not needed. Many of these experiments involve only one subject; if they involve more subjects, the response record for each subject is reported. Although some psychological experiments (for instance, those concerned specifically with interactions among groups or those that require special control groups) are not suited to the operant approach, the approach has certain advantages. One advantage is that the goal of research becomes one of predicting the behavior of an individual subject. As several psychologists (Skinner, 1953; Sidman, 1960) have demonstrated, the responses of a large group of subjects, expressed in statistical terms such as means or medians, do not necessarily tell us anything about the behavior of an individual subject.

RESPONSE RATE AS DEPENDENT VARIABLE

Those working in operant conditioning usually focus on the rate of a response; that is, they use response rate as a dependent variable. This approach has a number of advantages. First, the use of response rate simplifies analysis and interpretation of data. For instance, if the rate or frequency of a particular response is twice as much as it was before, we can accurately say that the "amount" of responding is twice as much. Second, the use of response rate as a measure of behavior is advantageous for statistical description. By definition, rate is derived from the observation of a number of responses occurring during a specific span of time. Any variability in the inter-response times is therefore averaged out by the use of the rate measure. Finally, changes in rate of responding (unlike measures obtained with mazes, memory drums, and jumping stands, which are extremely variable or "noisy" from trial to trial) show the uniformity expected of learning and other biological processes. If uniform changes in rate are not observed, the researcher usually assumes that he has failed to exercise sufficient experimental control. Thus, a sudden reduction in response rate is usually interpreted as resulting from some extraneous noise or malfunction of the programming equipment.

CONTROLLING SUBJECT'S BEHAVIOR

In addition to controlling a subject's responses by means of reinforcement, experimenters sometimes correlate discriminative stimuli with various *reinforcement schedules* (see Chapter 3) in order to establish *stimulus control over behavior* (Chapter 5). Excellent stimulus control is observed when the performance of a subject is appropriate to the reinforcement conditions associated with each stimulus. Furthermore, discriminative stimuli that are associated a number of times with positive reinforcement acquire reinforcing properties of their own. Such stimuli, called *conditioned reinforcers* (Chapter 4), can be used to establish or shape new responses. Behavioral control can also be established by aversive or punishing stimulation, resulting in escape or avoidance behavior, or in *conditioned suppression* (Chapter 6).

The technology of operant conditioning has been explored in psychological laboratories for the past thirty years. Many aspects of these procedures have been carefully studied, and certain principles of behavior have been identified. Some of these operant procedures, which will be discussed in more detail in subsequent chapters, have also been successfully employed in modifying human behavior outside the laboratory situation.

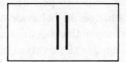

POSITIVE REINFORCEMENT

A positive reinforcer is a stimulus that, if presented after a response, will increase and/or maintain the organism's tendency to repeat that particular response. According to Hull (1943), three reward conditions are of prime importance in influencing instrumental responses: (1) the number of reinforced responses, (2) the quantity and quality of reward, and (3) the delay of reinforcement. Many operant conditioning experiments during the last two decades have examined one of these three reinforcement parameters, usually to determine whether such variables influence the actual learning of an operant response or whether they have only a temporary effect on performance. From your own experience, you are probably familiar with the distinction between "learning" and "performance." Confronted with an examination grade that was not as high as you expected, you may have remarked, "I could have done better than that," meaning how much you had learned.

In 1932, Tolman proposed that what is learned depends on an organism's sensory experience, including the rewarding and punishing stimuli provided by the environment. On the other hand, what is performed depends not only on what has been learned but also on the particular

motivation of the organism when it is tested and the particular rewarding and punishing features of the environment. Whereas performance
can be directly observed from the organism's behavior, learning must
be inferred from certain changes in performance. Learning is assumed
to have occurred when changes in behavior are *relatively permanent*.
Transitory changes in behavior that occur as a result of shifts in drive
or motivation (hours of hunger deprivation, drugs, etc.) are therefore
not considered to reflect learning. More subtle distinctions between
the concepts of learning and performance will become apparent as
we examine some of the parameters of reinforcement.

NUMBER OF REINFORCED RESPONSES

The most straightforward way of varying the conditions of reinforcement is to vary the number of times the subject's response is
reinforced. Typically, responding increases in a negatively accelerating
manner as the subject makes a greater number of reinforced responses
during the training. That is, the subject at first rapidly increases his
responses but then gradually reaches an asymptote or plateau with a
greater number of reinforcements. However, the shape of a response
record obtained during training reflects both learning and performance
factors. Therefore, psychologists have used the number of responses
made during an *extinction test* following training in order to assess
whether the number of reinforcements influences response strength
(how well a response is learned). Many such experiments (Williams,
1938; Perin, 1942; Harris & Nygaard, 1961; Dyal & Holland, 1963)
indicate a negatively accelerating relationship between the number of
reinforcements and the resistance to extinction. Harris and Nygaard,
for example, reinforced three groups of thirsty rats for lever pressing;
one group was given reinforcement (water) 45 times; another group,
90 times; and the third group, 360 times. The animals were given no
more than 45 reinforcements on a single day to ensure that they would
not become satiated. The three groups were then tested in extinction;
that is, when the lever pressing was no longer reinforced. Figure 2-1
shows the mean number of responses made to extinction for each of
the groups. The point on the curve for zero reinforcements was determined by fitting a curve to the other three points and extrapolating
it to the zero value. The shape of this curve is assumed to reflect

the gradual increase in response strength that occurs with repeated presentations of reinforcement.

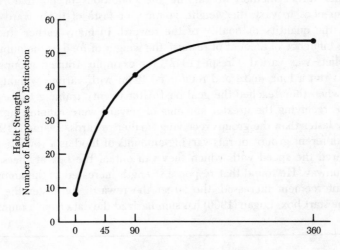

FIGURE 2-1.   The effect of number of reinforced trials on habit strength, as measured by resistance to extinction. (Reprinted with permission of author and publisher: Harris, P., & Nygaard, J. E. Resistance to extinction and number of reinforcements. *Psychological Reports*, 1961, 8, 233–234.)

Other learning theorists, (for instance, Spence, 1956) have argued that the learning curve should be S-shaped, with a gradual increase to a peak response frequency and then a tapering off in response rate. Others (for instance, Estes, 1960) claim that the process underlying learning is not incremental at all and that under strictly controlled conditions response strength should jump from a chance level to its maximal level. Still other researchers (North & Stimmel, 1960; Ison, 1962; Mackintosh, 1962; Walker, 1964) have observed a decrease in performance with extensive training. This decrease has been termed the *overlearning extinction effect*. According to Walker (1967), this effect reflects performance rather than learning. He claims that response strength (learning) remains level after a large number of reinforced trials but that performance decreases because there is a reduction in the "perceived" value of the incentive.

QUANTITY AND QUALITY OF REINFORCEMENT

Another direct method of varying the conditions of positive reinforcement is to vary the weight, volume, or taste of the reward—in
short, the quantity or quality of the reward. In many earlier studies
of the influence of amount of reward, the weight of food or the number
of pellets was varied. Crespi (1942), for example, trained groups of
rats to run a long maze and reinforced them with various weights of
food when they reached the goal box. After twenty training trials, the
groups receiving the greater amounts of reward were running significantly faster than the groups receiving smaller rewards. Zeaman (1949)
gave different groups of rats varying amounts of food as a reward and
measured the speed with which they ran out of the box at the start
of a runway. He found that response strength increased as the amount
of reinforcement increased; the larger the reward, the faster the rat
left the start box. Logan (1960) has summarized the data from a number

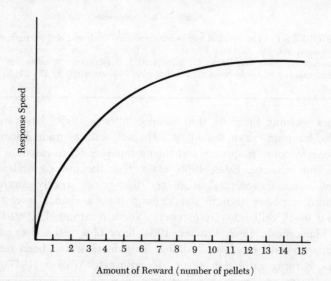

FIGURE 2-2.   Hypothetical curve showing the relationship between speed
of a particular response and amount of reinforcement (number of food
pellets or weight of food). (Adapted from *Incentive*, by Frank A. Logan.
Copyright 1960 by Yale University Press and reprinted by permission.)

of runway experiments. Figure 2-2 shows his hypothetical curve illustrating the relationship between amount of reinforcement (number of food pellets) and response speed.

Defining the amount of reinforcement in weight or number often leads to some difficulty in making precise conclusions. For example, large amounts of food look bigger, require more bites, and take longer to eat than smaller amounts of food. Thus, the perceived size of the reward and the time required to consume the reward may be more important characteristics of reinforcement than the weight or nutritional value of the reward. To eliminate some of the confounding factors involved in varying the size of the reward, Guttman (1954) used different concentrations of sucrose (sugar dissolved in water) as the reinforcer. He trained groups of rats to press a lever in a Skinner box to obtain a standard volume of water but varying amounts of sucrose concentrations (0, 2, 4, 12, 20, or 32 per cent) as the reward. Figure 2-3 shows the relationship that Guttman found between the rate of lever pressing during a ten-minute session and the concentration of

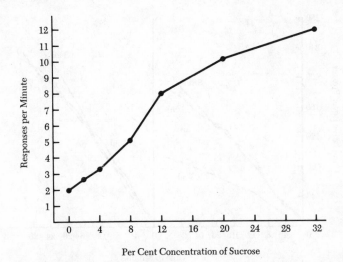

Per Cent Concentration of Sucrose

FIGURE 2-3. Effect of the percentage of concentration of sugar in water on the rate of responding in an operant chamber. (Adapted from Guttman, N., "Equal reinforcing values for sucrose and glucose solutions compared with sweetness values," *Journal of Comparative and Physiological Psychology*, 1954, **47**, 358–361. Copyright 1954 by the American Psychological Association, and reproduced by permission.)

the sucrose solution. Here again, response strength appears to increase in a negatively accelerating manner with an increase in the quality of the reward. The word *quality*, as opposed to *quantity*, is probably more appropriate here since the volume remains constant. Similar results have been reported by Smith and Capretta (1956), who used various concentrations of saccharin, a nonnutritive sweetener. This result indicates that reinforcing properties of sweet substances are due to taste factors as well as to stomach and drive-reducing factors.

Experimenters have also varied both the quantity (volume in milliliters) and the quality (per cent of sucrose concentration) of the sucrose solution. Collier and Myers (1961), for example, used varying concentrations of sucrose (either 4 or 32 per cent) and varying volumes of solution (either .03, .1, or .3 milliliters) as reward for lever pressing in two groups of rats. Figure 2-4 shows the cumulative number of lever responses as a function of concentration (quality) and volume (quantity). This figure illustrates that the relationship between quantity and quality, in terms of response strength, is very complex. When 4 per cent

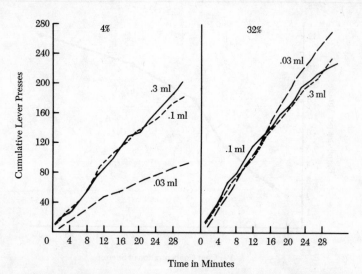

FIGURE 2-4.   Cumulative number of lever presses as a function of concentration (percentage of sucrose) and volume (milliliters of water). (Adapted from Collier, G., and Myers, L., "The loci of reinforcement," *Journal of Experimental Psychology*, 1961, **61**, 57–66. Copyright 1961 by the American Psychological Association, and reproduced by permission.)

sucrose was given, the response rate remained high throughout the entire thirty-minute session for the larger volumes of sucrose but was considerably lower for the .03-milliliter volume of reinforcement. In contrast, with the 32 per cent concentration of sucrose, the smaller volume (.03 ml) was more effective than the larger volumes in maintaining a high rate of responding throughout the session. This type of complex relationship between two variables is called an *interaction*. This particular interaction is probably explained by the fact that higher concentrations of sucrose make the animal quickly satiated; by the end of the session, therefore, the greater volumes of sucrose satiated the animal faster than the smaller volumes did. With the lower concentrations, however, satiation was not so critical and larger volumes were therefore preferred.

Tombaugh and Marx (1965) attempted to eliminate the effects of satiation in their study of the relationship between quality of reward and response strength. They varied the quality of reward by presenting four groups of rats with either 4, 8, 32, or 64 per cent concentrations of sucrose following each response. Reinforcement presentations were discontinued, however, during the last half of each sixteen-minute session. Each of the twenty-four sessions, therefore, included a reinforcement and a nonreinforcement period. The investigators assumed that satiation would affect lever responding during the periods of reinforcement but would have no effect on responding during the nonreinforcement periods. Figure 2-5 illustrates the mean number of responses made by each of the four groups during the reinforcement and nonreinforcement periods. As predicted, the performance during reinforcement increases and then decreases as the concentration of sucrose is increased and the animals consequently become satiated. In contrast, the performance during nonreinforcement, when satiation is not in effect, increases linearly with the sucrose concentration. Thus, the upper curve (reinforcement) indicates the relationship between quality of reinforcement and performance, whereas the lower curve (nonreinforcement) reflects the influence of quality of reinforcement on habit strength, or learning.

DELAY OF REINFORCEMENT

According to the results of most experiments on delay of reinforcement, there will be little learning unless the reward is presented soon after the response. But how long can reinforcement be delayed and still be

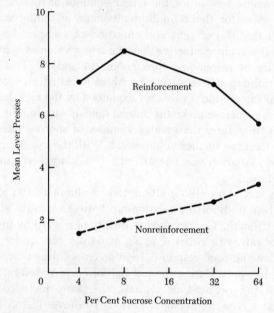

FIGURE 2-5.   Influence of percentage of sucrose on operant performance during periods of reinforcement and nonreinforcement. (Adapted from Tombaugh, T. N., and Marx, M. H. "Effects of ordered and constant sucrose concentrations on nonreinforced performance," *Journal of Experimental Psychology*, 1965, 59, 630–636. Copyright 1965 by the American Psychological Association, and reproduced by permission.)

effective for learning? Watson (1917) was the first psychologist to investigate this problem systematically. He trained two groups of rats to dig through sawdust to reach a cup containing food. One group was permitted to eat the food immediately. The other group was restrained from eating for thirty seconds. Watson found no difference in performance in the two groups. However, since his delayed group had remained in the vicinity of the food cup, where they could smell the food, and also knew that the cup contained food, they did have cues informing them of the future arrival of food. Such informative cues are called *conditioned* or *secondary reinforcers*. Secondary reinforcers are stimuli that acquire reinforcing properties by association with primary reinforcers (see Chapter 4).

In another delayed-reinforcement experiment (Wolfe, 1934), a rat was released from a start box into a T-maze, chose a goal box to approach, and then moved in that direction. Before he reached the entrance to the goal box, the doors in the maze were closed to prevent him from obtaining the reinforcement. Wolfe found that animals delayed from obtaining the reward for up to twenty minutes still would learn the correct response. Again, however, the delay box itself probably provided secondary reinforcement, since the rat always went from the delay box to the goal box, where he received food.

To investigate the effects of delay of reinforcement, Perin (1943) modified a Skinner box so that the movement of a lever to the right or left would produce a pellet of food. After the animals had learned to move the lever in both directions and displayed an individual preference for one direction, the procedure was changed so that a movement

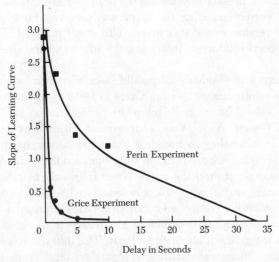

FIGURE 2-6.   Delay-of-reinforcement gradients obtained in two experiments. Grice's procedure effectively eliminated most of the conditioned reinforcement; as a result, his experiment shows little learning with delays of five seconds or more. (Adapted from Perin, C. T., "A quantitative investigation of the delay of reinforcement gradient," *Journal of Experimental Psychology*, 1943, **32**, 37–51. Copyright 1943 by the American Psychological Association, and reproduced by permission. Also, Grice, G. R., "The relation of secondary reinforcement to delayed reward in visual discrimination learning," *Journal of Experimental Psychology*, 1948, **38**, 1–16. Copyright 1948 by the American Psychological Association, and reproduced by permission.)

of the lever in the preferred direction would give no food, whereas moving it in the nonpreferred direction would cause food to be delivered. The crucial variable in this experiment was the time lapse between the "correct" response and reinforcement, which ranged from zero to thirty seconds for different groups of rats. Figure 2-6 presents the slope of the learning curve as a function of the delay intervals. Clearly, faster learning did occur with the shorter delays; virtually no learning occurred with delay intervals exceeding thirty seconds. This gradual tapering off of a response as a function of the delay interval is called a *gradient of reinforcement.*

Whereas Wolfe's subjects could learn a discrimination problem with delays up to twenty minutes, Perin's gradient of reinforcement extends only to thirty seconds of delay. The reason for this discrepancy is that Perin eliminated many of the secondary reinforcers that were present in Wolfe's study during the delay period. Nevertheless, secondary reinforcement is still present to some degree in Perin's experiment, because after every correct response the lever was removed for a period of time before reinforcement was given. This event undoubtedly served as a conditioned reinforcer, informing the subject of the presentation of food.

In an attempt to eliminate all possible secondary reinforcers during the delay-of-reinforcement period, Grice (1948) conducted an experiment that involved learning a black-white discrimination in a specially constructed T-maze. As in Wolfe's experiment, Grice kept his subjects in a delay box after they had made a choice. However, he shifted the reinforced and nonreinforced stimuli from side to side on different trials and also randomly shifted the delay boxes from side to side, so that one box would not be more strongly associated with reinforcement. Under these carefully controlled conditions, Grice obtained a delay-of-reinforcement gradient (also shown in Figure 2-6) that is clearly much steeper than the gradient obtained by Perin. This difference is explained by the fact that there was virtually no secondary reinforcement during the delay intervals in Grice's study.

Keesey (1964) reported similar findings. In his study, groups of rats were given electrical brain stimulation contingent upon lever pressing, with delays of either .0, .5, 1, 2, 3, or 5 seconds after the response. Following training, the subjects were tested in a chamber with two levers and a light over each lever. When the light was on over one of the levers (randomly selected), a response to that lever was reinforced by brain stimulation after the same delay that the animal had experienced during training. Responses made to the unlighted lever were

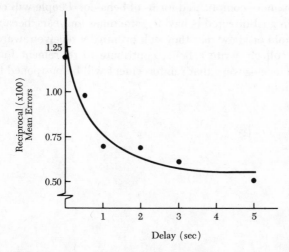

FIGURE 2-7. Rate of learning a discrimination problem in a Skinner box as a function of delay of electrical brain stimulation used as positive reward. (Adapted from Keesey, R. E., "Intercranial reward delay and the acquisition rate of a brightness discrimination," *Science*, 1964, **143**, 702–703. Copyright 1964 by the American Association for the Advancement of Science. Reprinted by permission.)

not reinforced. Following a response on either lever, the discriminative lights and the overhead (house) lights were turned off for ten seconds, so that the animals had time to recover from the brain stimulation and would make single responses on separate trials. The results are shown in Figure 2-7. Again, this curve is similar to the curves obtained by Grice (1948) and others. Keesey's study is particularly impressive because all possible conditioned reinforcers seem to have been eliminated during the delay interval. For instance, olfactory stimuli from food and proprioceptive (kinesthetic) feedback from consummatory responses were controlled by the use of electrical brain stimulation.

During delays before reinforcement, animals usually engage in some form of stereotyped, superstitious behavior—"superstitious" because it is in no way responsible for the presentation of the reward. For instance, a rat may vigorously preen himself, or a pigeon may perform a series of turning responses—because these activities occurred by chance immediately prior to reward and were therefore reinforced. These chains of superstitious behavior help the animal to pass the time while reinforcement is delayed. With humans, however, such time intervals are mediated by more complicated forms of behavior. People will continue to engage in goal-directed behavior, sometimes for years, because they have been told or know that they will eventually receive reward. They will go to college, write a book, contribute to retirement funds, get group insurance—aware that reinforcement will be postponed for long peiods of time.

SCHEDULES OF
POSITIVE REINFORCEMENT

Outside the laboratory, an individual is rarely reinforced for every response that he makes. For example, even though a boy repeatedly asks his parents for the use of the family car, his request is granted only occasionally; or a young man may have to telephone his girl several times before he gets any answer. When only a limited number of responses are reinforced, a *schedule of intermittent reinforcement* (Skinner, 1938; Ferster & Skinner, 1957) is said to be in operation. Since schedules of reinforcement have very reliable and very profound effects on behavior, the importance of reinforcement schedules in controlling behavior cannot be overemphasized.

In the laboratory, there are two basic ways of scheduling reinforcement. The first way is to require that a subject make a certain *number of responses* in succession before he receives reinforcement. For example, we might decide that only every tenth response made by an animal in a Skinner box will be reinforced or that the number of nonreinforced responses between successive reinforcements will be varied. Both of these schedules are referred to as *ratio schedules of reinforcement*. The faster the organism responds under a ratio schedule, the more reinforcements he will obtain. The second way is to establish a certain *time interval* between reinforcements. Thus, a timer might be set so that an animal in a Skinner box is rewarded only for responses made at intervals greater than one minute after the prior reinforcement. The time interval between reinforcements also can be variable rather than fixed. Both of these schedules are referred to as *interval schedules of reinforcement*. As with most operant conditioning paradigms, the subject in an interval schedule must make a response to receive reward. However, the number of responses that a subject makes is independent of the number of reinforcements he earns under an interval schedule.

SIMPLE SCHEDULES OF REINFORCEMENT

There are two simple ratio schedules (fixed ratio and variable ratio) and two simple interval schedules (fixed interval and variable interval). Figure 3-1 summarizes the precise requirements for presenting reinforcement under these ratio and interval schedules.

FIXED-RATIO (FR) SCHEDULES

Under a fixed-ratio reinforcement schedule, the subject receives reinforcement if he performs the operant response a fixed number of times. A fixed-ratio schedule requiring only one response is called a *continuous-reinforcement schedule* (CRF) or an FR 1 schedule. In contrast, a subject under an FR 10 schedule would have to respond ten times for each reward.

The effects of FR schedules on performance are quite different from those of CRF. Figure 3-2 illustrates the different response patterns in the cumulative record of animals given considerable training on one of the simple reinforcement schedules. Remember, the steeper the slope of the cumulative response record, the faster the rate of responding. As the figure shows, reinforcement on an FR schedule results in a high rate of responding—because the FR schedule places a premium on rapid responding. Higher response rates are also found for higher ratios. Thus, an animal on an FR 30 responds faster than an animal on an FR 5. Another characteristic of FR schedules is that an animal will usually pause for awhile (often as long as a minute or so) after he receives reinforcement. These so-called *postreinforcement pauses* are usually longer with higher fixed-ratio schedules. When these pauses are excluded, the cumulative record clearly shows that higher ratio schedules produce faster responding. (The factors influencing FR performance and postreinforcement pauses are discussed in more detail in the section on homogeneous chains in Chapter 4.)

A good example of a fixed-ratio schedule is the piecework system used as a basis for paying workers in some factories. Each time a fixed number of items is assembled or serviced, the money earned by the

SIMPLE SCHEDULES OF REINFORCEMENT

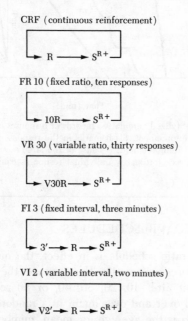

CRF (continuous reinforcement)

R $\longrightarrow$ S^{R+}

FR 10 (fixed ratio, ten responses)

10R $\longrightarrow$ S^{R+}

VR 30 (variable ratio, thirty responses)

V30R $\longrightarrow$ S^{R+}

FI 3 (fixed interval, three minutes)

3' $\longrightarrow$ R $\longrightarrow$ S^{R+}

VI 2 (variable interval, two minutes)

V2' $\longrightarrow$ R $\longrightarrow$ S^{R+}

FIGURE 3-1. Diagrams of the operations involved in the simple ratio and interval schedules of reinforcement. (Adapted from Mechner, Francis. A notational system for the description of behavioral procedures. *Journal of the Experimental Analysis of Behavior*, 1959, **2**, 133–150. Copyright 1959 by the Society for the Experimental Analysis of Behavior, Inc. Reprinted by permission.)

employee increases. Usually, people work rapidly under such a schedule, but they may take occasional breaks between each block of work.

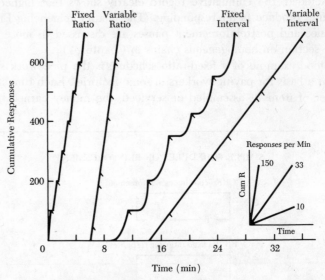

FIGURE 3-2.   Stylized cumulative records of responses under the simple schedules of reinforcement. Slash marks in the response records indicate presentations of reinforcement. Because of the large number of responses on the vertical axis (ordinate), individual responses cannot be detected in the records.

VARIABLE-RATIO (VR) SCHEDULES

When a variable-ratio schedule is in effect, the number of responses required for reinforcement varies. For instance, the experimenter may give reinforcement after 10, 20, 30, 40, or 50 responses—with this schedule repeated over and over again in a random order. The value of a variable ratio is the average, or mean, number of responses per reinforcement. The above example, then, would be a VR 30 schedule of reinforcement (see Figure 3-1).

Like the FR schedule, the VR schedule can generate a very high rate of responding. Figure 3-2 shows the steep slope of a cumulative record obtained from an animal given VR training. Notice that postreinforcement pauses do not appear in the response record. Because of the absence of these pauses, VR reinforcement schedules will usually lead to a higher rate of responding than comparable FR schedules. For instance, an animal will perform more responses during a one-hour session with a VR 15 schedule than with an FR 15 schedule.

A good example of a variable-ratio schedule is the operation of a slot machine programmed to pay off once for every fifty or so operations. It is impossible, however, to predict which plays will pay off. A person might win twice in succession, or he might have one hundred or more plays between payoffs. Interestingly, the persistent and vigorous playing of many gamblers is strikingly similar to the behavior pattern of very hungry animals, responding under a VR schedule for food.

FIXED-INTERVAL (FI) SCHEDULES

The fixed-interval schedule presents reinforcement on a fixed, or periodic, time schedule. For instance, if an animal is put on a fixed-interval three-minute schedule (FI 3), only responses made at least three minutes after the previous reinforcement are reinforced. During a thirty-minute session, the subject could receive no more than ten reinforcements. As Figure 3-1 shows, two conditions are necessary for the presentation of reinforcement: the fixed interval must have completely elapsed, and the subject must make a response.[1]

The stable performance of a subject under FI reinforcement is shown in Figure 3-2. Under this schedule, a subject usually emits a constant number of responses between successive reinforced responses. For example, if an animal makes an average of thirty responses for each reinforcement, and the reinforcement is given once every minute (FI 1), the average response rate is thirty responses per minute. If, however, reinforcement is given once every three minutes, (FI 3), the same thirty responses will be distributed over this interval, so that the response rate is only ten responses per minute. Skinner (1938, 1950) claims that with interval schedules of reinforcement the rate of responding usually is inversely proportional to the interval between reinforcements.

As Figure 3-2 shows, FI schedules generate very specific response patterns within each reinforcement interval. At the beginning of an interval, few if any responses are made; at the end of the interval, just prior to the reinforced response, a great many responses are made. Thus, a kind of scalloped pattern appears in the cumulative record. This pattern of responses indicates that the schedule is controlling the subject's behavior. Responses made immediately after FI reinforcement

---

[1]Sometimes a *limited-hold* (LH) schedule is used in conjunction with fixed- and variable-interval schedules. When LH is used, the subject receives reinforcement only if he responds within a specified period of time after the designated interval has elapsed. For example, "FI 3 LH 30 sec" means that only responses occurring during a thirty-second period following an interval of three minutes will be reinforced. Responses made prior to or after the thirty-second period will not be reinforced.

are gradually extinguished because they are never reinforced; however, as time passes and the animal anticipates a reward, his responses tend to pile up at the end of the interval. The degree to which the subject shows this scalloping effect is directly related to his ability to discriminate the passage of time. When, for instance, the size of the interval is varied for different subjects (Ferster & Skinner, 1957), scalloping becomes more apparent with the longer intervals; in other words, the subjects here could discriminate the extinction phase better with a longer interval.

Precise fixed-interval reinforcement is not found frequently outside the laboratory. However, approximations abound. For example, the glances a student makes at a clock during a one-hour lecture may result in a scalloped FI curve.

VARIABLE-INTERVAL (VI) SCHEDULES

Instead of reinforcing after a fixed or constant interval, we could reward a subject for responding at variable intervals. Thus, after an operant has been reinforced, we might wait for one minute before reinforcing the next response; and then we might wait three minutes before giving the next reinforcement; and so on. A beggar whose patrons appear irregularly could be said to receive money rewards on a variable-interval schedule.

The average time interval between reinforcements given during a session defines the particular VI schedule. The VI 2 schedule shown in Figure 3-1, for instance, might have inter-reinforcement times of 10 seconds, 50 seconds, 1 minute, 3 minutes, and 5 minutes, presented in random order. Under these conditions, the subject cannot learn the time intervals accurately. Therefore, he tends to respond at a relatively low but steady rate (see Figure 3-2). As with fixed-interval reinforcement, response rate during variable-interval sessions is inversely related to the size of the interval. There is faster responding when the interval is shorter and the reinforcement density is higher.

PERFORMANCE UNDER VR AND VI SCHEDULES

By means of an experimental design called *yoking*, a valid comparison can be made between performances on VR and VI schedules. (Because of variations in time intervals and in number of responses between reinforcements, comparisons among the other schedules cannot be made.) In a yoked experiment, pairs of subjects are simultaneously given training in separate Skinner boxes. In one box, the operant response is reinforced according to a VR schedule, whereas in the second box the subject's response is reinforced *only* when the first subject receives reward. The rate of responding of the first animal, on the VR schedule, therefore determines the number of reinforcements presented to both subjects. In this way, it is possible to equate the number of reinforcements and to have approximately the same inter-reinforcement interval for both subjects. The major procedural difference is that the first subject is being reinforced on a VR schedule, while the second subject is being reinforced according to a VI schedule.

Reynolds (1968) conducted an experiment of this type. His results are presented in Figure 3-3, which shows the cumulative records of two pigeons: one trained under VR and the other yoked on a VI schedule. These records were obtained after the performances of both subjects had stabilized. Although both pigeons made numerous responses and showed a relatively constant rate of responding, the VR bird responded about five times faster than the VI bird. Why were the response rates different, since both were given the same number of reinforcements at approximately the same times? Apparently, the bird on the VR schedule had learned that reinforcements were contingent on a high rate of responding, whereas the VI bird had learned that a high rate produced no more reinforcement than a slow steady rate.

RESISTANCE TO EXTINCTION ON SIMPLE SCHEDULES

The usual course of extinction for each of the previously described simple schedules is presented in Figure 3-4. All four of the intermittent schedules produce greater resistance to extinction than continuous reinforcement (CRF) does. This increase in resistance to extinction, following training with intermittent reinforcement, is referred to as the *partial-reinforcement effect* (PRE). The various intermittent schedules, however, show different patterns of responding during the initial period of extinction.

On an FR schedule, the postreinforcement pauses increase in time, and responses usually occur in bursts. Thus, the animal's response rate is sometimes the same as it was during training; at other times, it is zero; rarely is it at some intermediate level. During extinction, the interval between bursts of responses increases until it finally exceeds some arbitrary limit that the experimenter has used as his extinction criterion (for example, zero responses for three successive minutes).

On a VR schedule, animals typically emit a great many responses

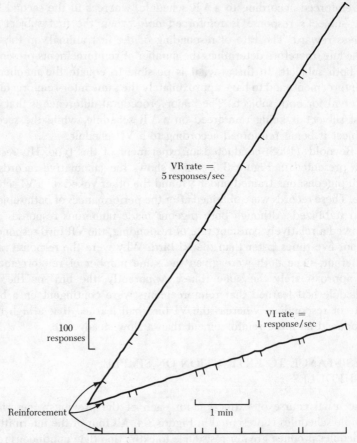

FIGURE 3-3.   Cumulative records of the performance of two pigeons, one trained on a variable-ratio (VR) schedule and the other yoked with a variable-interval (VI) schedule. Although both subjects received the same number of reinforcements at approximately the same times, the VR subject responded five times as fast as the VI subject. (Adapted from *A Primer of Operant Conditioning*, by G. S. Reynolds. Copyright © 1968 by Scott, Foresman and Company. Reprinted by permission.)

during extinction. As with extinction of FR performance, the high rate of responding that occurs with VR reinforcement continues to be found whenever the organism is responding in extinction and there is no intermediate response rate. When the average number of responses required for reinforcement is equal (for instance, VR 10 versus FR

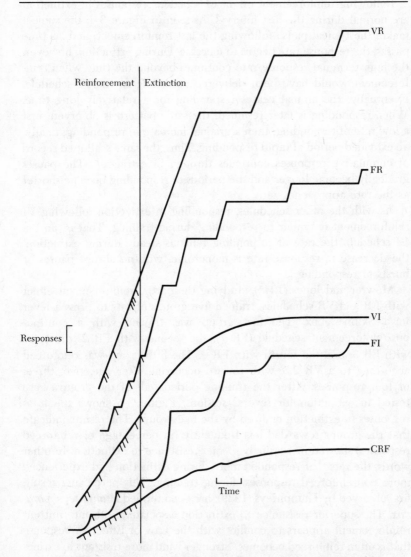

FIGURE 3-4. Stylized cumulative records of responses in extinction following reinforcement on each of the five simple schedules of reinforcement.

10), greater resistance to extinction usually is found for VR than for FR schedules.

Following reinforcement on an FI schedule, responses in extinction are normal during the first interval. As seen in Figure 3-4, the subject makes the typical pause following the last reinforcement; and, as time passes, the response rate begins to increase. During extinction, however, the high terminal response rate continues beyond the time when reinforcement would have been delivered according to the FI schedule. Eventually, the animal ceases responding for a relatively long time. When responding is later resumed, the same pattern is observed: first a low rate of responding; then a gradual increase in responding; finally, an extended period of rapid responding. Thus, the same scalloped record of cumulative responses continues throughout extinction. The pauses gradually become longer and the periods of responding become shorter as the rate approaches zero.

As with the other schedules, responding in extinction following VI reinforcement is similar to responding during training. That is, on the VI schedule the rate of responding remains steady during extinction; the decrease in response rate is monotonic, with no abrupt pauses or bursts of responding.

Mowrer and Jones (1945), studying the partial-reinforcement effect with FR and VR schedules, trained five groups of rats to press a lever in a Skinner box. The first group was trained with a continuous-reinforcement schedule (FR 1), the second with FR 2, the third with FR 3, and the fourth with FR 4. The fifth group was reinforced according to a VR 2.5, with reward occurring after one, two, three, or four responses. After the training periods, all of the groups were tested in extinction for several sessions. Figure 3-5 shows the total responses in extinction emitted by the five groups. The results indicate that the groups rewarded less frequently (in percentage of reinforced responses) showed increasingly *greater* resistance to extinction. In other words, the rats that responded more during extinction had experienced more nonreinforced responses during training. This perplexing result, first observed by Humphreys (1939), has been termed *Humphreys' paradox*. The superior resistance to extinction associated with intermittent reinforcement appears to conflict with the Law of Effect: A response that is often reinforced becomes "stronger" and more resistant to extinction than a response reinforced less often.

According to Mowrer and Jones, the results of their study do not contradict the Law of Effect if one analyzes their data in "response units" rather than individual lever responses. Thus, the FR 1 group was reinforced for each response, FR 2 for two responses, VR 2.5 for two and a half responses, FR 3 for three responses, and FR 4 for four

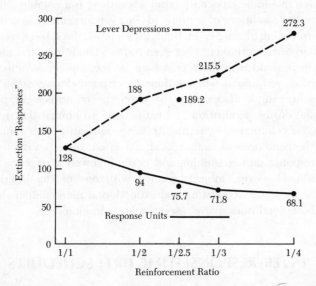

FIGURE 3-5.   Number of lever depressions made by five groups in extinction (upper curve) compared with number of response units in extinction
(bottom curve). (Adapted from Mowrer, O. H., and Jones, H. M., "Habit
strength as a function of the pattern of reinforcement," *Journal of Experimental Psychology*, 1945, **35**, 293–311. Copyright 1945 by the American
Psychological Association, and reproduced by permission.)

responses. Notice that the number of individual responses comprising
a response unit, or responses required for reinforcement, increases with
the larger ratios. Figure 3-5 shows the extinction data converted from
responses into response units. For example, the 188 responses emitted
in extinction by the FR 2 group were divided by 2 to give 94 response
units in extinction. According to the converted data, the groups rewarded less often show slightly less resistance to extinction. However, this
decline may be caused by fatigue or effort, rather than a decrease
in power of reinforcement.

The existence of the partial-reinforcement effect or Humphreys'
paradox in interval schedules, however, is difficult to account for on
the basis of the Mowrer-Jones response units. Responses are not as
tightly chained with the interval schedules, especially VI, as they are
with the ratio schedules. One theory that seems particularly applicable
in predicting the speed of extinction following interval reinforcement

is termed the *discrimination hypothesis*. According to this hypothesis, extinction should be especially rapid when there is a notable difference between the conditions of training (during reinforcement) and the conditions of testing (during extinction). Presumably, the subject recognizes this difference (discriminates between the two conditions) and therefore ceases to respond in extinction, where he receives no reinforcement. Specifically, an animal will continue to respond during extinction as long as he cannot discriminate between the reinforcement patterns (schedule) during acquisition and extinction. An animal that received continuous reinforcement during training can easily discriminate between the conditions of training and extinction, since reward followed every response during training and never followed a response during extinction. However, subjects trained with one of the intermittent schedules perceive acquisition and extinction as more similar, because under both conditions many responses are nonreinforced.

INTER-RESPONSE-TIME (IRT) SCHEDULES

Under an inter-response-time schedule, a subject receives reinforcement if the time between his responses is either shorter or longer than an interval selected by the experimenter. We will now examine the behavioral effects of three different kinds of inter-response-time reinforcement schedules: *differential reinforcement for high rates* (DRH), *differential reinforcement for low rates* (DRL), and *differential reinforcement for other behavior* (DRO).

DIFFERENTIAL REINFORCEMENT FOR HIGH RATES (DRH)

Under the DRH schedule, reinforcement is presented whenever the subject responds *before* a specified time period has elapsed. For example, a subject might be given reinforcement only when his IRT is five seconds or less. Figure 3-6 shows a diagram of a DRH five-second schedule. Notice that reinforcement is given if the subject responds during an interval of five seconds following the previous response. If the IRT is greater than five seconds, the response merely resets a timer for another five-second interval. For highly motivated organisms (such as rats deprived of food), exceedingly high response rates can be produced when the required IRT is short.

INTER-RESPONSE-TIME (IRT)
REINFORCEMENT SCHEDULES

DRH (differential reinforcement
of high rate)

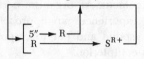

DRL (differential reinforcement
of low rate)

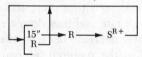

DRO (differential reinforcement
of other responses)

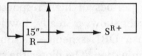

FIGURE 3-6. Diagrams of operations involved in the three inter-response-time (IRT) schedules of reinforcement. (Adapted from Mechner, 1959. Reprinted by permission.)

DIFFERENTIAL REINFORCEMENT FOR LOW RATES (DRL)

Under the DRL schedule, a response is reinforced only if it occurs *after* a fixed interval (for instance, fifteen seconds) following the last response (see Figure 3-6). If a response is made too early (before fifteen seconds has passed), no reinforcement is given and the timer controlling the interval is restarted. The subject is then required to pause again until the required interval has elapsed before a response will be reinforced. Notice that reinforcement is dependent upon a response, but the inter-response time must be at least the required interval. In the usual DRL schedule, there is no limit to the possible length of the IRT; however, a limited-hold (LH) schedule, much like the type used in either an FI or a VI schedule, can be added to the DRL schedule. Under this condition, responses are reinforced only if they occur, for instance, within five seconds *after* the interval of fifteen seconds.

The DRL schedule typically produces a very low rate of responding. Even so, because the subject is deprived and therefore strongly motivated to make the learned response, many of the responses are made too soon and therefore are not reinforced. But these errors gradually decrease in frequency because such responses result in postponing the opportunity for reinforcement. An organism performing under a DRL schedule undoubtedly experiences an approach—avoidance conflict (conflicting desire to respond and not to respond), especially as the required interval nears completion.

Performance under a DRL schedule is usually quite erratic during the initial training sessions. Animals are first trained on a CRF schedule and then on a DRL schedule with a short IRT requirement. At first, subjects respond at a high rate and thus do not receive reinforcement. Later, their response rates decrease because of extinction. Once their IRTs become longer than the required interval, the subjects receive reinforcement. These reinforcements, however, serve to reinstate the initial high response rate, so that again reinforcement is withheld. Gradually, these oscillating periods of high response rate and extinction disappear; and the subject shows a steady, low level of responding.

To perform well on a DRL schedule, a subject must learn some type of temporal discrimination. The closer the subject's IRTs approximate the required interval for reinforcement, the better is the subject's ability to discriminate the passage of time. Figure 3-7 shows the *frequency* of a subject's IRTs as a function of the duration of the IRT required for reinforcement. Here the only reinforced responses were IRTs of ten seconds or more; no holding schedule or upper limit was used. The frequencies of the IRTs are plotted in two-second intervals. The results show that the subject emitted responses far more frequently with long IRTs than with short IRTs. In general, however, the subject's responses indicate great accuracy in estimating the required interval, especially considering that time was estimated without the aid of a timer.

This curve resembles that of a cumulative record between FI reinforcements, in which fewer responses are emitted following reinforcement than at the end of the interval. However, there are two notable differences in the DRL schedule: (1) responses are made immediately after reinforcement; (2) the most frequent IRT is slightly longer than the required interval.

When subjects are required to time their responses to receive reinforcement, as in a DRL schedule, stereotyped response chains are often observed (Hodos, Ross, & Brady, 1962; Laties & Weiss, 1962). In one

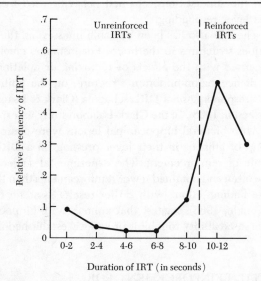

FIGURE 3-7.   Relative frequency distribution of inter-response times during performance of a ten-second DRL schedule. (Adapted from *A Primer
of Operant Conditioning* by G. S. Reynolds. Copyright © 1968 by Scott,
Foresman and Company. Reprinted by permission.)

study (Laties, Weiss, Clark, & Reynolds, 1965), a rat trained on a DRL
schedule chewed on his tail during the interval between reinforced
responses (twenty-two seconds). This chewing, in the opinion of the
investigators, served as a mediating behavior, providing discriminative
stimuli for lever responses with long IRTs. Thus, perhaps an animal
on a DRL schedule, instead of learning to make a temporal discrimination as such, simply learns to make a chain of responses that fill
up the interval.

Further support for this chaining interpretation comes from experiments (for instance, Segal, 1962) testing DRL-trained animals with stim-
ulants such as amphetamines, in dosages that might influence the subject's behavior but would not interfere with eating. The subjects in
these studies increased their response rates, which resulted in decreasing
the number of reinforcements they otherwise would have received.
Although this finding might mean that the subject's perception of time
was distorted by the drug, the chaining interpretation seems more ap-
pealing. That is, since amphetamines increase the rate of emission of
all behavior, it seems reasonable to assume that there would also be

an increase in the superstitious, chained behavior used by a subject to regulate his lever responding.

The DRL schedule also has been valuable in assessing the functions served by various structures in the brain. For instance, much research has been concerned with the effects of removing or oblating the hippocampus, a diencephalon-midbrain structure, on the ability of rats to inhibit their responding on a DRL schedule (Clark & Issacson, 1965; Schmaltz & Issacson, 1968). In the Clark-Isaacson study, an experimental group of rats with bilateral hippocampal lesions were compared with a control group of animals in their lever pressing on a DRL twenty-second schedule of reinforcement. The experimental subjects pressed the lever more often and obtained fewer reinforcements than the control subjects. These findings, along with earlier results (Issacson & Wickel-gren, 1962; Kimble, 1963), suggest that animals with hippocampal lesions show decreased ability to inhibit previously established instrumental responses.

DIFFERENTIAL REINFORCEMENT FOR OTHER BEHAVIORS (DRO)

Either delaying the presentation of reinforcement following a response (see Chapter 2) or requiring a given delay between successive responses (DRL schedule) seems to result in the appearance of chains of superstitious behavior. An even more effective way of establishing chains of superstitious responses is by a DRO schedule, on which responses other than the instrumental response are reinforced. A DRO fifteen-second schedule (see Figure 3-6) is similar to a DRL fifteen-second schedule. With the DRL schedule, however, the subject receives reinforcement *only* if he makes a response after a specified delay period; with the DRO schedule, the subject receives the reinforcement automatically (without having to respond), provided he has not responded for a given period of time.

An experiment reported by Ferster (1953) illustrates this type of reinforcement schedule. In this experiment, pigeons were trained to peck at a lighted key or disc on a VI schedule of reinforcement. The peck that produced a reward also turned out the light behind the key and started a clock for a one-minute period, after which the reward was automatically delivered. If the pigeon pecked at the dark key during the delay interval, the clock reset and the bird had to wait an additional minute. All subjects in this study showed considerable superstitious behavior during the delay intervals. One pigeon, for example, developed a circling response, making as many as forty turns during an eighty-second delay period. As we noted before, this behavior is integral to learning temporal discriminations.

DISCRIMINATION SCHEDULES

MULTIPLE (*MULT*) SCHEDULES

A multiple schedule consists of two or more simple schedules presented successively to the subject and correlated with exteroceptive discriminative stimuli. For example, a pigeon might be given successive presentations of blue, green, and red lights projected on a translucent response key. The blue stimulus might be associated with FI reinforcement, the green with FR, and the red with extinction. Figure 3-8 presents a diagram of the conditions presented under a *mult* FI 3 FR 10 ext. After the subject has received several sessions of training with this multiple schedule, he will show a scalloped pattern of responding during the blue stimulus, a high response rate during the green, and a very low rate during red. However, some interactions may exist among the components. In other words, a subject's performance during a specific

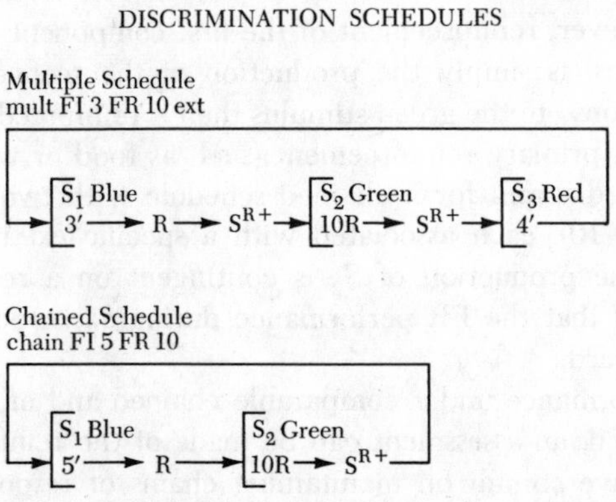

DISCRIMINATION SCHEDULES

Multiple Schedule
mult FI 3 FR 10 ext

Chained Schedule
chain FI 5 FR 10

FIGURE 3-8.   Diagrams of operations involved in multiple and chained schedules. Notice that each response component of the multiple schedule is followed by reinforcement, whereas only the final response component is reinforced in the chained schedule. (Adapted from Mechner, 1959. Reprinted by permission.)

---

component of a multiple schedule is influenced by his performance during the previous components.

The interacting effects in a multiple schedule have usually been studied experimentally by combining two simple schedules. The same operant response is used in each of the individual schedules. According to Reynolds (1968), two types of interactions are usually observed under these conditions. First, as mentioned before, the characteristic response pattern may be changed, but not to the point where it would be considered completely inappropriate for the schedule. For example, during a *mult* FI FR schedule, a dramatic burst of responding usually occurs at the end of the FI component—response at a higher rate than normally found on an isolated FI schedule; this interacting effect, however, still does not distort the scalloped FI response curve.

The second type of interaction is that the overall responses to all the components of a multiple schedule are often greater than the total responses in the individual schedules presented alone. This type of interaction, referred to as *behavioral contrast*, is further discussed in Chapter 5, in relation to the behavioral effects of discrimination training.

CHAINED (*CHAIN*) SCHEDULES

A chained schedule, like a multiple schedule, also consists of two or more stimuli presented successively to the subject. With the chained schedule, however, reinforcement of the first component (for instance, a blue stimulus) is simply the production of the second component (green); a response to the green stimulus then is reinforced, on a second schedule, with primary reinforcement (such as food or water). Figure 3-8 shows the diagram for a chained schedule with two components (FI 5 and FR 10), each associated with a specific external stimulus. Notice that the production of S_2 is contingent on a response made during S_1, and that the FR performance during S_2 is reinforced with a primary reward.

When performance under comparable chained and multiple schedules is examined, an assessment can be made of the reinforcing effect of discriminative stimuli on maintaining chains of responses. Ferster and Skinner (1957) studied the performance of pigeons—first under a multiple schedule and later under a chained schedule. The pigeons were first exposed to a *mult* ext FR 50. In the extinction component, an orange stimulus (S_1) was presented on a VI one-minute schedule, and no reinforcement was presented. At the end of this time, S_1 was turned off, and a blue stimulus (S_2) appeared. After a bird had made fifty responses in the blue light (S_2), reinforcement (food) was given. This cycle (orange stimulus followed by blue stimulus) was then repeated. After ten sessions on this schedule, the birds were making almost no responses under the orange light and rapid responses in the presence of the blue light.

The schedule was then changed to a chained schedule, *chain* VI 1 FR 50. After the birds were exposed to the orange light for approximately one minute, a *response* would cause the light to change from orange (S_1) to blue (S_2). As before, fifty responses under the blue light were required for reinforcement. Since S_2 presumably had become a conditioned reinforcer, as a consequence of its association with the primary reinforcer during the multiple schedule, its presentation in the chained schedule should have resulted in an increase in responding during the presentation of the first component of the schedule. The results of the Ferster-Skinner experiment support this prediction; the pigeons now responded at a stable, intermediate rate (typical of the performance under a VI schedule) during the S_1 segment, in which they had previously showed near-zero responding under the multiple schedule.

CONCURRENT (CONC) SCHEDULES

Concurrent reinforcement schedules involve two or more operant responses that are each reinforced by a separate schedule at the same time. For instance, a pigeon may be reinforced for responding to one of two keys on a VI 2 schedule and at the same time receive reinforcement on an FI 1 schedule for responding to the other key. This type of concurrent schedule, termed *conc* VI 2 FI 1, is diagramed in Figure 3-9. Another type of concurrent schedule is *conc* VI 2 FR 3 *pun*; here responses to one key are reinforced with food on a VI schedule, while responses to the second key are punished by a brief electrical shock. The diagram for this schedule is also presented in Figure 3-9, with S^{R-} representing an aversive stimulus.

Even though the individual components of a concurrent reinforcement schedule are independent, certain temporal and spatial contingencies may occur frequently enough to produce interacting effects between the component schedules. For instance, the subject may accidentally be reinforced when he switches from one response to the next. If such reinforcement occurs a number of times, the subject may

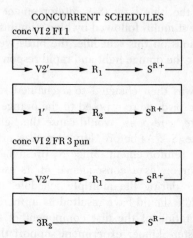

CONCURRENT SCHEDULES

conc VI 2 FI 1

conc VI 2 FR 3 pun

FIGURE 3-9. Diagrams of the operations involved in two concurrent schedules of reinforcement. Notice that with concurrent schedules more than one response can be performed in order to receive reinforcement. (Adapted from Mechner, 1959. Reprinted by permission.)

develop a sequence of making one response and switching to the other one. When such a chain is established, the rate of responding on the first key is usually somewhat higher than it would otherwise be, since the subject perceives such responses as a necessary part of a response chain for reward.

One way of ensuring the independence of the components is to introduce a *changeover delay* (COD), whereby a response is reinforced only after a certain interval of time (Herrnstein, 1961); thus, the COD often guarantees a separation in time, sometimes only a second or less, between the two types of responses. For example, if a one second COD is programmed with concurrent schedules of reinforcement, a pigeon's peck on a given key will not be reinforced until at least one second after the bird changes his responding from one key to another.

Even with the COD procedure, however, the rate of one operant is often influenced by the consequences of other operants. That is, the response rate of a particular operant is determined largely by the frequency with which the other operants are followed by reward or punishment.

Three types of interactions are found with concurrent operants. With the first type, involving similar reinforcers scheduled for each of the two concurrent responses, an increase in frequency of reinforcement for one operant produces a corresponding decrease in response rate of the other operant (Catania, 1961). Some responses are still made, however, to the less frequently rewarded key. Apparently, the subjects—instead of responding only to the key that yields the most frequent reinforcements—try to maximize their chances for reward by dividing their responses between the alternatives according to their reinforcement frequency. Certain concurrent schedules are more compatible than others in allowing the subject to maximize his opportunity for reward. For instance, if a subject is given a concurrent FI-FR schedule, he can share his responding between the two components in a very efficient manner (Catania, 1963).

The second type of interacting effect occurs when one of the responses results in punishment. When punishment (for instance, shock) results from a response, that rate of responding decreases. This decrease, however, is often accompanied by an increase in the rate of responding for the concurrent operants (Hearst & Sidman, 1961). This facilitating or compensating effect of punishment on unpunished behavior is a form of *behavior contrast*, further examined in Chapters 5 and 6. The use of punishment in suppressing or eliminating a particular response in humans has also been found more effective if the concurrent operants are reinforced (Herman & Azrin, 1964).

A third type of interaction occurs when reinforcement is scheduled for one operant while the concurrent operant enables the subject to avoid an aversive stimulus. Under these conditions, an increase in intensity or frequency of the aversive stimulus increases the probability of avoidance behavior but decreases the response rate of the first operant (Catania, 1966).

Concurrent reinforcement schedules may be useful in studying many different problems. For instance, the effects of various drugs can be examined precisely by the use of concurrent schedules known to produce conflict and frustration. Concurrent schedules are also relevant to the problems of eliminating or reducing the response rate of certain undesirable operants.

The use of schedules of reinforcement is rapidly expanding, and many other types of schedules have been developed (see Appendix). Presently, schedules are being used in the study of motor skills, psychophysics, motivation, physiology, problem solving, and other areas of research. Techniques involving schedules have also been adapted to a wide variety of species. Surprisingly similar performance, especially with complex schedules, has been demonstrated in the pigeon, mouse, rat, cat, and monkey. At the human level, as will be discussed in Chapters 7 and 8, many types of reinforcement schedules are being used in the design of educational techniques and in the treatment of mental illness.

CONDITIONED REINFORCEMENT AND CHAINING BEHAVIOR

Operant responses are usually conditioned by means of unconditioned, or primary, reinforcers such as food and water. However, since behavior is also influenced by *conditioned,* or *secondary, reinforcers,* such as money, psychologists include the concept of conditioned reinforcement in their attempts to explain how organisms learn new responses. Conditioned reinforcers also may be used to prolong responding during periods of extinction, when primary reinforcement is absent. Finally, conditioned reinforcers are considered important in the acquisition and maintenance of long sequences or chains of responses.

CONDITIONED REINFORCEMENT

Conditioned reinforcers are stimuli that possess reinforcing properties because they have been associated with previously demonstrated reinforcing stimuli (either a primary reinforcer or a powerful secondary reinforcer). The specific operations that might be used to establish a conditioned reinforcer are shown in Figure 4-1. A neutral (conditioned) stimulus is paired with a primary reinforcer (unconditioned stimulus) over a series of trials. Eventually, the neutral stimulus acquires certain properties of the primary reinforcer. (Since this same set of operations is used in classical conditioning, there seems reason to believe that the learning processes underlying classical conditioning and secondary reinforcement are very similar.)

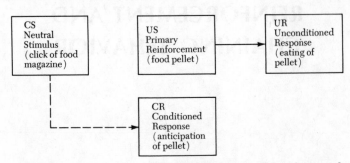

FIGURE 4-1.   Procedure used in establishment of a conditioned or second-ary reinforcer. The CS typically precedes the US by a short interval. The solid line represents an unlearned, or reflexive, association between the stimulus and the response; the dashed line represents a learned association.

Psychologists have devised a number of techniques to test for the reinforcing power of potential conditioned reinforcers.

The first of these techniques is called the *new-learning method.* Here a stimulus is paired with a primary reinforcer in one learning situation; later, a test is done to determine whether that stimulus reinforces a new response in a different learning situation. An experiment using this type of procedure was conducted by Saltzman (1949). He first trained rats to run down a straight-alley maze to obtain food. The food was found in either a black or a white goal box, depending on the condition to which the subject was assigned. The rats were then tested in a T-maze with one path leading to a black goal box and the other leading to a white goal box but with no food reinforcement in the boxes. Even without the primary reinforcement, all the animals still learned to take the path leading to the previously baited goal box.

The basic design of a second technique, the *relearning method,* is as follows: Animals first are trained to press a lever for food, and then their responses are extinguished (that is, food is withheld). The animals then are placed in a Skinner box from which the lever has been removed and are given brief presentations of tone followed by food. When the animals are again placed in the box with the lever, they still have a slight tendency to press the lever (because of the phenomenon of spontaneous recovery); responses to the lever are now followed by brief presentations of tone (conditioned reinforcement) for half of the subjects. These subjects usually relearn the lever-pressing response, whereas the other subjects make very few responses.

A third technique is referred to as the *resistance-to-extinction method.* An experiment by Bugelski (1938) provides a good example of a study using this technique. Bugelski first trained rats to press a lever for food reinforcement; the presentations of food were preceded by a distinct click of the magazine mechanism. Half of the rats (the control subjects) then were placed in boxes with the food mechanism disconnected, thus eliminating both the food and the clicking noise; for the remaining subjects (the experimental subjects), the food magazine was connected but empty, thus providing a click but no food reinforcement. The experimental subjects made 30 per cent more responses in extinction than the control subjects. Thus, the clicking sound, which prior to training had been a neutral stimulus, was found to be a reinforcing stimulus after training, since it increased resistance to extinction.

A fourth technique for assessing the power of a conditioned reinforcer is referred to as the *chaining method.* A chain of behavior usually consists of a sequence of different responses that eventually leads to primary reinforcement. Conditioned reinforcers are responsible for the acquisition of new responses in the chain and also function to maintain the strength of the chain until primary reinforcement is received. Basic extensions of chained schedules are the use of *concurrent chained schedules* (Autor, 1960), wherein the subject makes a choice between two chained schedules, and the *observing-response technique,* wherein the subject makes a response different from the primary reinforced response for the purpose of producing stimuli associated with primary reinforcers. (For a more complete description and critique of these and other methods used to measure conditioned reinforcements, see Hendry, 1969.)

VARIABLES CONTROLLING STRENGTH OF CONDITIONED REINFORCERS

Since conditioned reinforcers are established by the procedure of classical conditioning, we would expect their strength to be influenced by all the variables known to affect the strength of a conditioned response. Such variables would include the number of presentations of primary reinforcement, the magnitude of reinforcement, the delay of reinforcement, and the level of motivation, to name only a few.

Number of Presentations of Primary Reinforcement.   Several investigators (Hall, 1951a; Bersh, 1951; Miles, 1956) have demonstrated that the strength of a secondary reinforcer is related to the frequency with which it has been paired with primary reinforcement. Miles, for instance, conditioned six groups of rats in a Skinner box; the groups received food either 0, 10, 20, 40, 80, or 160 times. The conditioned reinforcer, presented after the response, was the click of the food magazine plus the presentation of a dim light. After training, the lever-pressing response was extinguished. For half of the rats, a lever-pressing response during extinction was followed by the click-light stimulus; for the other subjects performance of the lever-pressing response had no effect. As Figure 4-2 shows, all the groups receiving the click-light

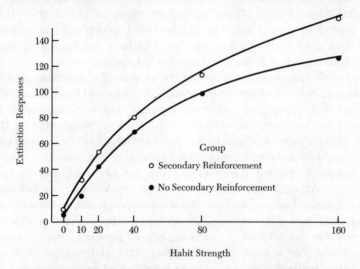

FIGURE 4-2.   Median number of responses in extinction as a function of number of primary reinforcements (habit strength). The secondary-reinforcement groups received the click-light stimulation during extinction; the control groups received no secondary reinforcement. (Adapted from Miles, R. C., "The relative effectiveness of secondary reinforcers throughout deprivation and habit strength parameters," *Journal of Comparative and Physiological Psychology*, 1956, **49**, 126–130. Copyright 1956 by the American Psychological Association, and reproduced by permission.)

combination emitted more responses in extinction than those given the same training but tested without the click and the light.

Magnitude of Primary Reinforcement. The magnitude of primary reward, as a variable affecting the strength of conditioned reinforcement, has been studied by means of two experimental procedures: the *differential method* and the *absolute method*.

The differential method is one in which a subject learns to associate one particular stimulus with a large reward and another stimulus with a small reward. By means of the differential technique, D'Amato (1955) showed that the strength of a conditioned reinforcer is a direct function of the amount of primary reinforcement given during training. In his experiment, rats were trained to run down a straight-alley maze and receive reward in a goal box. When the goal box was white (black for half of the subjects), it was baited with five pellets of food; when it was black (white for half of the subjects), only one pellet of food was given. Following training, the animals were tested in a T-maze with the five-pellet goal box placed on one side and the one-pellet goal box on the other. The animals were given fifteen test trials in the T-maze *without* the food pellets. The results indicated that the mean number of responses to the five-pellet box was significantly greater than chance. In fact, eighteen of the twenty subjects made eight or more responses to the five-pellet box. Thus, "new" responses are acquired more strongly if the conditioned reinforcer is associated with the large reward.

The absolute method is one in which several groups of subjects learn to associate a single stimulus with a different amount of reward. Such a method was employed by Butter and Thomas (1958). In their study, rats learned to associate the click of the reinforcement mechanism with their approach to a dispenser containing sugar water. The concentration of the sucrose solution was 8 per cent for one group and 24 per cent for the other group. Following training, a lever was introduced into the box; all lever-pressing responses were now reinforced by the click alone, which served as a secondary reinforcer. The rats who had received the 24 per cent solution made significantly more lever responses than the 8 per cent group. Again, as with the differential method, the larger the magnitude of the primary reinforcer, the stronger the conditioned reinforcer.

Delay of Primary Reinforcement. Both Jenkins (1950) and Bersh (1951) have demonstrated that the strength of a conditioned reinforcer depends upon the duration of the interval between the presentation of the neutral stimulus and the primary reward; specifically, as the interstimulus interval is increased, the stimulus becomes a weaker conditioned reinforcer. In the study by Bersh, subjects were given a pellet of food 0, .5, 1, 2, 4, or 10 seconds after the onset of a light. After 160 pairings of light and food, a lever was made available in the Skinner box; conditions were now arranged so that a lever response turned the light on for one second, but no food was presented. The mean number of responses emitted during the first ten minutes of this test are shown in Figure 4-3 for each of the interstimulus intervals. The function plotted in this figure closely resembles the one typically found in classical conditioning experiments where the interval between the conditioned and unconditioned stimulus is systematically varied. According to Figure 4-3, conditioning is greatest when the interstimulus interval is approximately .5 seconds and decreases as the interval becomes longer.

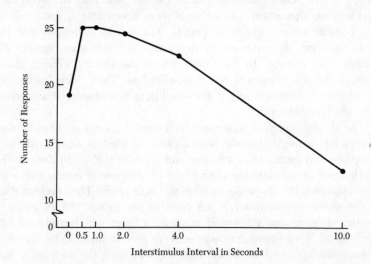

FIGURE 4-3. Strength of secondary reinforcement as a function of interstimulus interval during training. The response measure is the mean number of responses emitted during the first ten minutes of the test session. (Adapted from Bersh, P. J., "The influence of two variables upon the establishment of a secondary reinforcer for operant responses," *Journal of Experimental Psychology*, 1951, 41, 62–73. Copyright 1951 by the American Psychological Association, and reproduced by permission.)

Reinforcement Schedules and Conditioned Reinforcement.   There are two places in the secondary-reinforcement training sequence where an intermittent schedule can be introduced: (1) between the response and the neutral stimulus; (2) between the stimulus and the reward. D'Amato, Lachman, and Kivy (1958) compared the effects of continuous versus intermittent presentations of *primary* reward on the strength of conditioned reinforcement. In this study, rats were given runway training in which one goal box (black or white) provided intermittent reinforcement and the other goal box provided continuous reinforcement. The subjects were then tested in a T-maze with the black and white goal boxes placed at opposite ends of the maze; presentations of food were discontinued. The rats made a significantly greater number of entries into the goal box associated with continuous reinforcement.

In a second experiment, these investigators gave continuous reinforcement to one group of rats and intermittent reinforcement to another. For both groups, a black goal box contained the reinforcement. Following runway training, both groups were tested in a T-maze with the black goal box on one side and a neutral goal box on the other. The groups were given fifteen trials per day on two successive days. The results of the testing phase of this experiment are shown in Figure 4-4. During the first day of testing, both groups showed a preference for the goal box associated with food. On the second day, however, the partial-reinforcement group made a significantly higher percentage of responses to that goal box than the continuous-reinforcement group did. Thus, when separate groups are used during training, it appears that intermittently reinforced stimuli have stronger reinforcing properties than continuously reinforced stimuli. Similar findings have been reported by Armus and Garlich (1961).

What happens when a conditioned reinforcer is intermittently presented during testing? Zimmerman (1957, 1959) conducted experiments concerning this question. In the 1957 study, rats were trained to press a lever to receive water; the delivery of water was always preceded by a two-second presentation of a buzzer. As training progressed, water reinforcements were frequently omitted; thus, the schedule of primary reinforcement was gradually changed from continuous to partial, until the ratio of unreinforced to reinforced trials was 10:1. Following this training procedure, an intermittent schedule was employed for the buzzer. Thus, the subjects were required to make a number of lever-pressing responses before the buzzer would be presented. Zimmerman found such a procedure very effective in maintaining high rates of responding during long sessions of extinction, when the primary reward was discontinued. Apparently, then, when conditioned reinforcers are

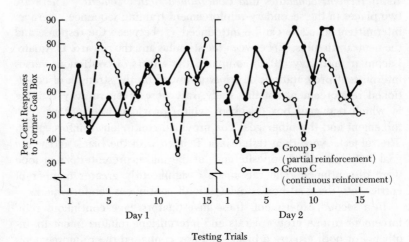

FIGURE 4-4. T-maze performance during extinction, with the former goal box on one side and a neutral goal box on the other. During training, group P was partially reinforced in the goal box; group C was continuously reinforced. (Adapted from D'Amato, M. R., Lachman, R., and Kivy, P., "Secondary reinforcement as affected by reward schedule and the testing situation," *Journal of Comparative and Physiological Psychology*, 1958, **51**, 737-741. Copyright 1958 by the American Psychological Association, and reproduced by permission.)

associated with intermittent schedules, these reinforcers have a powerful influence on behavior.

Drive and Conditioned Reinforcement. Are conditioned reinforcers capable of reducing a drive state—a state established by depriving an organism of a primary reinforcer such as food or water? Several experiments (Simon, Wickens, Brown, & Pennock, 1951; Calvin, Bicknell, & Sperling, 1953; Williams, 1970) have shown that a conditioned reinforcer does not reduce a primary drive. For example, thirsty rats whose lever-pressing responses were associated with secondary reinforcement drank about the same amount of water as rats whose responses were not paired with conditioned reinforcement (Simon et al., 1951).

Other studies have tried to determine the influence of drive on the acquisition of a conditioned reinforcer. In such studies, groups of subjects are deprived of food to varying degrees and are given pairings between a neutral stimulus and the reward; during the test phase, however, the groups are equally deprived, and their responses produce the conditioned reinforcer. Investigators (Brown, 1956; Hall, 1951b) have found that a subject's drive condition at the time of training has very little effect on his responding during subsequent testing.

Finally, how does drive at the time of testing affect secondary reinforcement? To answer this question, investigators have used groups of subjects with the same level of deprivation during training; later, the subjects are tested with the conditioned reinforcer under different levels of deprivation. In one such study (Miles, 1956), rats pressed a lever for food, which was preceded by the presentation of a click-light stimulus. After eighty consecutive reinforced responses, their lever-pressing response was extinguished, half of the subjects with and half without the secondary reinforcer, under 0, 2.5, 5, 10, 20, or 40 hours of food deprivation. Figure 4-5 shows the difference in responding during extinction between the secondary-reinforcement and the control groups as a function of deprivation during testing. The figure indicates that, as the hours of deprivation increased, the secondary-reinforcement groups responded considerably more than the control groups.

Apparently, then, when the drive level at the time of testing is very low, there is very little responding for secondary reinforcement. But

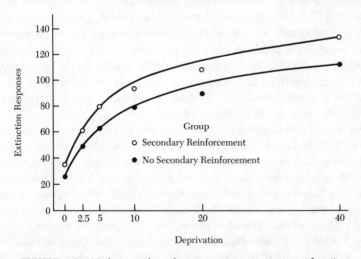

FIGURE 4-5. Median number of responses in extinction as a function of hours of deprivation during the test. The secondary-reinforcement groups received click-light stimulation during extinction; the control groups received no secondary reinforcement. (Adapted from Miles, 1956, by permission.)

does a conditioned reinforcer have any effect at all when the organism is satiated? Two experimental approaches have been used to investigate this problem. The first method has been to test animals when their drives are minimized as much as possible. Testing in a straight-alley maze, Wike and Casey (1954) found that satiated rats ran faster if they were rewarded for entering a goal box containing food, which they did not eat, than for entering an empty goal box. Apparently, the sight and smell of the food was sufficiently reinforcing to maintain the running behavior.

The second approach to this problem has been to train subjects under one drive condition (for instance, thirst) and then test them when they are satiated but experiencing some other drive condition (hunger). Estes (1949), in an experiment of this type, reinforced three groups of thirsty rats with water after lever pressing. For two groups, the sound of a tone was associated with the presentations of water; the third group, a control group, was given lever-pressing training with no secondary reinforcement. In a subsequent test session, the rats were satiated with water but were deprived of food (one experimental group for six hours; the other experimental group and the control group for twenty-three hours). All three groups received the tone after pressing the lever during testing. The hungrier experimental group made more responses than either the six-hour experimental group or the control group—suggesting that a conditioned reinforcer can influence behavior even when the drive involved is different from the one used during training. A study by Grice and Davis (1957), however, casts doubt on the assumption that hunger and thirst are independent drives. According to these investigators, a subject deprived of water is probably also hungry, since he will decrease his food consumption.

As several investigators (Reid & Sliviniski, 1954; Wike & McNamara, 1955; Wike & Barrientos, 1958; Wunderlich, 1961) have demonstrated, a stimulus that is associated with a number of different drives and rewards is a stronger conditioned reinforcer than a stimulus associated with only one reinforcer and drive. Skinner (1953), who was also aware of this phenomenon, termed such stimuli *generalized conditioned reinforcers*. A good example of a generalized reinforcer is money, which is associated with the reduction of many types of drives. For example, money may be used to obtain a hamburger when one is hungry or to buy a ticket to a movie when one is bored.

Stimulus Generalization of Conditioned Reinforcement. Stimulus generalization is usually defined as the tendency for an organism to respond *to* discriminative stimuli that are similar but not identical to the one used during training. With regard to secondary reinforcement, stimulus generalization occurs when organisms increase their responses *in order to produce* stimuli that are similar but not identical to the stimulus previously established as a conditioned reinforcer.

Several studies (Denny, 1948; Ehrenfreund, 1954; Saltzman, 1950) have shown that stimulus generalization occurs with secondary reinforcers presented in the maze situation. More recently, Williams (1963) and Thomas and Williams (1963a) have determined the precise slope of the generalization gradient of conditioned reinforcement in the operant setting. In this experiment, forty pigeons were trained to peck at a disc or key in a Skinner box to receive a two-second exposure to a 550-mμ (greenish-yellow) light, which was immediately followed by the presentation of food. The birds were *not* required to peck at the key, when it was illuminated, to receive the food reinforcement. Eventually, the birds were reinforced according to a variable-interval (VI 30 sec) schedule, with the 550-mμ stimulus followed by food. After training, the subjects were tested for resistance to extinction with two-second exposures of light at wavelengths of either 550 mμ (yellow-green), 530 mμ (green-yellow), 510 mμ (green), or no light on the key. During the test, no food reinforcement was given, but the stimulus exposures were presented according to the same VI schedule used in training. The testing was continued until each bird ceased responding for a period of five consecutive minutes.

Even though the subjects were not required to respond to the conditioned reinforcing stimulus to receive reward, all birds developed superstitious responding to the stimulus during its presentation. These responses, as opposed to those given to the unlighted key, are not indicative of the reinforcing function but rather the discriminative function of the stimulus. (When reinforced responses are made *in the presence* of a stimulus, it is considered to be a discriminative stimulus; when responses are made *in order to produce* a stimulus, it is termed a reinforcing stimulus.)

Figure 4-6 presents the mean number of responses made to the unlighted key (between stimulus exposures) and the minutes to extinction for each of the four test conditions. Stimulus-generalization gradients were observed with both of these response measures. That is, the more similar the stimulus values were to the 550-mμ value of the conditioned reinforcer, the more responses were made and the longer was the time to reach the extinction criterion.

The superstitious responses to the colored stimuli were also recorded

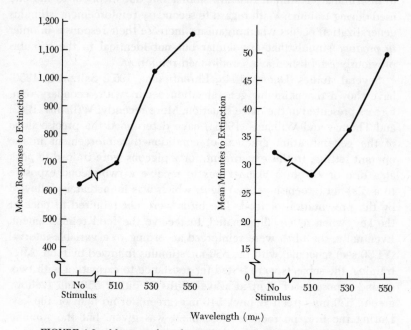

Wavelength (mμ)

FIGURE 4-6.   Mean number of responses made to the unlighted key and
the mean number of minutes to extinction for each of four test conditions.
The 550-mμ value was paired with food reinforcement during training.
The gradients indicate the generalization of the reinforcing function of
the training stimulus, 550μ. (Adpated from Thomas, D. R., and Williams,
J. L., "Stimulus generalization of a positive conditioned reinforcer,"
Science, 1963, **142**, 172–173. Copyright 1963 by the American Association
for the Advancement of Science. Reprinted by permission.)

to determine the generalization gradient of the *discriminative-stimulus
function* (that is, the degree to which a response occurs during the
presence of a specific stimulus value as compared to the absence of
that value). Because the time to extinction varied for the four groups
of subjects, they did not receive an equal number of presentations of
the test values. Therefore, the response data were converted into the
mean number of responses per minute during each stimulus exposure.
These results are shown in Figure 4-7. The gradient here is steeper
than the gradient of conditioned reinforcement (shown in Figure 4-6).
A possible difference between these two stimulus functions may be
in the specificity with which their physical characteristics exert control
over behavior. The most obvious reason for reduced stimulus control

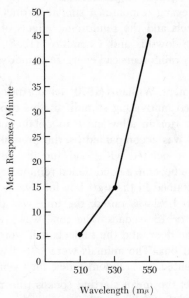

FIGURE 4-7.   Mean number of responses per minute during each of the stimulus exposures. The gradients indicate the generalization of the discriminative function of the training stimulus, 550mμ. (Adpated from Thomas and Williams, 1963, by permission.)

in conditioned reinforcement is that the subject's responses are made to the "memory" of the stimulus rather than to the actual stimulus.

THEORETICAL INTERPRETATIONS OF CONDITIONED REINFORCEMENT

What exactly are the processes underlying conditioned reinforcement? And under what specific conditions does a neutral stimulus become a secondary reinforcer? Various hypotheses or explanations of these questions have been proposed.

Elicitation Hypothesis.   In the previously described study by Bugelski (1938), rats extinguished with a magazine click produced about 30 per cent more lever responses than a control group extinguished without the click. Apparently, the click had acquired reinforcing properties. Later, however, Bugelski (1956) rejected this explanation. The conditioned-reinforcement group, he now claimed, made more responses *not* because the click strengthened a previous response but because it elicited the next lever-pressing response. A similar distinction between the eliciting or cue effects and the reinforcing effects of a stimulus was made by Wycoff, Sidowski, and Chambliss (1958), who also suggested that secondary reinforcers can energize or motivate instrumental behavior.

In a recent experiment, Williams (1970) demonstrated that secondary reinforcers are indeed motivating stimuli. In this experiment, sixteen rats were trained to run an alley maze to obtain sucrose as a reinforcement; the food was accompanied by the presentation of a tone. Since the tone was associated with food and the consummatory response, it should have become a conditioned reinforcer. During testing, the animals were detained in the start box for twenty seconds; before the door of the start box was raised, the tone was presented for an interval of 0, .5, 5, or 15 seconds. The tone was always terminated by the opening of the door, and the subjects still were given the tone and food in the goal box. The animals were tested with each of the tone durations, presented in a random order, for twenty-four trials.

Figure 4-8 depicts the mean starting speeds (the time it took the subjects to leave the start box) for the various tone conditions over blocks of twelve trials. As can be observed, the animals started faster when a tone was presented than when there was no tone. The tone, then, which had been established as a secondary reinforcer, did energize or motivate the animals' behavior. Furthermore, the longer the subjects were exposed to the tone in the start box, the faster their starting speeds. This activating effect occurred during the initial test trials and did not decrease significantly with repeated testing.

Figure 4-8 also illustrates the mean running speed for the various tone conditions over the two blocks of twelve test trials. An abrupt increase in running speed is observed between the no-tone and the tone conditions. The various tone durations, however, appear not to have had any differential effect on the running response. Possibly the starting response was more sensitive to motivational effects because it was made sooner after the tone.

According to Williams (1970), *frustration* perhaps provides the best explanation for the motivating effect of conditioned reinforcers. The subjects in his experiment, when they were detained in the start box, were being blocked from making the response; furthermore, they were being exposed to the stimulus previously associated with reward. Thus, the operational definitions of secondary reinforcement and frustration are virtually identical.

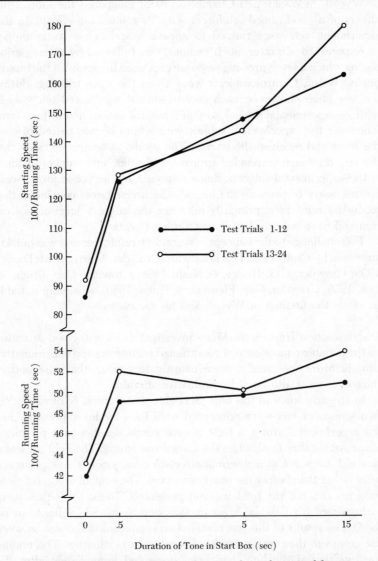

FIGURE 4-8.   Mean starting and running speeds as a function of duration of tone presented in the start box over two blocks of twelve test trials each. (Adpated from Williams, J. L., "Effects of the duration of a secondary reinforcer on subsequent instrumental responses," *Journal of Experimental Psychology*, 1970, 483, 348–351. Copyright 1970 by the American Psychological Association, and reproduced by permission.)

Wycoff, Sidowski, and Chambliss (1958) compared the motivating effects of a conditioned reinforcer with its reinforcing effects. In this experiment, rats were trained to approach and lick a water dipper in response to a buzzer. Such training was followed by a test period during which a lever-pressing response produced the sound of the buzzer but no water. Control subjects were given the same training; during the test phase, however, each control animal was paired or "yoked" with an experimental subject, so that a control subject heard the buzzer whenever the experimental subject with whom he was paired pressed the lever and received the buzzer. The results of testing revealed that the yoked subjects responded approximately the same number of times as the experimental subjects. Since responses by the yoked group were not necessary to produce the buzzer, the investigators concluded that secondary reinforcers primarily influence the subjects' level of motivation and have only negligible reinforcing effects.

This challenge to the concept of secondary reinforcement was quickly answered by Crowder and his associates (Crowder, Morris, & McDaniel, 1959; Crowder, Gill, Hodge, & Nash, 1959; Crowder, Gay, Bright, & Lee, 1959; Crowder, Gay, Fleming, & Hurst, 1959), who were not able to verify the findings of Wycoff and his associates.

Discrimination Hypothesis. Many investigators have focused attention on the possible equivalence of conditioned reinforcers and discriminative stimuli. More specifically, these investigators claim that a secondary reinforcer must also be a discriminative stimulus.

In an early study in this area (Schoenfeld, Antonitis, & Bersh, 1950), two groups of rats were reinforced with food for lever pressing. For the experimental group, a light of one-second duration was presented immediately after food, while the animal was eating. The light presentation did not serve as a discriminative stimulus, since it was presented *after* rather than before the onset of reward. The control group received food reward, but the light was not presented. The animals then were extinguished (that is, the lever presses were followed by light but no food). The results of this test revealed no significant difference between the groups in their total number of responses to extinction. This finding suggests that if the light had been presented immediately after the response but before the reward, it would have become *both* a discriminative stimulus for the response of approaching the food cup and a conditioned reinforcer for lever responding. Thus, the investigators concluded that the light failed to be a conditioned reinforcer because it had not been established as a discriminative stimulus.

Corroboration of this conclusion is found in a study by Marx and Knarr (1963). In this experiment, the possible reinforcing function of a light was established over a long period of training, given according to three conditions: (1) light stimulation regularly preceding every presentation of food in a dark cage; (2) light and food presented simultaneously; (3) an independent relationship, with a minimal temporal association between light and food. Subsequent testing was conducted in extinction, with lever presses producing the light only. The group for which the light preceded food responded more than the other two groups, especially on the initial test session. This result seems to indicate that there is some similarity between the discriminative and the reinforcing functions of stimuli.

A number of other investigators (Dinsmoor, 1950; Webb & Nolan, 1953; McGuigan & Crockett, 1958; Myers & Myers, 1962) support the position that some type of discrimination training is necessary before a neutral stimulus can become a secondary reinforcer.

Several experiments have cast some doubt on the discriminative-stimulus hypothesis. In a study by Ratner (1956), a click immediately preceded the delivery of water to thirsty rats throughout magazine training. During testing, all responses by the experimental subjects produced a click, while the responses of control subjects had no effect. Both lever presses and approaches to the dipper were recorded during the test session. A conditioned-reinforcing effect was demonstrated by the fact that the experimental subjects showed more lever pressing in extinction than the control subjects, but the two groups did not differ in number of approaches to the water dipper. The latter response was assumed by Ratner to reflect the discriminative function of the click. These results suggest that the conditioned-reinforcing function of a stimulus is independent of the discriminative function of the stimulus.

An experiment employing the new-learning method was reported by Stein (1958). This study is unique in that electrical stimulation of the midbrains of rats was used as the primary reinforcement. Brain stimulation was selected as a reinforcer because it requires no approach or consummatory response. Because this experiment has important implications for the discrimination hypothesis, its procedure will be described in detail.

In the first phase of the study, eighteen rats were given a series of six one-hour sessions in a Skinner box with two separate response levers. Responses to one of the levers produced a one-second tone; responses to the other lever had no effect. The responses that each animal made to the separate levers were recorded in order to determine which lever the animals preferred. In the second phase, the rats were presented with the tone followed by five seconds of positive brain stimulation. During this phase, one hundred trials per day for four consecutive days, the levers in the Skinner boxes were removed. The tone should have acquired reinforcing properties because of its close association to the brain stimulation; since the tone did not "set the occasion for a response" (Skinner, 1938), it is *not* considered a discriminative stimulus. In the third phase, the levers were reintroduced into the chamber. During this phase, one-hour sessions each day for three days, responses on one lever produced the tone, but responses on the other lever did not. In order to determine the reinforcing power of the tone, the investigators recorded the mean number of responses to each of the levers. In the final phase of the experiment, one lever was removed; responses on the remaining lever produced brain stimulation with no tones. Responding in this phase indicated whether the brain stimulation was indeed a positive reinforcer or a neutral stimulus, depending upon how accurately the electrodes had been inserted in the hypothalamic area of the brain.

The results are shown in Figure 4-9 for the thirteen subjects for whom the brain stimulation was positively reinforcing and for the five subjects for whom it was a neutral stimulus. The thirteen subjects made about equal responses to each of the levers during the first phase of the study, before the pairings of tone and brain stimulation were given. During the third phase (after pairings), however, the subjects showed a significant preference for the lever to which a response resulted in the tone. In contrast, no such preference was shown by the animals for whom the brain stimulation was apparently a neutral stimulus.

As mentioned, the important theoretical implication of this study is that the primary reinforcement (brain stimulation) in the second phase did not require any specific consummatory response in order to be experienced; therefore, the tone was not technically a discriminative stimulus. This result suggests that conditioned reinforcers can be acquired without necessarily being discriminative stimuli and thus contradicts the discrimination hypothesis of conditioned reinforcement.

Egger and Miller (1962, 1963) extended the discriminative-stimulus hypothesis by claiming that a stimulus can function as a conditioned reinforcer only if it provides "information" about the occurrence of primary reinforcement. In contrast, if a stimulus is redundant (that is, if it provides the organism with no additional information about the presentation of reward), it will not become an effective conditioned reinforcer.

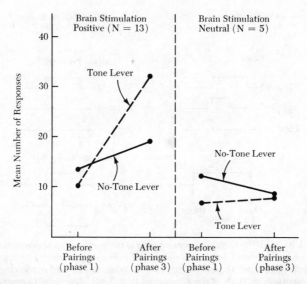

FIGURE 4-9.   Mean number of responses on the two levers during the experimental sessions before and after the pairing of tone with positive brain stimulation. (Adapted from Stein, L., "Secondary reinforcement established with subcortical stimulation," *Science*, 1958, **127**, 466–467. Reprinted by permission of the American Association for the Advancement of Science.)

In the 1962 study, albino rats were trained to press a lever for food. The rats were then divided randomly into two groups and given 135 trials in the same Skinner boxes with the levers removed. During this phase of the experiment, two stimuli (S_1, light; and S_2, tone) were presented; these stimuli ended at the same time and always preceded the presentation of food. For one condition of training (Condition A), the shorter stimulus (S_2) was always redundant because the longer stimulus (S_1) had already provided reliable information about the presentation of food (see Figure 4-10). S_2 should therefore acquire very little reinforcing power, even though it is a discriminative stimulus and its onset is closer than S_1 to the time of the delivery of reward. For a second condition (Condition B), S_2 was made informative because S_1 sometimes was presented alone and not followed by food (B_1), and sometimes was accompanied by S_2 and food (B_2). It was predicted that S_2 would be the only reliable predictor and therefore a more effective secondary reinforcer than S_1 for Condition B.

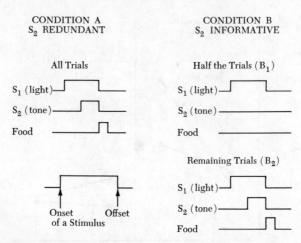

FIGURE 4-10.   Schematic representation of the presentation of two stimuli, along with reward, for the redundant and informative conditions. (Adapted from Egger, M. D., and Miller, N. E., "When is a reward reinforcing?
An experimental study of the information hypothesis," *Journal of Comparative Physiological Psychology*, 1963, **56**, 132–137. Copyright 1963 by the
American Psychological Association, and reproduced by permission.)

Following training, all the subjects were tested in the boxes with
the lever reinserted and with every third response (FR 3) reinforced
with food. Once their response rates stabilized, the lever was disconnected and ten minutes of extinction given. At the end of the extinction
period, the lever was again operative, but it delivered a brief presentation of light or tone on the same FR 3 schedule. This relearning phase,
following experimental extinction, was used to measure the second-
ary-reinforcing strength of the two stimuli. The subjects were tested
in two consecutive sessions, with one of the two stimuli occurring after
every third response. Half of the subjects were tested with S_1 and
then S_2, and the remaining subjects were tested with S_2 and then S_1.
Throughout the course of the ten-minute extinction phase and the subsequent "pressing-for-stimuli" sessions, the cumulative number of responses for each subject was recorded.

Table 4-1 shows the mean number of responses made during the
extinction and the pressing-for-stimuli sessions. There were no significant
differences in total responses made during the ten minutes of extinction
preceding the test. Thus, the response strength, independent of second-

TABLE 4-1

Mean Responses during Extinction and "Pressing for Stimuli"

Condition	Ext.	S_1 Pressing	Ext.	S_2 Pressing	$S_1 + S_2$
A	110.8	115.1	101.9	65.8	90.5
B	112.1	76.1	112.0	82.6	79.4
		95.6		74.2	

(Adapted from Egger and Miller, 1963. Reprinted by permission.)

ary reinforcement, was comparable for all the subjects. The subjects trained under Condition B, for whom S_2 was informative, pressed more for S_2 than the subjects trained under Condition A, for whom S_2 was redundant (82.6 vs. 65.8). Furthermore, Condition-A subjects responded more for S_1, which was both a reliable and an informative predictor of reinforcement, than did condition-B subjects, for whom S_1 was unreliable (115.1 vs. 76.1). Finally, S_1 was a much more effective conditioned reinforcer than S_2 for Condition-A subjects (115.1 vs. 65.8).

The research of Egger and Miller clearly suggests that conditioned reinforcement can best be explained as the processes whereby an organism is informed of the arrival of primary reinforcement. This interpretation also accounts for much of the effectiveness of primary reinforcement in the acquisition of a new response. More specifically, the drive-reducing function of most rewards is usually preceded by the presentation of certain stimuli related to the reward (for instance, the smell and taste of food and water). Based on past experience, these conditioned reinforcers (or discriminative stimuli) in some sense inform the organism that his condition of hunger or thirst will be alleviated. Probably the only type of reward that would not have conditioned reinforcers normally associated with it is electrical brain stimulation. Although brain stimulation produces very high rates of responding, it is not very effective in maintaining behavior during intermittent-reinforcement schedules and extinction, where the role of secondary reinforcement is important.

The information hypothesis has also been proposed by several psychologists (Bilodeau, 1966; Fitts & Posner, 1967) who have been mainly concerned with human learning. These investigators claim that "knowledge of results" or "response feedback" is reinforcing for an individual in that it provides him with information about whether or not the appropriate response was performed. Thus, saying "That's right" to a person after he has made the correct response appears to be functionally similar to presenting an animal with a secondary reinforcer following an instrumental response.

CHAINING BEHAVIOR

Psychologists have long been interested in studying the development and the maintenance of ordered sequences of responses. Numerous examples of such sequences are found in human behavior. Relatively simple motor skills, such as throwing a ball, tying one's shoe, or making a bed, are often performed automatically and require very little thought or concentration. On the other hand, considerable practice and attention are required for more advanced skills, such as typing or playing the violin. The area of study concerned with the processes underlying the learning of such response sequences is termed *chaining*, and the response sequences themselves are called *chains*.

Psychologists have categorized chained behavior as either heterogeneous or homogeneous. In a heterogeneous chain, several different types of responses must be made in a prescribed order before reinforcement is given. For example, a rat learns to press a lever in a Skinner box, approach the food tray, and finally ingest the food; or a man starts a car by turning on the ignition key, pressing the accelerator, and operating the gear shift. In a homogeneous chain, the same response is repeated for a given number of times. For example, an animal under a fixed-ratio or a variable-ratio schedule presses a lever a certain number of times before reinforcement is given; or a man makes the same response repeatedly when he is hammering a nail, raking leaves, or walking across campus.

HETEROGENEOUS CHAINS

In order to establish a heterogeneous chain of responses, an experimenter begins with the last member of the chain and works backward. For example, when a pigeon is being trained to peck at a small button or key in a Skinner box, he must first be magazine trained (that is, trained to approach the food dispenser every time the food is presented by the experimenter). Once this approach behavior occurs consistently, it is assumed that the clicking sound of the magazine has become a discriminative stimulus for approaching the food hopper. The bird is then shaped, by the method of successive approximations, to orient toward the illuminated key and eventually to peck at it. The sight of the illuminated key then becomes a discriminative stimulus for the pecking response, which in turn produces the sound of the food dispenser, which leads to an approach response, and so forth. Notice that the sound of the dispenser mechanism serves two functions in this chain: it is a discriminative stimulus for approaching the hopper; it is also a conditioned reinforcer for the key-pecking response. Thus, the sound of the dispenser is important in that it bridges the gap or interval in time between the pecking response and the presentation of food.

In order to establish a longer chain of the heterogeneous responses, the experimenter would continue in the same way, adding links in front of those previously established. For example, after the animal has completely turned around in the cage, the experimenter might illuminate the key. The turning response would therefore be reinforced by the onset of the light on the key. In this way, one could continue to add new members in a backward order until the length of the chain becomes so long that the reinforcing power of the maintaining stimuli is ineffective.

A popular demonstration of a complex heterogeneous chain was reported by Pierrel and Sherman (1963). These investigators used a stimulus for each link in the chain to establish the following sequence of responses: The rat first responded to a light by climbing a wire-mesh staircase. After he reached a platform, he pushed down a drawbridge and crossed it to another platform. He then climbed a tall ladder. Next, he pulled a string connected to a small cart or trunk, climbed inside it, and moved it along a track by treading a paddlewheel with his forepaws. At the end of this ride, he climbed up a flight of stairs and squeezed through a tunnel, which led to a small elevator. For the grand finale, the rat raised the Columbia University flag and lowered himself to the ground level again, where he pressed a lever to obtain food.

HOMOGENEOUS CHAINS

When a schedule involves repeating the *same* response in order to receive reinforcement, it is called a *homogeneous* chained schedule. In this schedule, the rate of responding is often examined at different points during a series of stimulus presentations. For example, when a pigeon responds to a blue light, one of his responses will change the color of the light from blue to yellow; then one of his responses will change the yellow to red; finally, one of his responses to the red stimulus will produce food as a reinforcer.

Typically, each of the successive stimuli in a chained schedule is associated with a different reinforcement schedule. That is, a fixed-interval schedule may be in effect when the pigeon is responding to blue, a variable-ratio schedule when he is responding to yellow, and so forth. If a fixed-interval schedule is in effect during a certain color, a pigeon's cumulative record will show the usual scalloped pattern—indicating temporal discrimination during that particular stimulus. If a given color is associated with a variable-interval schedule, the pigeon will respond at a steady rate. If a variable or fixed number of responses is required, he will respond at a rapid rate until the response requirement for a stimulus change is met. These findings illustrate that the stimuli comprising a chain are both discriminative stimuli (because the subject's performance differs according to the particular stimulus that is present) and reinforcing stimuli (since they produce the appropriate response patterns without primary reward, except for the last link in the chain).

Using a chained schedule, Gollub (1958) showed that an interesting change in performance occurs if two stimuli (colors) are associated with exactly the same reinforcement schedule (fixed-interval schedule). Initially (because the second stimulus was the discriminative stimulus associated with the primary reward), the rate of responding was faster during the presence of the second stimulus than during the first stimulus. With further training, the response rate during the first stimulus gradually increased—although it never equaled the rate observed during the second stimulus. This finding illustrates that effectiveness of a particular stimulus in a chain depends on its proximity to the primary reinforcer and the amount of experience the subject has had with the chained schedule.

Another type of homogeneous chaining involves the repetition of the same response to obtain reinforcement; in this case, however, responses do not produce changes in discriminative stimuli. In the laboratory, chains of this type are studied by means of either a variable-ratio schedule or a fixed-ratio schedule. The general procedure used to establish ratio schedules is similar to that employed in other types of chains. For example, when an animal is trained on an FR 25 schedule, he is first given reinforcement according to a continuous schedule; then he is given successive sessions of FR 2, FR 4, FR 6, FR 10, FR 15, FR 20, and finally FR 25. Thus, additional response members gradually are added to the chain, so that the animal must increase his responses throughout the course of training. If too many responses are required for reinforcement, the subject will express *response strain* by making long pauses in responding or possibly by ceasing to respond altogether.

After a subject has received considerable training on a fixed-ratio schedule, his performance becomes stereotyped (that is, he adopts a consistent pattern of responding). If the ratio is low, the response rate is high and fairly steady, except for intervals when the subject is consuming the reinforcement. If the ratio is high, the response rate remains high until reinforcement is given; then a postreinforcement pause is usually observed. Figure 4-11 shows the cumulative records of two pigeons trained under two different fixed-ratio schedules, FR 50 and FR 200. In contrast to the FR 50 subject, the FR 200 subject shows numerous postreinforcement pauses—possibly because it is easier for a subject under a higher ratio schedule to learn that the responses made following reward are never reinforced.

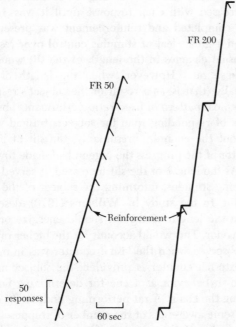

FIGURE 4-11.   Performance generated by two different fixed-ratio schedules. Note that the postreinforcement pause is observed for FR 200, but not for FR 50.

The role of the various stimuli in a homogeneous chain is not as obvious as it is in a heterogeneous chain. Each response in an FR schedule brings the number of responses one step closer to that required for the presentation of reward. Outside the laboratory setting, each response usually produces a change in the stimulus situation, which informs the subject of the approximate number of responses still to be performed. For instance, a trailer of furniture becomes emptier as each item is carried into the house, or the height of a stack of term papers on a professor's desk decreases as he spends time grading them. In the Skinner box, an animal under a fixed-ratio schedule typically does not receive this type of information. In order to inform an animal of how far he has progressed in a homogeneous chain, an external counter of some sort can be presented in the operant chamber.

Ferster and Skinner (1957) were the first investigators to study effects of an external counter on an animal's behavior. They projected a slit of light on a darkened key in a Skinner box for pigeons. When the bird started the ratio, the slit was only 1/16 inch long; the length of the slit increased with each response until it was 3/8 inch when the ratio was completed and reinforcement was presented. This slit of light exerted a great deal of stimulus control over responding. Any sudden or unusual changes in the length of the slit would change the pigeon's response rate. However, when the length of the slit was changed normally (that is, as a result of the subject's responses), it did not alter the typical pattern of fixed-ratio performance, but it did result in higher rates of responding than for subjects trained with the same schedule without the counter. Presumably, the slit of light served as a visual indicator of the progress the pigeon had made toward completing the ratio. As the length of the slit increased, it served as a discriminative-reinforcing stimulus, informing the subject of the arrival of reward. According to the study by Williams (1970), described earlier, the increase in the length of the slit should energize or motivate instrumental behavior. This would account for the higher rate of responding that was observed when the visual counter was in operation.

When no external counter is provided, the subject must use some aspect of his own behavior as a cue for determining how far he has progressed along the chain. A rat performing under a fixed-ratio schedule must have some awareness of the number of responses still required for reward and also of the number of responses already performed. Mechner (1958) has shown that a rat can "count," or in some way discriminate fairly accurately the number of responses he has emitted. The rats in this study were tested in a two-lever Skinner box. In order to obtain reinforcement, the animal was required to complete a particular ratio schedule on one lever and then to make a single response on the other lever. There was no external counter for these subjects. If the rat made fewer responses than required for the ratio, he was penalized by having to begin the fixed-ratio performance all over again. No such penalty was in effect when the subject made more responses than required for the ratio.

Figure 4-12 shows frequency distributions of the number of lever-pressing responses of one subject under an FR 4, FR 8, FR 12, and FR 16 schedule. In each case, the peak of the distribution is located near the required number, although the subject tended to overrespond when tested with the FR 12 and the FR 16 ratios. The findings suggest that the rat was somehow able to judge when he had made a sufficient number of responses on the first lever. Similar results were obtained by Rilling (1967), with pigeons as subjects.

Experimental findings indicate that the individual units comprising the homogeneous chain are virtually indestructible. For example, once

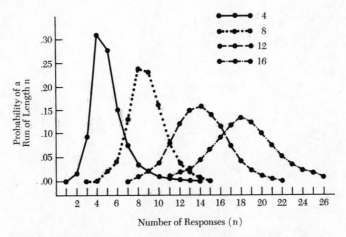

FIGURE 4-12. Probability distributions of response runs as a function of the number of responses subject has already emitted. The different distributions represent the number of responses required for the presentation of reward (FR 4, FR 8, FR 12, and FR 16). (Adapted from Mechner, Francis. Probability relations within response sequences under ratio reinforcement. *Journal of the Experimental Analysis of Behavior*, 1958, 1, 109–121. Copyright 1958 by the Society for the Experimental Analysis of Behavior, Inc. Reprinted by permission.)

the subject resumes responding after being reinforced on a fixed-ratio schedule, he will almost always continue to respond at a high rate until a ratio run is completed. If he does perform some other response, it is usually done during the postreinforcement pauses rather than during the ratio run. Once the initial response has been made, satiation (Sidman & Stebbins, 1954) and punishment (Azrin, 1959) may increase the length of the postreinforcement pauses but have virtually no disruptive effect on responding. Finally, the ratio runs are unchanged even during periods when the reinforcement is withheld (Ferster and Skinner, 1957).

V

STIMULUS CONTROL: GENERALIZATION AND DISCRIMINATION

The presentation of reinforcement following operant response has two major effects: (1) it increases the probability of recurrence of the response, and (2) it influences the extent to which stimuli at the same time of reinforcement exercise control over behavior. A stimulus is assumed to control behavior if the conditioned response occurs more often during its presence than during its absence.. Thus, if a dog frequently sits when his master says "Heel," this response is considered to be under the control of a specific verbal stimulus. Since, however, the controlling stimulus does not *always* result in the conditioned response, the stimulus is assumed merely to "set the occasion" during which the operant response was previously reinforced. Let us now examine some of the operant methods used in studies of stimulus control.

STIMULUS GENERALIZATION AND
STIMULUS CONTROL

When a response is reinforced in the presence of one stimulus, a subject tends to respond not only to that stimulus but also to similar stimuli; that is, the subject tends to generalize among stimuli. A baby, for instance, says "Dada" to any man who approaches him, even though his father was the only one who reinforced this response.

In most instances, the probability that the response will occur is greatest in the presence of the original conditioned stimulus (CS) and decreases with stimulus values of increasing remoteness from this CS. The function relating the obtained response probabilities to their respective stimulus values is called a *generalization gradient*. The slope of a generalization gradient is assumed to reflect the controlling power of the conditioned stimulus along a particular dimension. A generalization gradient with a slope of zero indicates 100 per cent generalization and no stimulus control. As the slope of the generalization gradient increases, or becomes steeper, the degree of stimulus control is considered to increase.

Investigators have demonstrated stimulus generalization by training groups of subjects with the same CS and testing them separately with different test values. Guttman and Kalish (1956), however, developed a method for obtaining reliable gradients from individual subjects during a single test session. They trained six pigeons in a Skinner box to peck at a translucent disc, which was illuminated from outside the box with a monochromatic (nearly pure) source of 550 mμ (a wavelength that appears yellow-green to humans). After the pecking to the discriminative stimulus had been well established under the continuous-reinforcement schedule, a VI 1 schedule was used. By the end of ten days of training (in half-hour daily sessions) a steady rate of pecking behavior was generated. Thus, the investigators could test each subject for generalization in a subsequent extinction session by presenting, in a random sequence, many short exposures to a wide range of wavelength values. Specifically, eleven test stimuli (490, 510, 520, 530, 540, 550, 560, 570, 580, 590, and 610 mμ) were given during generalization testing. Note that one of the stimulus values in the series was the original training stimulus, whereas the remaining values were new.

Figure 5-1 shows the percentages of the total number of responses made by the six birds (550-mμ group) in each of the test values. The largest number of responses occurred during the presentation of the

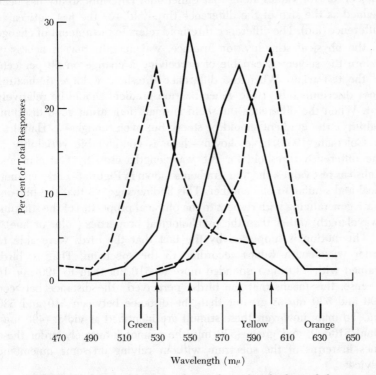

FIGURE 5-1. Generalization gradients of wavelength obtained during extinction from four groups of pigeons trained to respond to stimuli of different wavelengths. (Adapted from Guttman, N., and Kalish, H. I., "Discriminability and stimulus generalization," *Journal of Experimental Psychology*, 1956, **51**, 79–88. Copyright 1956 by the American Psychological Association, and reproduced by permission.)

conditioned stimulus (550 mμ); progressively fewer responses were emitted to stimuli of decreasing similarity. This figure also shows the generalization gradients obtained from three other groups of birds—previously trained with 530, 580, and 600 mμ as the training stimulus. In each group, the generalization gradients show peak responding to the conditioned stimulus, and all the gradients are bidirectional and relatively symmetrical.

One of the major objectives of the Guttman-Kalish study was to determine whether there is an inverse relationship between the slope of generalization gradient and the degree of *discriminability* that a subject has for values along that dimension. Discriminability has been defined as the size of the difference threshold—or the just noticeable difference (jnd). The difference threshold refers to the amount of change in the physical stimulus (for instance, wavelength) that is necessary before the subject is capable of perceiving a change on 50 per cent of the test trials. When the difference threshold is large (indicating poor discriminability), the generalization gradient should be relatively flat. When the difference threshold is small (indicating good discriminability), the gradient should be steep. But even though—as Hamilton & Coleman (1933) have shown—there is considerable variability in the difference threshold for the wavelengths used by Guttman and Kalish as test values, the four gradients shown in Figure 5-1 are symmetrical and similar to one another. This finding suggests that the pigeons were generalizing with respect to the physical properties of the stimulus (wavelength) rather than the psychological properties (color or hue).

This notion is supported by the fact that the birds were able to order wavelength values according to the spectrum. That is, birds trained with 530 mμ responded more to 510 mμ than to 490 mμ. In a sense, this means that the birds "perceived" the distance between 490 and 530 mμ as greater than the distance between 510 and 530 mμ. To man, however, these stimuli are identified as violet (490 mμ), blue (510mμ), and green (530 mμ); he cannot intuitively order these hues in terms of the spectrum without relying on some mnemonic device.

Although the Guttman-Kalish results suggest that discriminability and generalization are not related; another study (Kalish, 1958) indicates that they are. In this experiment, college students rather than pigeons were used as subjects. The procedure consisted of presenting a standard stimulus and instructing the subject to try to remember it. Values of 500, 530, 560, and 580 mμ served as standard stimuli for different groups. During testing, each subject was shown a random sequence of various wavelengths and was told to lift his hand from a telegraph key only when he considered the test stimulus to be the same as the standard. In this study, the presentation of the standard was functionally equivalent to the training conditions that the pigeons received in the Guttman-Kalish experiment. Likewise, the response that the human subjects were supposed to make when they recognized the stimulus was equivalent to the high rate of responding that the pigeons emitted during testing. The resulting generalization gradients were predictable from the discriminability functions that had been obtained from other subjects. This evidence supports the hypothesis that the processes of generalization and discrimination, as they are generally defined, bear an inverse relationship to each other.

Thomas and Mitchell (1962) virtually replicated Kalish's study and found similar results; and Ganz (1962) has reported that, with monkeys as subjects, the obtained generalization gradients for wavelengths are clearly related to the wavelength-discriminability function. These findings suggest that pigeons are unique in responding solely to some physical property (such as frequency) of the stimulus and that for them generalization and discrimination are separate or independent processes. This conclusion, however, has been challenged by Shepard (1965), who showed that the wavelength-discriminability function could be derived from the generalization gradients found by Guttman and Kalish. On the basis of Shepard's reanalysis of the data, it now appears that generalization and discrimination have a common origin and in a sense can be considered as complementary processes.

DISCRIMINABILITY AND STIMULUS CONTROL

Since stimulus control can be measured by means of generalization, techniques for determining discriminability should also be valid is assessing stimulus control. Numerous psychological techniques have been developed for obtaining discriminability data.

By the use of operant techniques, Blough (1956) developed an ingenious method for studying psychophysical problems in animals. His method involved two critical features. First, he trained pigeons to learn a discrimination problem. The birds were confronted with two response keys (A and B) and a white stimulus patch (see Figure 5-2). According to a random schedule, pecking responses made to key A closed a shutter and blocked out the stimulus patch; responses to key B when the patch was dark were reinforced with food. Stated another way, the pigeon pecked key A to turn off the white light and then pecked key B to get reward. Although only a limited number of responses were reinforced, all birds gradually learned the discrimination task of pecking key A when the white patch of light was visible and pecking key B when it was not.

The second critical feature of this experimental procedure was that the bird's responses on each of the keys also controlled the intensity of the light projected on the stimulus patch. Before each session, a pigeon was kept in darkness for one hour; then his head was inserted

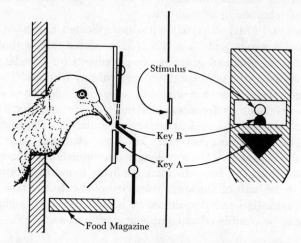

FIGURE 5-2. Response chamber of the adaptation box. *Left:* side view, showing pigeon, food magazine, response keys, and stimulus patch. *Right:* front view, showing keys and stimulus patch as seen by the pigeon. (From Blough, D. S., "Spectral sensitivity in the pigeon," *Journal of the Optical Society of America*, 1957, **47**, 827–833, with permission of the American Institute of Physics, Inc.)

in a lighted pre-exposure globe for one minute. The bird was then placed in the dim operant chamber. Responses emitted to key A, indicating that the light was visible to the bird, resulted in reducing the intensity of the light. After continuous pecking at key A, the subject could no longer see the stimulus patch—not because the shutter was closed but because the light intensity had apparently decreased below the bird's absolute visual threshold. Once the stimulus light was no longer visible, the bird immediately began pecking key B. All nonreinforced responses made to this key resulted in increasing the intensity of the light. When the stimulus intensity was above threshold, the bird again responded to key A; all responses to this key decreased the stimulus intensity. Thus, as a result of the subject's response selection, the stimulus intensity was continually oscillating about the bird's theoretical absolute threshold. As dark adaptation occurred during the course of the session, the pigeon naturally became more sensitive to weaker intensities of light and "tracked" his own dark-adaptation curve (decreasing threshold function).

A typical dark-adaptation curve found by Blough for one of his birds

is seen in the upper portion of Figure 5-3. This curve is strikingly
similar to the human dark-adaptation curve (lower portion of Figure

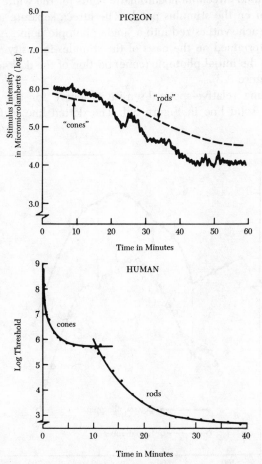

FIGURE 5-3.   *Upper figure:* pigeon dark-adaptation curve, with dotted
lines indicating the theoretical curves for rod and cone receptors. *Lower
figure:* human dark-adaptation curve. These adaptation curves are similar,
even with regard to the segments corresponding to rod and cone receptors.
The pigeon curve was determined by the use of Blough's operant conditioning technique; the human curve was obtained by a psychophysical technique. (Adapted from Blough, D. S., "Dark adaptation in the pigeon,"
Journal of Comparative and Physiological Psychology, 1956, **49,** 425–430.
Copyright 1956 by the American Psychological Association, and reproduced by permission.)

5-3), even with respect to the segments for cone (photopic or hue) and rod (scotopic or achromatic) reception. In order to assess the degree of discriminability that the pigeon has for various wavelengths, Blough (1957) substituted fifteen monochromatic lights for the white light previously shown on the stimulus patch. The fifteen separate adaptation curves were each synthesized into a single photopic point. A photopic point was determined on the basis of the stimulus-intensity values obtained during the initial photopic (cone) portion of the dark-adaptation curve (see Figure 5-3).

The resulting relative-spectral-sensitivity curve for the pigeon is shown as the solid line in Figure 5-4. The dotted line in this figure

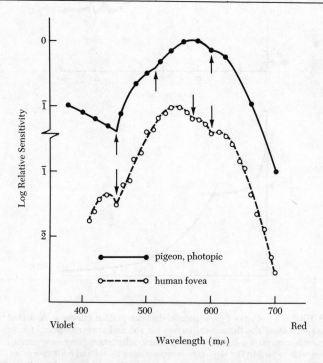

FIGURE 5-4. Relative sensitivity of various wavelengths for photopic vision in pigeons and for foveal vision in humans. Inflections of possible significance are indicated by arrows. (Adapted from Blough, 1957, by permission.)

depicts the relative-spectral-sensitivity curve obtained from human subjects with only foveal (color) vision. The two curves are similar in that the degree of discriminability is best between 500 and 600 mμ. Both the pigeon and the human curves also exhibit discontinuities, or inflections, suggesting that the photopic curve in both species is a composite of several underlying color-vision mechanisms. One of the major differences between the spectral sensitivity of pigeons and man is found in the violet and ultraviolet regions, where pigeons are capable of making better discriminations than man.

CONDITIONS FOR ESTABLISHING STIMULUS CONTROL

Why do generalization gradients occur when no explicit differential training has been given? For example, why did the subjects in the Guttman-Kalish experiment show steep generalization gradients when they had never received explicit wavelength-discrimination training? Several studies dealing with this question examine the extent to which generalization gradients occur when differential reinforcement and experience with values along the test dimension are never given to the subject during his life history. If generalization decrements are observed under these conditions, then we must assume that differential stimulation along the test dimension is not a necessary condition for establishing stimulus control. According to the theories of Spence (1936, 1937) and Hull (1943), gradients should occur even without discrimination training because "an increase in response strength occurs not only with respect to the stimulus associated with reinforcement but also to a lesser degree to adjacent stimuli" (p. 149). On the other hand, if a gradient of generalization is not found under these conditions, then we must assume that the subject will not display stimulus control unless he has an opportunity to experience more than one value along the dimension. Lashley and Wade (1946) accept this view; "A dimension of a stimulus does not exist for an organism until established by differential learning" (p. 7).

Peterson (1962) was one of the first to investigate the influence of experience on stimulus control. In his experiment, ducklings were raised in white-walled cages illuminated by a monochromatic light of 589 mμ. Thus, these animals were exposed to a very narrow range of colors. Other ducklings were raised in cages illuminated by a lamp with a tungsten filament. Both groups were trained in their home cages to peck at a key that was transilluminated by a light of 589 mμ. After fifteen days of training on a variable-interval three-minute (VI 3) schedule of reinforcement, a test for stimulus generalization was conducted; in this test, eight different wavelengths (ranging from 490 mμ to 650 mμ) were used to illuminate the response key. The results of the generalization tests for both groups are shown in Figure 5-5. As can be seen, the ducklings raised in the monochromatic light (represented by the dotted line) yielded a relatively flat gradient, whereas a typical generalization gradient was obtained from the other group. These results indicate that when an organism has an opportunity to experience variations along a stimulus dimension, stimulus control (a gradient of generalization) will be observed. Several other investigators, however, (Malott, 1968; Rudolph, Honig, & Gerry, 1969), have attempted to replicate Peterson's results—all without success.

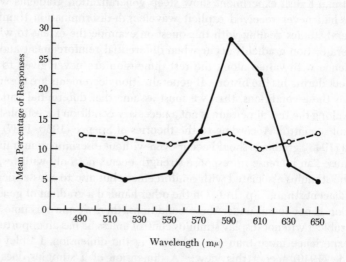

FIGURE 5-5. Generalization gradients obtained from birds raised in a monochromatic environment (dotted line) and from birds raised in a laboratory environment in which chromaticity was not controlled (solid line). (Adapted from Peterson, N., "Effect of monochromatic rearing on the control of responding by wavelength," *Science*, 1962, **136,** 774–775. Copyright 1962 by the American Association for the Advancement of Science. Reprinted by permission.)

Another study of the influence of experience on the slope of the generalization gradient was done by Ganz and Riesen (1962). In this experiment, infant monkeys were reared in total darkness, whereas other monkeys were raised in a typical laboratory setting. After ten weeks, both groups were trained to press a key for sucrose reinforcement. Exactly the same conditioning procedure was used for both groups. The subjects were brought to the training apparatus in a light-tight cage. During training, the left eye of the subject was covered by an opaque cup, and light to the right eye was projected through a mono-chromatic filter. In the presence of the monochromatic light, key-pressing responses were reinforced according to a VI schedule; during periods when there was no light, responses were not reinforced. After numerous training sessions, generalization tests were administered for a period of seven days. During each of these sessions, six wavelength values, in addition to the reinforced value, were presented as test stimuli.

Figure 5-6 shows the number of key presses made to each of the wavelength values during the successive days of testing. For Day 1, the results of this experiment are similar to those found by Peterson; that is, the group raised in darkness produced a somewhat flatter gradient than did the normal group. During ensuing generalization tests, however, the gradients obtained from the dark-reared group became steeper—indicating that the receptors of these monkeys were not atrophied or permanently damaged; in fact, by the end of testing, the light-deprived group showed a steeper generalization decrement than the control group.

The above findings indicate that a history of varied stimulation is an important condition for obtaining stimulus control. Such a history, however, appears not to be a sufficient condition. In addition, as numerous other studies have suggested, some form of discrimination training must be given.

Jenkins and Harrison (1960) examined the role of discrimination training in establishing stimulus control with auditory frequency. In this experiment, pigeons (a control group) were trained to peck at a key on a VI reinforcement schedule during the continuous presentation of a 1,000-cps tone. The experimental birds were given discrimination training, during which periods of a 1,000-cps tone (S^D) were associated with reinforcement and periods of no tone (S^Δ) were associated with no reinforcement. After the number of responses during the S^D presentation was four times greater than responses during the S^Δ presentations, testing for generalization was conducted. Seven tones (300, 450, 670,

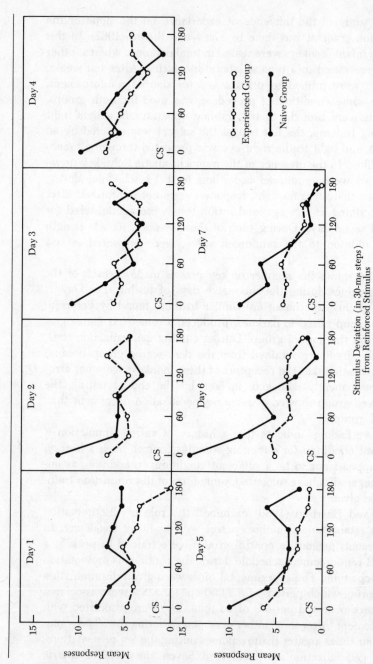

FIGURE 5-6. Generalization gradients for visually experienced and naïve (visually deprived) groups of monkeys on seven testing days. (Adapted from Ganz, L., and Riesen, A. H., "Stimulus generalization to hue in the dark-reared macaque," *Journal of Comparative and Physiological Psychology*, 1962, **55**, 92–99. Copyright 1962 by the American Psychological Association, and reproduced by permission.)

1,000, 1,500, 2,250, and 3,500 cps), equally spaced along a logarithmic scale, were used as test values. Periods of no tone were also presented during the test.

The generalization gradients for each of the subjects in both groups are shown in Figure 5-7. As the figure indicates, every subject who had had differential training yielded a bidirectional generalization gradient, whereas none of the control subjects produced such a gradient. Thus, discrimination training, involving the presence or absence of the training stimulus, is a sufficient condition for the establishment of stimulus control. More recently, Thomas, Mariner, and Sherry (1969) have shown that prior experience with a single tone as a feeding cue is sufficient to produce stimulus control.

Heinemann and Rudolph (1963) claimed that in a situation where the training stimulus is localized in space (for instance, a response key in a Skinner box), responses that are accidentally made to the background area are not reinforced, and therefore inadvertent or accidental differential training is in effect. To demonstrate that inadvertent discrimination can occur under certain conditions, these investigators conducted an experiment in which the size of a ring surrounding the response key in a Skinner box was systematically varied. In this experiment, three groups of pigeons were reinforced for responding to a key and surround, which had a total area of either 5.5, 6.5, or 19.2 square inches. Both the key and the surround were of the same reflectance (luminance of 10 ml). Each group was then divided into three subgroups and tested in extinction with the same key and surround that they had had during training but with one of three possible reflectances (luminance of 1.5, 10, or 15 ml). Groups trained and tested in the presence of the smaller surround showed steeper generalization gradients than groups trained and tested with the larger surround. Heinemann and Rudolph believe that this result occurred because of inadvertent discrimination:

Some discrimination training must inevitably occur in any situation in which the stimulus is a fairly small visual area and the required response is a movement that is directed with respect to the stimulus, such as pecking at the stimulus, or walking or jumping through a door upon which the stimulus appears, or turning at a choice point marked by the stimulus [p. 657].

The stimulus control gained from inadvertent discrimination training may therefore account for the observed generalization decrements in those studies involving no explicit differential reinforcement (for in-

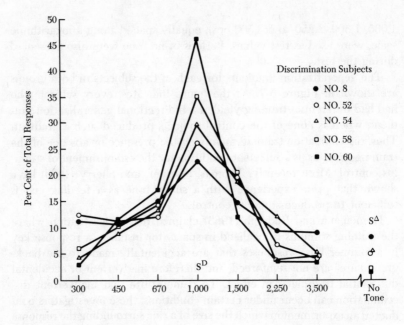

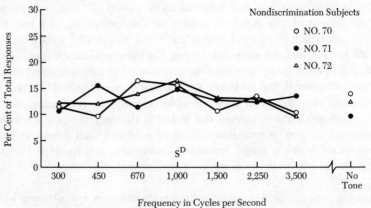

Frequency in Cycles per Second

FIGURE 5-7. Individual generalization gradients of tonal frequency obtained from pigeons following two training conditions. *Upper figure:* gradients obtained from five birds following discrimination training in which S^D was a 1,000-cps tone and S^Δ was no tone. *Lower figure:* results from three birds given nondifferential training in which S^D (1,000-cps tone) was continuously present. (Adapted from Jenkins, H. M., and Harrison, R. H., "Effect of discrimination training on auditory generalization," *Journal of Experimental Psychology,* 1960, **59,** 246–253. Copyright 1960 by the American Psychological Association, and reproduced by permission.)

stance, Guttman & Kalish, 1956; Peterson, 1962). Likewise, stimulus control can be established when subjects are given discrete training trials prior to generalization testing (Pavlov, 1927; Bass & Hull, 1934; Brown, Bilodeau, & Baron, 1951). In these training trials, the responses emitted during the intervals between trials (when the training stimulus is not present) are not reinforced, so that some discrimination training is possible at such times.

In conclusion, the results of Peterson (1962) and Ganz and Riesen (1962) suggest that differential stimulation is an important condition for obtaining a generalization gradient. However, the findings of Jenkins and Harrison (1960) and Heinemann and Rudolph (1963) clearly indicate that some form of discrimination training, even if it is simply the presence versus the absence of the training stimulus, is also required in order to observe stimulus control. The latter two groups of investigators have also shown that conditions of differential reinforcement frequently are present in situations where the experimenter believed he was employing a nondifferential training procedure. Finally, several other studies (Malott, 1968; Rudolph, Honig, & Gerry, 1969; Thomas, Mariner, & Sherry, 1969) suggest that differential stimulation and reinforcement may not be *necessary* conditions for establishing stimulus control. It is assumed in these later studies that specific discrimination training on one dimension will increase stimulus control on other dimensions. Experimental evidence supporting this hypothesis will be discussed later.

SHARPENING OF STIMULUS CONTROL

EFFECTS OF DISCRIMINATION TRAINING ON GENERALIZATION

How can explicit discrimination training be used to enhance or sharpen the controlling power of a particular stimulus? More specifically, how does discrimination training influence the generalization gradient—its slope, its shape, the location of its peak? In one of the first studies in this area, Hanson (1959) trained pigeons to respond to one of two successively presented monochromatic stimuli for VI reinforcement. No reinforcement was given for responses made when the other stimulus was present. A generalization test, administered during extinction after completion of discrimination training, revealed a displacement of the mode (peak) of responding away from the positive stimulus (S+, reinforced value) in the direction opposite the negative stimulus (S−, nonreinforced value). In addition, discrimination training produced an elevation of this peak, an increased steepness of the gradient in the region of the S⁻, and a low value of the gradient in this region. These aspects of the postdiscrimination gradient have also been reported by others (Honig, Thomas, & Guttman, 1959; Guttman & Kalish, 1956; Thomas, Ost, & Thomas, 1960).

In a subsequent study, Hanson (1961) demonstrated that the control exercised by the training stimulus can be greatly increased if adjacent stimulus values (values on either side of the reinforced stimulus) are not reinforced. In Hanson's study, pigeons were given discrimination training in which 550-mμ light served as the reinforced stimulus, but responses made to either 540-mμ or 560-mμ light were not rewarded. Thus, these subjects were trained on a three-stimulus discrimination problem involving one positive stimulus and two negative stimuli. Discrimination training was given until the subjects showed complete suppression of responding to each of the negative stimuli for three successive stimulus presentations. A nondifferential control group was also reinforced for responding to the 550-mμ light but did not receive discrimination training with the two negative stimuli. Following training, twelve generalization test series were given. Each series consisted of the random presentation of exposures to stimuli ranging from 490 to 610 mμ. Responding during these sessions was not reinforced.

Responses emitted to each of the test values during generalization testing are shown in Figure 5-8. As can be seen, relatively symmetrical generalization gradients were obtained from both groups. Responses by the experimental group, however, were restricted to the stimulus values between the two negative (nonreinforced) stimuli. In addition, the number of responses to the original training stimulus (550 mμ) was much greater for the experimental group than it was for the control.

In an experiment closely paralleling Hanson's procedure, Thomas and Williams (1963) employed a single negative stimulus surrounded by two positive stimuli. More specifically, their experimental pigeons were reinforced for responding to a 540-mμ and a 580-mμ light but not for responding to a 560-mμ stimulus. Two nondifferential control groups (one matched with the experimental group for number of training sessions and the other for number of reinforcements) were also trained to respond to the two positive stimuli but were not presented with the negative value.

Following ten sessions of training, generalization tests with thirteen stimuli ranging from 500 mμ through 620 mμ were given in eight successive test series. This testing was done during extinction. Figure 5-9 presents the generalization gradients for the experimental and con-

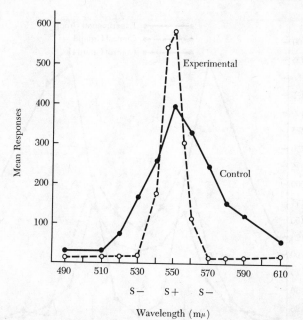

FIGURE 5-8. Generalization gradients for a group not given discrimination training (control group) and a group trained on a discrimination
with 550-mμ stimulus reinforced and 540-mμ and 560-mμ stimuli not reinforced (experimental group). Adapted from Hanson, H. M., "Stimulus generalization following three-stimulus discrimination training," *Journal of
Comparative and Physiological Psychology*, 1961, **54**, 181–185. Copyright
1961 by the American Psychological Association, and reproduced by permission.)

trol groups. Both of the gradients from the control groups show that
training to the two positive stimuli produces a peak of responding for
each of these values. The number of responses decreases to stimuli
"outside" the positive values (that is, to wavelengths shorter than 540
mμ and longer than 580 mμ) as well as to stimuli located between
the reinforced stimuli. However, some summation of generalized response strength is observed for the middle values. The only difference
between the two control gradients is that Control Group II, which
received more training (but the same number of reinforcements), emitted less total responses during the test; but this difference was not
statistically significant.

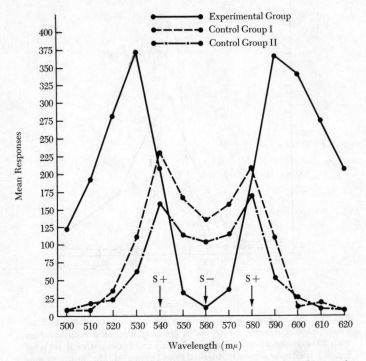

FIGURE 5-9. Generalization gradients of experimental and control groups of pigeons. The control groups were not given discrimination training and were reinforced for responding to both 540-mμ and 580-mμ stimuli. The experimental group was given discrimination training in which it was reinforced during the presentation of 540-mμ and 580-mμ but not during 560-mμ stimulus. (Adapted from Thomas, D. R., and Williams, J. L. A further study of stimulus generalization following three-stimulus discrimination training. *Journal of the Experimental Analysis of Behavior,* 1963, 6, 171–176. Copyright 1963 by the Society for the Experimental Analysis of Behavior, Inc. Reprinted by permission.)

The experimental group, as seen in Figure 5-9, showed a postdiscrimination generalization gradient with both of its peaks displaced from the positive stimulus values in the direction away from the negative stimulus. In addition, few responses were made to the negative value, with increased steepness of the slope of the gradient in the middle region. Finally, the experimental group responded much more than the control groups to values located "beyond" the two reinforced stimuli, in the direction away from the negative stimulus. This finding is consistent with Hanson's (1959, 1961) results, described previously.

The results of the three experiments just described are relevant to Spence's (1936, 1937) theory of discrimination learning. This theory involves the following assumptions: (1) that every reinforcement leads to an increment in the (excitatory) tendency to repeat the reinforced response, (2) that every nonreinforcement leads to an increment in the (inhibitory) tendency not to respond, (3) that both of these tendencies generalize to other stimuli, (4) that the magnitude of the inhibitory tendencies is less than that of the excitatory tendency (otherwise learning could not occur in any partial-reinforcement situation, where reinforced and nonreinforced trials occur in a ratio of 1:1 or less), (5) that the excitatory and inhibitory tendencies summate algebraically, to determine the postdiscriminatory responses made to the various stimulus values.

The algebraic summation of gradients of excitation and inhibition would account for many of the findings in the previously described studies of Hanson (1959, 1961) and Thomas and Williams (1963b). Such findings include the peak shifts, the increased steepness of the gradient, and the low value of responding in the region of the S⁻. However, Spence's theory of discrimination learning does not account for the fact that the postdiscrimination gradient for differentially trained subjects is higher than the gradient obtained from nondifferential (control) subjects. Instead, his theory predicts that the postdiscrimination gradient should be some fraction of the nondifferential gradient. Thus, Spence's theory is in error in failing to consider that extinction has excitatory as well as inhibitory effects. The excitatory effects resulting from extinction (or discrimination training) are best explained by the concept of *behavioral contrast*.

BEHAVIORAL-CONTRAST EFFECTS

In the three previous studies, discrimination training was shown to sharpen stimulus control. Differential reinforcement also appears to produce contrast effects. The factors responsible for the development of behavioral-contrast effects in subjects have been investigated by Reynolds. In one of his studies (1961a), pigeons were first trained on a *mult* VI 3 VI 3 schedule. As noted in Chapter 3, a multiple schedule consists of two or more independent schedules presented successively, each associated with a specific discriminative stimulus. In this case, the separate components were associated with a red and a green light, but the identical reinforcement schedule (VI 3 min) was in effect for both stimulus hues. The birds were then trained to discriminate between the red light, which was correlated with extinction (*mult* VI 3 ext schedule). After this discrimination schedule had been established, the subjects were again trained under the *mult* VI 3 VI 3 schedule.

Figure 5-10 presents the rate of responding by two birds to each of the stimuli during all three phases of the experiment. Notice that the response rates to the two stimuli are comparable during Phase I (nondifferential reinforcement). During Phase II (differential rein- forcement), however, response rates to the red light (VI 3) increase considerably as the subjects learn to suppress their responses to the green light (ext); in this phase, then, behavioral contrast is seen. A contrast effect due to a shift in the frequency of the reward is also seen in the final phase of the experiment; that is, the response-rate curves for the two stimuli cross each other rather than converging to the same asymptote.

On the basis of these results and those of other studies (Reynolds, 1961b, 1961c), Reynolds concluded that the condition necessary for the occurrence of behavioral contrast is a "change in the relative fre- quency of reinforcement associated with one of several successive stimu- li" (Reynolds, 1961b, p. 70). This explanation, however, seems to over- look one finding in all of Reynolds' studies—namely, that the relative frequency of reinforcement was positively correlated with response rate. It is possible, therefore, that the necessary condition for a contrast effect is a difference in response rates between two stimuli rather than a difference in the frequency of reinforcement.

ERRORLESS-DISCRIMINATION LEARNING

Explicit discrimination training increases stimulus control because dis- crimination involves inhibition responses during presentation of the nonreinforced stimulus (S^Δ or S^-). This inhibition, in turn, is responsible for the increase in the slope of the postdiscrimination generalization gradient. Furthermore, responses made to the S^Δ are not reinforced and therefore produce frustration, which serves to motivate behavior in the presence of the S^D. Thus, behavioral contrast occurs because of the frustrating consequences of the nonreinforced responses emitted to the S^Δ.

In order to examine the validity of the above interpretation, Terrace (1961, 1963a, 1963b) devised a procedure for training subjects to form a perfect discrimination without making an error (without responding

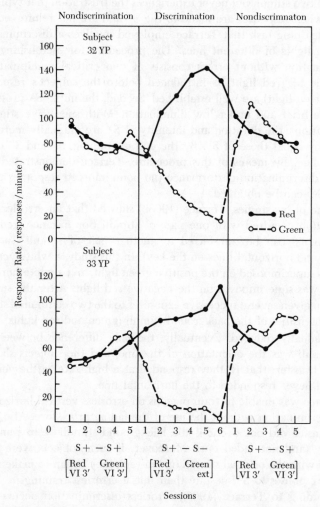

FIGURE 5-10.   Rates of responding to alternative discriminative stimuli during three phases of experiment: nondifferential training (VI 3' VI 3'), differential training (VI ext), and nondifferential training (again VI 3' VI 3'). The development of behavioral contrast is observed during the differential reinforcement phase. (Adapted from Reynolds, G. Behavioral contrast. *Journal of the Experimental Analysis of Behavior*, 1961, 4, 57–71. Copyright 1961 by the Society for the Experimental Analysis of Behavior, Inc. Reprinted by permission.)

to the S^Δ). A bird trained under this procedure thus learns to discriminate between two stimuli but never experiences the frustration that typically occurs when responses are made to the S^Δ and are not reinforced.

The learning task that Terrace employed involves a discrimination between lights of different hues. The procedure for establishing this discrimination without errors consists of two critical manipulations. First, the S^Δ (red light) is introduced before the subject's responses to S^D (green light) are well established. Second, the initial S^Δ presentations are brief and under low illumination. With successive stimulus presentations, the duration and intensity of S^Δ are gradually increased until they equal those of S^D. By the end of training, S^Δ and S^D differ only in hue. By means of this procedure, Terrace demonstrated that perfect discrimination performance (no nonreinforced responses made to the S^Δ) can be obtained.

In one of his studies, Terrace (1963b) showed that an errorless discrimination acquired with one pair of stimuli (for instance, red and green lights) can be transferred to another pair of stimuli (such as vertical and horizontal lines on the key). In this study, a white vertical line was superimposed on the positive green light, and a white horizontal line was superimposed on the negative red light. After the subject had been given several successive exposures to the two compound stimuli, the intensities of the background stimuli (green and red lights) were then gradually reduced. Eventually, the only difference between the two stimuli was the orientation of the line, and the subjects showed perfect transfer; that is, they responded at a high rate to the vertical line and never responded to the horizontal line.

Terrace was unable to train pigeons on errorless vertical-horizontal-line discrimination without the use of the fading procedure. Also, perfect transfer did not occur if the background stimuli were removed abruptly (and not faded out). Moreover, if such subjects were later retested with the original stimuli (green-red), they began to make more errors (responses to S^Δ) despite their initial errorless training.

According to Terrace (1966), errorless discrimination occurs as a result of contiguity conditioning of the last response emitted before the termination of the discriminative stimulus. Typically, pigeons do not peck—and may actually show a slight withdrawal response—at a key that is suddenly darkened (Herrnstein, 1955). Since, in the errorless-discrimination procedure, the S^Δ is at first presented dimly and for a very brief duration, a pigeon usually backs away from the key and never emits a pecking response. The withdrawal response, therefore, becomes conditioned because it was the last response performed in the presence of the S^Δ.

Terrace (1966) also found that pigeons not trained with the errorless procedure display considerable emotional behavior (wing flapping, turning away from the key) when the S^Δ is presented. Since these responses do not occur with errorless-trained birds, it seems likely that the S^Δ functions differently under the two discrimination procedures: for birds not trained in errorless discrimination, it appears to be an aversive stimulus; for trained birds, it is a completely neutral stimulus.

In still another study, Terrace (1964) found that errorless-trained subjects—in contrast to the subjects in previously described studies (Hanson, 1959, 1961; Thomas & Williams, 1963b; Reynolds, 1961a)—do not show peak shifts or behavioral contrast in their generalization gradients. Terrace replicated Hanson's (1959) procedure but used different discriminative stimuli: 580 mμ (S^D) and 540 mμ (S^Δ). One group was trained without errors on this problem, and another group was trained with errors. Still another group (the nondifferential group) was not trained on the discrimination task but was simply reinforced for responding to 580 mμ. Following training, the three groups were tested in extinction for stimulus generalization with a random presentation of stimulus. Figure 5-11 shows the gradients obtained from each of the groups.

The gradient from Group I (the group given nondifferential training) appears to be the flattest, indicating very little stimulus control. In contrast, the discrimination groups show considerable stimulus control, with no responses to the S^Δ. Group III, however (the one that learned the discrimination with errors), shows a definite peak shift and a greater behavioral contrast than Group II (the errorless-discrimination group).

These findings support the notion that the S^Δ functions as an aversive stimulus if nonreinforced responses (errors) are made during its presentation. Thus, the shift in the peak of the gradient for the groups trained with errors can be described as a shift "in preference" away from the aversive stimulus. Furthermore, as the discrimination training with errors was extended, both the extent of the peak shift and the amount of behavioral contrast were reduced—again suggesting that such phenomena are related to the emotional consequences of not receiving reinforcement for responding to the S^Δ. After responding to the S^Δ is completely suppressed, the aversive effects of the S^Δ should then disappear.

Terrace (1966) has also demonstrated that an errorless-trained bird

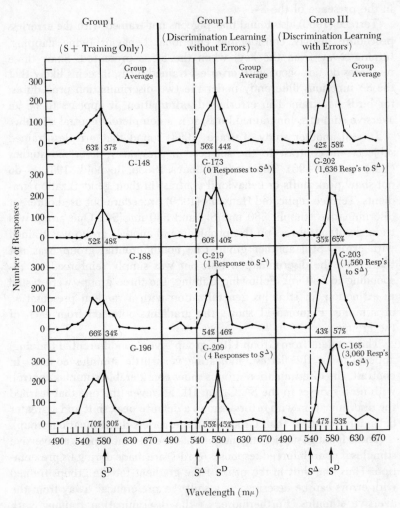

FIGURE 5-11.   Generalization gradients of wavelength following different training conditions. The top three figures show average gradients for each training condition; below these are shown data for the three subjects comprising each of the groups. Numbers to the right and left of the vertical lines, drawn at the S^D values, represent the percentage of total area under the gradient that lies above and below the S^D. (Adapted from Terrace, H. S.,."Wavelength generalization after discrimination learning with and without errors," *Science*, 1964, **144**, 78–80. Copyright 1964 by the American Association for the Advancement of Science. Reprinted by permission.)

induced to start making errors during the transfer training (by an abrupt removal of the background stimulus instead of fading) shows a shift in the peak of its generalization gradient in the direction away from the S^Δ and a consequent behavioral contrast. Again, the S^Δ, under discriminations established with the errors, appears to be an aversive stimulus responsible for the peak shift and the behavioral-contrast effects observed in postdiscrimination generalization gradients.

As a further test of this hypothesis, Terrace (1963c) gave tranquilizers to pigeons while they were trained on a discrimination problem. Some of the pigeons were trained to perform an errorless horizontal-vertical-line discrimination by means of the transfer-fading method. Others learned this same problem by a regular discrimination procedure, but they made a large number of errors. Tranquilizer injections (which presumably would reduce the aversiveness of S^Δ) did not lead to significant changes in performance of the group trained with the errorless procedure; however, the drugs greatly disrupted the perfect performance that had been eventually established in the group trained with errors. The absence of drug effect in the errorless group indicates that the discrimination had been learned without emotional reaction to the S^Δ. Under the usual discrimination procedure, according to Terrace, responses to the S^Δ produce frustration because reinforcement is not given. When this frustration is reduced by tranquilizers, a decrement in discrimination performance could be expected.

STIMULUS CONTROL AND ATTENTION

Certain organisms show greater responsiveness to some modalities than to others. For example, rats are apparently more responsive to olfactory than to visual stimuli; monkeys are more responsive to visual than to auditory stimuli; and humans are more responsive to visual stimuli than to either auditory or olfactory cues. Even within the visual modality, adult humans appear to respond more readily to the form of an object than to its color. In other words, each species apparently possesses a unique hierarchy of stimulus cues and modalities to which it attends. In this connection, we will focus on two major problems: (1) How can we operationally assess the stimulus-attending or utilization hierarchies of various organisms? (2) Can the arrangement of such attending hierarchies be modified through differential training?

One way to assess the attending hierarchy of a given organism is to investigate the slopes of generalization gradients for a number of

different dimensions. As mentioned, dimensions yielding steep generalization gradients indicate considerable stimulus control, whereas dimensions yielding relatively flat gradients indicate very little stimulus control. Furthermore, stimulus control appears to be a valid index of the
degree to which a subject attends to or utilizes a particular stimulus
dimension during training. Thus, by comparing the relative slopes of
generalization gradients for a variety of stimulus dimensions, we should
theoretically be able to determine an organism's *attending hierarchy*
of cues.

INTERACTION OF STIMULUS DIMENSIONS

Although numerous studies have investigated the properties of stimulus
generalization (and stimulus control), very little attention has been
directed to the extent to which generalization occurs when the test
stimulus is varied along two or more dimensions, as compared with a
single dimension. Experiments of this type are important because they
enable us to determine whether two stimuli exhibit independent or
interacting effects. Butter (1963) was the first investigator to conduct
an experiment concerned with multidimensional generalization. In this
study, pigeons were reinforced on a variable-interval schedule to respond to a key. On this key was displayed a band of 550-mμ light
oriented in a vertical position (90°). During a single training session,
thirty such presentations of light occurred for durations of fifty-five
seconds each. A fifteen-second interval of light-off, during which no
responses were reinforced, separated each of the periods of light-on.
After ten days of such training, the subjects were given generalization
tests with stimuli differing in either one or two dimensions from the
training stimulus; that is, three wavelength values (520, 550, and
580 mμ) were paired in all possible combinations with values of angular
orientation of the band of light (40°, 90°, and 140° rotated to the
right of horizontal). In addition, 0° (horizontal) was paired with 550
mμ, making a total of ten different stimulus combinations.

Figure 5-12 shows the mean total responses to stimuli of various
wavelengths and angular orientations. The obtained gradients appear
to be similar to those generated in tests in which the test stimuli are
varied only on a single dimension. The results demonstrate that generalization to stimuli varied in two dimensions is less than generalization
to stimuli varied in either dimension alone. Furthermore, these data
suggest that multidimensional generalization is not simply the result
of the linear summation of the generalization decrements for all of

the component dimensions of the training stimulus. According to Butter (p. 342):

The form of the gradients suggests that relative generalization along one dimension is equal at different levels of the second dimension. Thus, for example, if R_t = responses to the training stimulus, R_a = responses to the stimulus varied only in angular orientation, R_w = responses to a stimulus varied only in wavelength, and R_{aw} = responses to a stimulus varied in both, then

$$\frac{R_a}{R_t} = \frac{R_{aw}}{R_w}$$

and

$$R_{aw} = \frac{R_a \times R_w}{R_t}$$

Dividing both sides of the equation by R_t

$$\frac{R_{aw}}{R_t} = \frac{R_a \times R_w}{R_t \times R_t}$$

According to the last equation, the relative amount of generalization to a stimulus varied in both dimensions (R_{aw}) equals the product of the values of relative generalization to the two stimuli when tested separately along a single dimension (R_a and R_w). By means of the above formula, Butter was able to predict with a fair degree of accuracy the shape of multidimensional generalization gradients of a different group of subjects tested with a new set of stimulus values.

From the results of the above study and another by Butter and Guttman (1957), it appears that differential training is not necessary to obtain gradients of angularity with a stimulus consisting of a *colored line* on a dark surround. In contrast, according to Newman and Baron (1965), a *white line* on a colored surround requires discrimination training in order for generalization gradients to be found.

Other findings (Newman and Baron, 1965) suggest that nondifferentially trained subjects, even though exposed to all aspects of the conditioned stimulus, will primarily utilize or respond to those that are high-

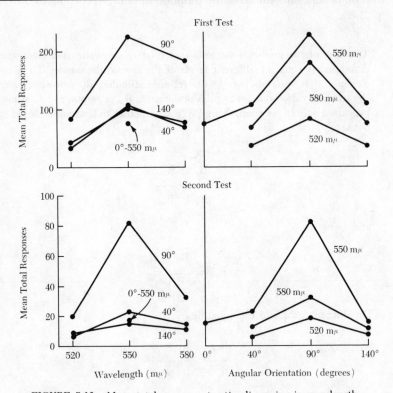

FIGURE 5-12. Mean total responses to stimuli varying in wavelength and angular orientation from the training value (550 mμ and 90°) on the first and second generalization tests. (Adapted from Butter, C. M., "Stimulus generalization along one and two dimensions in pigeons," *Journal of Experimental Psychology*, 1963, 65, 339–346. Copyright 1963 by the American Psychological Association, and reproduced by permission.)

est in their attending hierarchy. Thus, differential training may be necessary for a weak component of the conditioned stimulus to gain response control over a stronger component.

The above hypothesis was specifically tested by Newman and Benefield (1968), who trained three groups of pigeons to respond on a chained schedule: pecking responses on a blank key intermittently producing a stimulus on the key and simultaneous presentation of reward. The stimuli differed for the three groups. For Group I, a white vertical line on a green surround (positive secondary reinforcer, S^{r+}) was consistently paired with reward. For Group II, responses sometimes produced the white vertical line on green surround paired with reward but occasionally produced a green surround without the vertical line (nonreinforcing stimulus, S^{r-}), which was never followed by reinforcement. Thus, Group I received nondifferential training with the line on a green surround, whereas Group II received differential training with the line either present or absent on a green surround. Group III was given the same differential training as Group II except that the S^{r+} and the S^{r-} values were reversed.

Following training, the investigators—using the Guttman-Kalish (1956) method—conducted stimulus-generalization tests in extinction, with seven different angular-orientation values of the white line. Half the subjects in each group were tested with the surround constantly green; the remaining subjects were tested with an achromatic surround. Figure 5-13 shows the mean number of responses made to each of the test values for the three groups tested with the achromatic surround. The gradients for Groups I and II are similar in their symmetry and slope. This result suggests that the subjects, whether they received differential or nondifferential training, were attending to the line component of S^{r+}. In contrast, no gradient was obtained from Group III.

Figure 5-14 shows the mean number of responses made to each of the test values for the groups tested with a constant green surround. The groups tested under this condition show considerably different gradients from those tested under the achromatic condition (seen in Figure 5-13). The gradient for the differentially trained subjects (Group II) is steep and symmetrical, with a peak of responding at the vertical value; the gradient for the nondifferentially trained subjects (Group I) is much flatter and does not peak at the training value. These data suggest that the presence of the green surround interfered with the stimulus control exerted by the line. Furthermore, the results support the original hypothesis that specific differential training directed at the weaker component (line orientation) can overcome this interference and bring about stimulus control. According to the previously described notion of a stimulus-attending hierarchy, these findings can be interpreted as a shifting of the line-orientation dimension further up the hierarchy as a result of discrimination training.

Finally, Newman and Benefield noted that the presentation of the line, in all orientations, tended to inhibit responding—as demonstrated by the fact that Group III consistently gave fewer responses than the other two groups during tests with either the achromatic (Figure 5-13) or the green (Figure 5-14) surround.

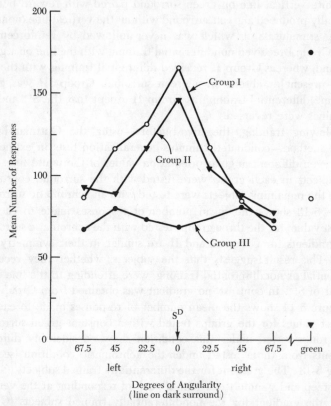

FIGURE 5-13.   Generalization gradients of three groups of pigeons following training. Test stimuli consisted of varying the angular orientation of a white line on a dark surround. (Adapted from Newman, F. L., and Benefield, R. L., "Stimulus control, utilization and attention: Effects of discrimination training," *Journal of Comparative and Physiological Psychology*, 1968, 66, 101–104. Copyright 1968 by the American Psychological Association, and reproduced by permission.)

SELECTIVE ATTENTION

Some learning theorists (Hull, 1943; Spence, 1936, 1956) believe that all aspects of a stimulus acquire increments of association with the response. Others, however, claim that only those cues that the subject is attending to (Lashley, 1942) or that are relevant to the subject's "hypothesis" (Krechevsky, 1938) during the trial will be involved in

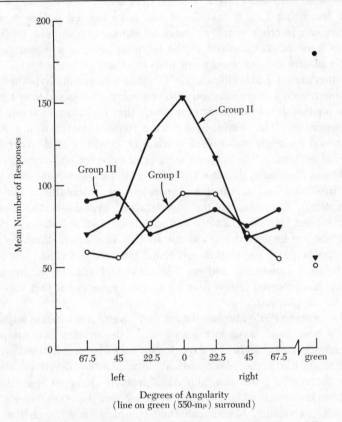

FIGURE 5-14.   Generalization gradients of three groups of pigeons following training. Test stimuli consisted of varying the angular orientation of
a white line on a surround of 550 mμ. (Adapted from Newman and Benefield, 1968, by permission.)

the learning process. These latter theorists claim that attention to various
dimensions of the conditioned stimulus is in some sense selective.

After reviewing experiments concerned with the problem of attention, Mackintosh (1965) concluded that a compromise position must
be accepted. According to his view, a subject does pay attention to
the various aspects of a conditioned stimulus, but he pays more attention
to some aspects than to others. Moreover, the more he utilizes or attends
to his input in one way, the less he will utilize this information in
another. For instance, if the subject is attending predominantly to Cue

A, he will learn more about Cue A than about Cue B; and he will learn less about Cue B than he would have learned if Cue A were not present. In other words, although all aspects of a stimulus probably are to some extent involved in the learning process, a subject might simply attend to some cues more than to others.

Sutherland and Mackintosh (1964) tested this specific hypothesis by training rats on a discrimination with two relevant cues and later testing them for transfer, to discover how much they had learned about each cue separately. The stimuli used during training consisted of a white horizontal rectangle and a black vertical rectangle located on separate doors of a T-maze. The subjects were reinforced for responding to the brightness dimension (black-white). Later, the subjects were tested on the irrelevant or incidental dimension of orientation (horizontal-vertical). According to the investigators' hypothesis, the more a given subject learned about one of the dimensions (for instance, brightness), the less he should learn about another cue (orientation). As predicted, a negative correlation was found between individual scores on the training dimension and on the incidental dimension. Reynolds (1961c) has reported results from an operant experiment that also support this hypothesis.

Mackintosh (1965) also has shown that investigators can manipulate exactly how much a subject learns about the various dimensions of the training stimulus. In this experiment, subjects were trained on the same white-horizontal/black-vertical discrimination described above. Prior to receiving this discrimination problem, some of the subjects had been trained on a black-white discrimination; the others were given no such pretraining. Mackintosh then compared how much the two groups learned about line orientation. During testing, the black-white pretrained group learned significantly less about line orientation than did the other group. Thus, attention to one dimension of the training stimulus appears to reduce the amount of incidental learning of another stimulus dimension. Similar findings have been reported with octopuses as subjects (Sutherland, Mackintosh, & Mackintosh, 1963) and with human subjects (Eckstrand & Wickens, 1954; Egeth, 1967).

According to Mackintosh (1965), two separate stages are involved in the solving of a discrimination problem. First, the subject must learn which features of the stimulus situation are relevant and should be utilized. Second, the subject must learn to make the correct (reinforced) choice between two relevant stimuli.

An experimental finding that supports the two-stage model of discrimination learning is the *overlearning reversal effect* (ORE). In most studies of the ORE, two groups of subjects (one given training trials until it reaches asymptotic performance; the other given additional training trials) learn a particular discrimination problem; both groups are then given another discrimination problem—this time with the positive and negative stimuli reversed. According to Mackintosh (1969), overlearning appears to facilitate reversal learning under certain conditions—namely, when the discrimination problem is relatively difficult and when a large amount of reinforcement is used. Overlearning, under these conditions, increases the probability of the subject's attending to the appropriate dimension, even though his choice performance remains at an asymptotic level. During reversal, then, the overtrained subjects will continue to attend to the relevant dimension and need only extinguish their original choice and learn a new one. In contrast, subjects who are not overtrained will extinguish their attending behavior to the relevant stimulus more rapidly—and hence will require more trials to learn the reversal. This explanation of the ORE was first proposed by Sutherland (1959) and has been stated more formally by Lovejoy (1965) and by Mackintosh (1969).

A number of operant procedures have been used to investigate selective attention in animals. Most of these experiments involve two stimulus dimensions: wavelength of light and angle of line orientation. Typically, a monochromatic light is used as the positive stimulus, and a white vertical line on a black surround is used as the negative stimulus (or vice versa). These two dimensions, as noted previously, are ideal for investigating attentional processes because they can be independently manipulated and also can be presented simultaneously on the same response key.

Using these stimuli, Switalski, Lyons, and Thomas (1966) tested the effects of interdimensional nondifferential and differential training on the slope of a generalization gradient. The term *interdimensional* training refers to the fact that the negative stimulus in this study was completely independent of the dimension along which the positive stimulus was varied during generalization testing. More specifically, two groups of pigeons were tested twice for wavelength generalization in extinction. The first test was administered following single-stimulus training to respond to a key illuminated by a 555-mμ light. Next, the subjects in Group I were given twelve days of nondifferential training, with reinforcement presented according to a variable-interval schedule. During this training, presentations of the 555-mμ light and a white vertical line on a black surround were alternated randomly on the key. In contrast, subjects in Group II received discrimination training following the first generalization test. For the discrimination test, responses made to 555-mμ stimulus were reinforced, and responses to the orthogonal stimulus of a white vertical line were not reinforced. Following this training, both groups were again tested for generalization along the wavelength dimension.

Figure 5-15 indicates the mean generalization gradients obtained from the subjects in Group I on tests 1 and 2. Decremental gradients around the value of 555 mμ occurred in both tests. The gradient obtained after interdimensional nondifferential training, however, is reliably flatter than the gradient previously found (Test 1) after single-stimulus training. This same finding was observed when the absolute gradients were transformed in relative generalization gradients (percentage of responses) to the test values.

Figure 5-15 also presents the mean generalization gradients on both tests for Group II. Both of the resulting gradients are symmetrical and peak at the training value of 555 mμ. The gradient obtained after interdimensional-discrimination training was reliably steeper than the gra-

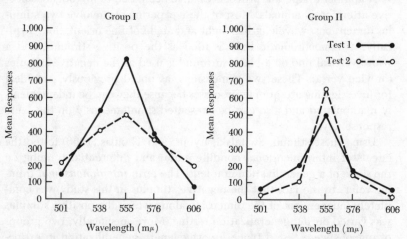

FIGURE 5-15.   Generalization gradients obtained during Test 1, following nondifferential training with 555 mμ as S^D. Also shown are the generalization gradients obtained during Test 2, given after nondifferential training (Group I) and differential training (Group II). (Adapted from Switalski, R. W., Lyons, J., and Thomas, D. R., "Effects of interdimensional training on stimulus generalization," *Journal of Experimental Psychology*, 1966, 72, 661–666. Copyright 1966 by the American Psychological Association, and reproduced by permission.)

dient previously found after the single-stimulus condition. This same result was found when the absolute gradients were transformed into relative generalization gradients. These findings suggest that interdimensional-discrimination training increases "attention" or "stimulus control," whereas nondifferential training has the opposite effect. Switalski, Lyons, and Thomas claim that interdimensional-discrimination training increases stimulus control because the subject acquires a "set to discriminate" during such training.

Another type of discrimination procedure, one that is becoming more frequently used to study the process of attention, is *extradimensional training*. In extradimensional training, the training dimension is clearly specified and completely independent of the dimension tested with regard to stimulus generalization. The basic question explored by this procedure is whether discrimination training along one dimension has any effect on the stimulus control (steepness of the generalization gradient) observed with another dimension.

Honig (1969) was one of the first investigators to employ the extradimensional procedure in the operant situation. For one group of pigeons in his experiment, successive discrimination training was given between two colors (white versus pink). For a second group of birds, *pseudo-discrimination training* was given; that is, the two colors were presented in the same sequence as for the first group, but reinforcement was given during half of each of the stimulus presentations. Thus, both groups were given the same number of stimulus and reinforcment presentations; but the reinforcements of the true-discrimination (TD) group were associated with only one stimulus, whereas those of the pseudo-discrimination (PD) group were associated randomly and equally with both stimuli. A third group, which served as a control group, was given blackout periods in the box instead of the S⁻. Pigeons do not usually respond during blackouts when extinction is in effect.

After a TD subject had learned the color discrimination, he—along with a PD and a control subject—was given single-stimulus training. In this phase of the experiment, the birds were reinforced for responding to a white vertical line on a black key. After several days of training, Honig tested all three groups for stimulus generalization, varying the angularity or orientation of the line. From the results of the generalization test, the TD group showed the steepest gradient; the PD group showed the flattest; and the control group's gradient was intermediate between the two. These results seem to contradict the selective-attention hypothesis proposed by Mackintosh (1965) and Sutherland (1964). It appears that discrimination training on one dimension increases stimulus control not only along that dimension but also along other dimensions.

In a recent paper (Thomas, Freeman, Svinicki, Burr, & Lyons, 1970), steepened generalization gradients were observed following extradimensional-discrimination training when the training and test dimensions were in a different sense modality. All the pigeons in this study were first trained to peck at a key illuminated with a 555-mμ value; the floor of the box was in the normal horizontal position. The subjects were then divided into subgroups. Subjects in the TD group were given discrimination training with the horizontal floor as S$^+$ and a ten-degree clockwise floor tilt as S$^-$. Short periods of blackout were given during the time that the floor was to be moved. The subjects assigned to the PD group received the same sequence of floor-tilt conditions as did the TD group, but the reinforcement contingency was in effect during half of the presentations of the zero tilt and half of the presentations of the ten-degree tilt, determined on a random basis. Thus, as in Honig's (1969) study, the number of stimulus and reinforcement presentations was identical for both the TD and PD groups. After each TD subject reached a criterion of tilt-discrimination learning, he and his PD partner were tested in extinction for generalization along the wavelength dimension.

The mean relative and absolute generalization gradients of the TD and the PD groups are presented in Figure 5-16. The relative gradients indicate the percentage of total responses made by each subject to the separate test values. Both the relative and the absolute set of gradients suggest that the TD condition yields more stimulus control (steeper gradients) than the PD condition.

Although the differences in the steepness of the gradients for TD training compared with PD training are relatively small, they are extremely consistent. Thomas and his associates have shown that extradimensional TD training steepens gradients, whether the test dimension is line angle (Hanson, 1959) or wavelength; whether the test dimension is present during discrimination training or is introduced later, and whether the training and test dimension is of the same modality as the training dimension or a different one.

It will be recalled that Sutherland (1959) and Mackintosh (1965) stressed the selective nature of attention. They claimed that the amount of attention given to one dimension of a stimulus is negatively correlated with the amount of attention given to the other dimensions. The basic assumption of this position is that the perceptual field of the subject is fixed and that, if the subject is reinforced for attending to one dimen-

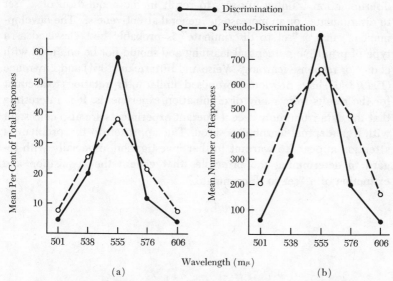

FIGURE 5-16. Relative (a) and absolute (b) generalization gradients of discrimination and pseudo-discrimination groups trained along floor tilt and tested along wavelength dimensions. (Adapted from Thomas, D. R., Freeman, F., Svinicki, J. G., Burr, D. E. S., and Lyons, J., "Effects of extradimensional training on stimulus generalization," *Journal of Experimental Psychology*, 1970, 83, 1–21. Copyright 1970 by the American Psychological Association, and reproduced by permission.)

sion, he must do so at the cost of ignoring other dimensions. This same assumption has also been held by many investigators working in the area of human performance (for instance, Fitts & Posner, 1967), who claim that individuals have a fixed "channel capacity" with which to process information. Other theorists (for instance, Easterbrook, 1959) take a similar position but hypothesize that certain variables (such as motivation) can influence the total size of the perceptual field (or the rate of processing information).

Other findings (Switalski, Lyons, & Thomas, 1966; Honig, 1969; Thomas, Freeman, Svinicki, Burr, & Lyons, 1970) clearly indicate that both interdimensional and extradimensional training steepen gradients of generalization along irrelevant dimensions. If one is willing to assume that attention can be measured by the steepness of generalization gradients (stimulus control), then the traditional positions of selective attention must be reevaluated. Instead of narrowing the perceptual field, discrimination training appears to result in the acquisition of a "set to discriminate" or an increase in "general attentiveness." The development of such a "set to discriminate" is probably best classified as a type of primitive perceptual learning and should not be confused with choice or response learning. Weise and Bitterman (1951) and Lawrence (1949, 1963) have previously proposed similar interpretations to account for the results from many discrimination experiments. It is interesting that the data from more recent operant experiments are also consistent with a perceptual-learning position. This approach to the problem of attention appears to warrant further investigation, especially with regard to determining the principles that govern the acquisition and extinction of a "set to discriminate."

VI

AVERSIVE CONTROL: ESCAPE, AVOIDANCE, PUNISHMENT

The previous chapters were concerned primarily with the influence of reinforcing stimuli on operant behavior. As was noted, the *presentation* of such stimuli generally increases the probability of future occurrence of the response. When we turn to the influence of aversive stimuli on operant responding, we find that the *withdrawal* of such stimuli generally increases response rates. The process of maintaining behavior by withdrawing aversive stimulation is called *negative reinforcement*.

There are two paradigms involving aversive stimulation: *escape* and *avoidance*. In the escape paradigm, the response terminates an aversive stimulus after it has begun. Under this procedure, the subject can free himself from prolonged exposure to the noxious stimulus, but he cannot completely avoid experiencing it. With the avoidance paradigm, however, the subject's response prevents or postpones the presentation of the aversive event. Usually, an organism first learns how to escape from the noxious stimulus; later he finds a way to avoid the stimulus. For example, if a young child burns his finger with a flaming match, he will learn that he can escape from pain by blowing out the match or withdrawing his finger. With more experience, the child will eventually learn approximately how much time he can allow the match to burn before he must extinguish it.

Another experimental paradigm involving aversive stimulation is called *punishment*. In punishment, the aversive stimulus follows and is contingent upon an operant response. The effect of the punishment procedure, in contrast to the effect of escape and avoidance, is to *reduce* or *suppress* the rate of responding.

The experimental setting in which the aversive control of operant behavior is studied is typically a modified Skinner box—modified to permit delivery of the aversive stimulus. Several types of aversive stimuli have been used: a blast of air with cats and a toy snake with monkeys (Masserman, 1946); a lever that slaps the paws of a rat (Skinner, 1938); and high intensities of noise with humans (Azrin, 1958). The most extensively used aversive stimulus, however, is electric shock—mainly because the physical parameters of shock (duration, frequency, voltage, waveform, amperage) can be most easily regulated. In the Skinner box, the subject usually is given electric shock through the grid floor of the box. One disadvantage of this method is that the subject can reduce the aversiveness of the shock by jumping up and down on the grid or by lying on his back. Azrin and Holtz (1966) claim that a more reliable technique for delivering shock is to use electrodes implanted slightly under the skin of the animal. If these electrodes are secure and make good electrical contact with the subject, the duration and intensity of the shock that the subject receives can be accurately controlled by the experimenter.

ESCAPE BEHAVIOR

When a subject first receives an aversive stimulus, such as shock, he responds reflexively—perhaps by leaping in the air and vigorously running around the box. While engaging in this respondent behavior, he may accidentally hit the lever in the box and thus succeed in turning off the shock. The first escape response made by the animal, therefore, is usually a respondent and not an operant. Why, then, do we refer to escape behavior as an example of operant conditioning? We do so because the removal of the aversive stimulus is made contingent upon the subject's response, and this response tends to occur earlier during subsequent shock presentations.

Escape behavior is maintained by a similar set of variables that are known to affect other operant behaviors. An increase in intensity of shock results in a higher rate of escape responding, just as an increase in amount of food will facilitate operant responding for a hungry animal. To demonstrate this effect, Dinsmoor and Winograd (1958) trained rats to press a lever and thus turn off a shock for a two-minute period. Since a variable-interval schedule of shock offset was used to reinforce the response, the subjects were given relatively long periods of shock. The intensity of the shock, measured in microammeters (ma), was varied randomly for given periods of time at six different levels during each session (0, 50, 100, 200, 300, and 400 ma). Figure 6-1 shows a cumulative record for one of these sessions.

According to this figure, the intensity of shock affected the rate of escape responding, with higher intensities producing faster responding. Furthermore, when the intensity of shock was changed, the transition to a new rate occurred almost immediately. Shock intensity apparently exerts this precise control over escape behavior because it provides motivation for the escape response and is also present *prior*

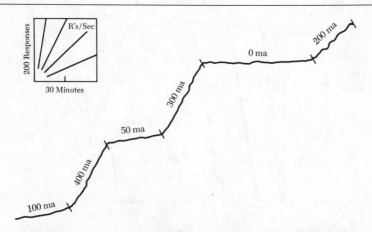

FIGURE 6-1. Cumulative record showing acquisition of an escape response by a rat. The intensity of the shock—measured in microammeters (ma)—from which the animal escaped was randomly varied. (Adapted from Dinsmoor, J. A., and Winograd, E. Shock intensity in variable-interval escape schedules. *Journal of the Experimental Analysis of Behavior,* 1958, 1, 145–148. Copyright 1958 by the Society for the Experimental Analysis of Behavior, Inc. Reprinted by permission.)

to the occurrence of the response. In contrast, in the positive-reinforcement paradigm, subjects do not know how much positive
reinforcement will be delivered until after they have made the response.

Escape behavior has also been demonstrated with conditioned aversive stimuli as well as with primary negative reinforcers. Using squirrel
monkeys as subjects, Azrin, Holtz, and Hake (1962) conditioned lever-
pressing behavior by having these responses turn off a light associated
with intermittent shock. The escape responses were reinforced by light
offset on various fixed-ratio schedules. Sample cumulative records of
a monkey's lever responding under various ratio schedules are shown
in Figure 6-2. The cumulative records are remarkably similar to those
reported in studies involving fixed-ratio schedules of positive reinforcement (Ferster and Skinner, 1957). For example, they show that
the length of the pause following reinforcement increases as the fixed-
ratio requirement increases. The same effect on postreinforcement
pauses is found with fixed-ratio schedules involving positive reward.
Additional research, indicating the parallel functions of positive and
negative rewards, is needed to further our understanding of the concept
of reinforcement.

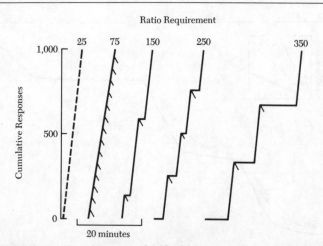

FIGURE 6-2.   Cumulative records of fixed-ratio escape from a conditioned
aversive stimulus (light paired with shock) by a monkey. The diagonal
lines indicate two-minute escape periods from the light (the recording
paper did not move during these intervals). (Adapted from Azrin, N. H.,
et al., "Intermittent reinforcement by removal of a conditioned aversive
stimulus," *Science*, 1962, **136**, 781–782. Copyright 1962 by the American
Association for the Advancement of Science. Reprinted by permission.)

AVOIDANCE BEHAVIOR

As mentioned, avoidance behavior usually occurs after escape behavior has been acquired. When avoidance conditioning is complete, the organism consistently makes an instrumental response (in a maze or shuttlebox) or an operant response (in a Skinner box) before the actual presentation of the aversive stimulus. In the literature, two types of avoidance-conditioning procedures have been reported: (1) *discriminated avoidance*, in which a particular stimulus (for instance, a tone or a light) warns the animal of impending aversive stimulation; (2) nondiscriminated or *free-operant avoidance*, in which the organism learns to make an avoidance response without a prior warning signal.

DISCRIMINATED AVOIDANCE

Discriminated Avoidance in Instrumental Conditioning. Solomon and Wynne (1953) conducted an experiment representative of the discriminated-avoidance procedure. Dogs were used as subjects in this study, and the apparatus consisted of a shuttle box with two sections separated by a barrier (see Figure 6-3). The warning cues were lights over each compartment. A dog was placed in one section of the box but could

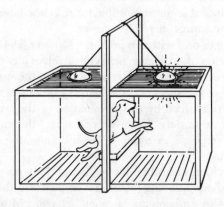

FIGURE 6-3.   Drawing of a shuttle box used to train dogs to avoid traumatic shock. (Adapted from Solomon, R. L., and Wynne, L. C., "Traumatic avoidance learning: Acquisition in normal dogs," *Psychological Monographs*, 1953, **61**, #354. Copyright 1953 by the American Psychological Association, and reproduced by permission.)

jump over the barrier into the other section. During a training trial, the light above the dog's section was turned off, whereas the light over the other section remained on. If the dog failed to jump over the barrier (make the avoidance response) within ten seconds following the change in illumination, he received a very intense (subtetanizing) shock. If the intensity of this shock had been any greater, the animal would have displayed muscular tetany and would have been unable to move. The dog could avoid this shock by leaping from one side of the box to the other within the ten-second interval.

During the initial training trials, the dogs displayed a tremendous amount of emotional behavior—rapid breathing, urination, and defecation. Eventually, they learned to jump over the barrier to escape from the shock. On subsequent trials, they escaped from the shock more and more rapidly (that is, the response latency decreased). When the latency of the response following the warning stimulus was less than ten seconds, the animals avoided the shock. Thus, they began to anticipate the shock following the warning stimulus and jumped before it was programmed to occur.

Figure 6-4 shows the acquisition curve of one of the dogs and illustrates the transition from escape to avoidance behavior. Notice that once the subject made his initial avoidance response, he successfully avoided the shock on *all* subsequent trials. Also, the latencies of avoidance responses continued to decrease even though the animal was no longer given shocks. The latter result is often referred to as the *avoidance paradox*, since it seems impossible for response latency to decrease when there is no source of reinforcement.

In attempting to deal with this problem, Mowrer (1947) hypothesized that the acquisition of avoidance behavior involves a two-stage process: (1) the classical conditioning of fear or anxiety to the warning stimulus, presented prior to the shock; (2) the learning of an instrumental avoidance response, reinforced by the termination of the warning stimulus and a reduction in anxiety. In the second stage, the animal is making the avoidance response in order to escape from the fear-producing warning stimulus.

In a later revision of his two-factor theory, Mowrer (1960) dropped the instrumental conditioning factor and emphasized the role of conditioned emotions in explaining avoidance behavior. Mowrer still maintained that conditioned fear occurs during the presentation of the warning stimulus, but he added that classical conditioning of another kind of emotion takes place. More specifically, he postulated that when the warning stimulus goes off, the subject should show a conditioned "relief"

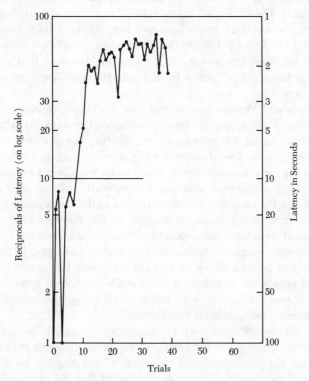

FIGURE 6-4.   Acquisition curve of a dog's jumping response to avoid an intense shock. When the latency of the response was less than ten seconds from the onset of the light, the dog avoided shock. (Adapted from Solomon and Wynne, 1953, by permission.)

response because this event indicates the end of the danger period. Thus, the subject learns that an avoidance response can provide escape from a fear-producing stimulus; after making the response, therefore, he will exhibit a relief-from-fear reaction. Bower, Starr, and Lazarovitz (1965) have found that the conditioned-relief reaction actually does exist and can be measured.

Returning now to the Solomon-Wynne study, the barrier-jumping avoidance response persisted without apparent diminution for over five hundred trials, even though shocks were no longer presented. This kind of avoidance response is virtually impossible to extinguish because, according to Solomon and Wynne, the avoidance response is made so quickly that fear is conserved and never has an opportunity to be extinguished. The only time that a subject would experience fear prior to making an avoidance response is on a long latency trial. Interestingly the results in Figure 6-4 show that long latency trials are consistently followed by short latency trials. Presumably, the fear that develops on a long latency trial serves to motivate the avoidance response on a subsequent trial.

Solomon and Wynne have found that avoidance responses can be extinguished by the use of a number of special procedures other than the ordinary extinction procedure of omitting the aversive stimulus. One method, called *forced reality testing*, involves putting a glass barrier between the two compartments. Thus, when the CS is presented, the dog is forced to discover that shock presentations have been discontinued. Since the animal is forced to remain in the fear-inducing setting and the shock is not given, extinction of the fear response and its concomitant avoidance behavior therefore occurs. A second method for suppressing avoidance behavior is through punishment. In this case, the subject is given a shock every time he makes the previously non-punished avoidance response. A third method involves a combination of the first two techniques, with the avoidance response being blocked on some trials and punished on others.

Although psychologists are understandably reluctant to use traumatic shock on human subjects, the results of avoidance-learning studies have great potential importance for the areas of personality development and clinical psychology. These results suggest that the mechanisms underlying neurotic behavior are conditioned responses, which the individual performs in order to reduce some learned fear or anxiety. Furthermore, they suggest that individuals with severe anxiety may never be able to rid themselves of this anxiety unless special therapeutic procedures are employed.

Another avoidance-conditioning study with possible relevance to clinical problems was conducted by two of Solomon's associates, Seligman and Maier (1967). These investigators demonstrated that animals who receive inescapable punishment cannot learn escape behavior later. More specifically, the experiment involved two groups of dogs. One group learned to press a panel in a harness to escape from shock; for the second group, however, (a yoked group), the panel was not present; therefore, the dogs could not escape the shock. Thus, the number and duration of shocks were equal for both groups; but one group had control over the situation, and the other group did not. After the first group had learned to escape the shock, both groups were trained in a shuttle box to escape and then avoid shock. The group that had previously learned to escape the shock showed normal acquisition of escape/avoidance behavior in the shuttle box. The other subjects failed to perform the escape response in the shuttle box—even when a seven-day rest was given between sessions of inescapable shock and shuttle-box testing. These data suggest that the yoked groups had learned "helplessness," which interfered with their ability to acquire future escape behavior. Apparently, they had learned that the termination of shock did not depend on their behavior. Further research may result in the discovery of methods or techniques that will enable a subject who has learned to be helpless to extinguish this behavior and to develop escape and avoidance responses, which are usually more adaptive ways of dealing with aversive situations.

Discriminated Avoidance in Operant Conditioning.   The paradigm for discriminated operant avoidance corresponds closely to the instrumental avoidance procedure previously described. A neutral stimulus is scheduled to precede or serve as a warning stimulus for the occurrence of an aversive stimulus. If the subject emits the appropriate operant response (a lever press) during the warning period, he can avoid the aversive stimulus.

Figure 6-5 shows the stimulus-response relationships that exist for a typical discriminated operant experiment. After the CS (the warning stimulus) has been given for a predetermined period of time, the aversive stimulus (shock) is scheduled to occur. An operant response made during the presentation of the CS and the shock is an escape response and will turn off both stimuli. The latency of the escape response is the time between the onset of the shock and the termination of the CS and shock. The right-hand side of the figure shows an example of avoidance behavior. The latency of the avoidance response (from the onset of the CS) is shorter than the duration of the warning period. This response has two effects: it terminates the CS, and it prevents the presentation of the shock. The inter-trial interval refers to the duration of time between successive CS presentations; this interval is usually varied in order to eliminate temporal conditioning. Responses usually are recorded during the inter-trial interval in order to measure the degree of stimulus control exerted by the warning stimulus.

Several investigators (Estes & Skinner, 1941; Brady & Hunt, 1955) have reported that when a neutral stimulus is consistently followed by an unavoidable aversive stimulus (such as shock), subsequent presentations of that stimulus will result in a striking reduction in the ongoing rate of responding for positive reinforcement. The degree to which this *conditioned suppression* occurs is often considered an accurate index of the magnitude of the emotional response elicited by the warning stimulus.

An experiment using both the discriminated-avoidance and the conditioned-suppression procedures was done by Hoffman and Fleshler (1962). This particularly ingenious study investigates the acquisition of avoidance behavior and also measures the degree of emotionality that the subjects showed throughout the course of training. In this study, rats were trained to press a lever to escape presentations of shock. The shocks were then discontinued and the animals trained to press a plate on the floor of the cage to receive food as a positive reward. The animals were deprived of food before each session, and the plate-pressing response for food was maintained on a variable-interval schedule. After the rate of responding for food had stabilized, one-minute tone (1,000 cps) presentations were given every ten minutes. If a rat pressed the lever when the tone was on, the tone was turned off. Plate presses were still reinforced with the positive reward according to the VI schedule. This phase of the experiment was done in order to allow

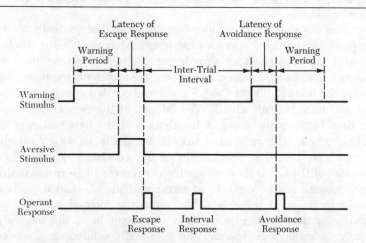

FIGURE 6-5. Schematic representation of stimulus-response relationships in a typical discriminated-avoidance experiment. (Adapted from Hoffman, 1966. In: *Operant Behavior: Areas of Research and Application.* Walter Honig; Editor. Copyright ©1966 by Meredith Publishing Company. Reprinted by permission of Appleton-Century-Crofts, Educational Division, Meredith Corporation.)

the subjects to adapt to the onset and offset of the tone. After two such adaptation sessions, the subjects were given shocks after the presentation of the tone, which now served as a warning stimulus. A subject could turn off the tone and avoid the shock if he pressed the lever before the warning period terminated. Otherwise, he received both tone and shock until he pressed the lever and thereby escaped the tone and the shock. Throughout the entire experiment, the plate-pressing response was scheduled to give positive reward.

Section A of Figure 6-6 shows the percentage and latency of the avoidance responses made per session. It also shows the percentage of one-minute intervals, prior to the tone, in which one or more lever responses were made. The mean values for the two adaptation (AD) sessions indicate that very few lever responses were made. Furthermore, as Sections B and C indicate, the animals spent most of their time pressing the plate for food throughout the AD sessions. During the subsequent sessions with shock, however, the percentage of avoidance responses increased, while the latency of these responses decreased. In addition, the number of inter-trial responses decreased across successive sessions, suggesting that the tone was gradually acquiring more stimulus control over the avoidance behavior.

Now let us examine the changes in emotionality over the sessions. As previously stated, emotionality or fear was measured in this study by means of conditioned suppression of the ongoing plate-pressing response. Hoffman and Fleshler quantified the degree of suppression by forming *suppression ratios* (shown in Section B and C). They calculated the ratios in Section B by obtaining the *rate* of plate pressing that occurred during the tone and dividing this rate by the rate of plate pressing made during a one-minute period prior to the tone. Thus, ratios with values near 1.00 indicate no response suppression and little emotionality, whereas values near zero indicate considerable response suppression and emotionality. To calculate the suppression ratios presented in Section C, the investigators took the ratio of plate pressing during the one-minute period following the offset of tone (and shock on nonavoidance trials) and divided this rate by the plate-pressing rate for the minute-period preceding the tone. The suppression ratios during both tone and post-tone periods were calculated separately for avoidance and nonavoidance trials.

As was noted earlier, the avoidance behavior was acquired very gradually over successive training trials. In contrast, the plate-pressing response (Section B) was rapidly suppressed when shock was paired with tone. In fact, this response was almost completely suppressed by

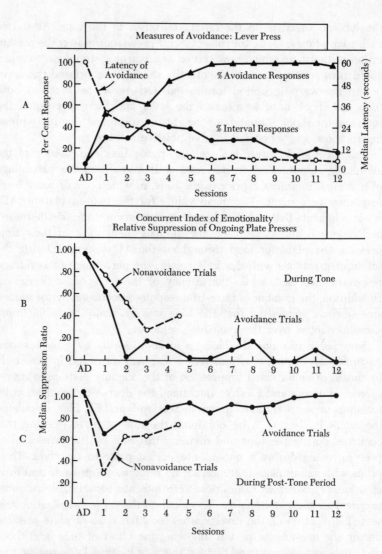

FIGURE 6-6. Measures of avoidance responses (Section A) and concurrent indices of emotionality during the tone (Section B) and following the tone (Section C). AD refers to the final adaptation session to tone. Shock-avoidance training was given on Sessions 1 through 12. (Adapted from Hoffman, H. S., and Fleshler, M., "The course of emotionality in the development of avoidance," *Journal of Experimental Psychology*, 1962, 64, 288–294. Copyright 1962 by the American Psychological Association, and reproduced by permission.)

Session 2, when the performance of the avoidance response was not yet optimal. These results suggest that the acquisition of fear *preceded*, and perhaps could have been responsible for, the avoidance response. In addition, conditioned suppression was significantly greater on trials during which the subjects made the avoidance response than on trials where they failed to avoid the shock. Again, this finding suggests that emotionality, as measured by conditioned suppression, plays an important role in establishing avoidance behavior. Both of these findings are consistent with the previously discussed two-factor theory of avoidance learning (Mowrer, 1947, 1960), which claims that the fear elicited by the CS provides the necessary motivation for the avoidance response to be performed.

As Section C of Figure 6-6 shows, suppression on avoidance trials was significantly less during the post-tone period than on the nonavoidance trials. This result also supports the two-factor theory, which assumes that the basis for reinforcement of an avoidance response is the reduction of fear.

The two-factor interpretation of these data, however, is subject to a number of criticisms. First, the fact the conditioned suppression occurred several sessions before the avoidance response does not necessarily mean that the suppression *caused* the avoidance response. Avoidance behavior may have required more training sessions than conditioned suppression because avoidance responding involves the acquisition of a specific response (lever pressing), whereas conditioned suppression consists of engaging in any type of behavior other than the reinforced response (plate pressing). A second criticism concerns the physical arrangement of the lever and plate in the experimental chamber. These two responses are incompatible in that they cannot be performed at the same time. If a subject makes an avoidance response during presentation of the tone, he naturally is unable to maintain his rate of plate pressing. Thus, suppression of the plate-pressing response would naturally be greater on avoidance trials than on nonavoidance trials, even though there might be no difference in amounts of emotionality experienced on these trials.

A third criticism concerns the suppression of the post-tone response. The fact that there was less suppression following the offset of tone on avoidance does not necessarily imply that there was greater fear reduction. Instead, the difference between these trials probably occurred because the emotionality was greater after nonavoidance trials, in which tone and shock were given, than after avoidance trials, in which only the tone was presented.

In addition to the major findings discussed above, Hoffman and
Fleshler revealed an interesting phenomenon when analyzing their subjects' changes in responses within and between sessions. The percentage
of avoidance responses made for each of the five trials per session,
over twelve successive sessions, is presented in Figure 6-7. During the
four trials of the adaptation session, there was no significant increase in
tendency to press the lever. With the introduction of the shock on
Session 1, there was an increase in the percentage of avoidance responses, which reached asymptote after about the fifth session. During
the initial sessions, there was a striking improvement over the four
trials given during each session. This improvement, however, was coun-
teracted by a between-session decrement. That is, the percentage of
avoidance responses was always smaller on the first trial of a given
session than on the last trial of the previous session. This phenomenon,
termed a *warm-up effect*, is strictly a motivational phenomenon, since
it does not lead to a permanent change in behavior.

Besides the temporal variables, the physical characteristics of the
warning stimulus play an important role in the conditioning of fear
and long-term maintenance of aversive control. As was previously
shown, when a warning stimulus precedes shock, subjects will show
conditioned suppression in their ongoing response rate. By using the
conditioned-suppression paradigm, Hoffman, Fleshler, and Jensen
(1963) were able to investigate the degree to which this emotional

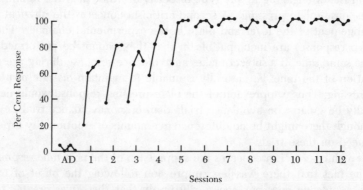

FIGURE 6-7. Percentage of avoidance responses performed during four
trials of each of twelve discriminated-avoidance sessions. AD refers to the
final adaptation session, in which the tone was not paired with shock.
(Adapted from Hoffman, 1966, by permission.)

reaction is restricted to stimuli similar to the CS. In this study, pigeons were trained to peck at a disc for food on a VI schedule; then a 1,000-cps tone was given for forty-eight seconds—after which unavoidable shock was presented. After several trials, the pigeons showed no pecking when the tone was presented. At this point, the shocks were discontinued, and tones of various frequencies were randomly presented to the subjects. The amount of response suppression given to each tone was calculated. Suppression ratios then were determined in the following way: First, the number of responses made during the initial forty seconds of tone was subtracted from the number of responses made during the forty seconds prior to the onset of tone. Next, this difference was divided by the number of responses made during the forty seconds prior to the tone. A ratio of 1.00, therefore, represents complete suppression; and zero indicates that there was no change in the rate of responding between the time prior to the tone and during its presentation.

The solid line in Figure 6-8 shows the mean suppression ratios found for the various frequencies. These results depict the phenomenon of stimulus generalization; that is, most of the response suppression occurs when the CS (1,000-cps tone) is presented, and there is less suppression to values that differ in frequency from the CS. Thus, conditioned suppression, like positively reinforced behavior, shows a considerable degree of stimulus control.

For a second group of pigeons, who received the identical conditioned-suppression training, generalization tests with various frequencies were given two and a half years following training. During this interruption, the animals were maintained under normal conditions and were not used in any experiments. The dashed line in Figure 6-8 shows the mean response suppression obtained from these subjects. By the end of the generalization testing, in which no shocks were given, the extinction process had progressed to the point where the emotional effects of suppression were scarcely discernible. This final extinction gradient is indicated by the dotted line in the figure.

Hoffman and his associates then addressed themselves to the following problem: What would happen if these subjects were again placed in a condition of emotional stress? Would the effects of emotionality be restricted to tones of similar frequency to the CS? In order to investigate this problem, they gave additional generalization testing to the birds just tested in extinction for stimulus generalization (dotted line). These tests were the same as those given before—except that there were periods of complete darkness between tone presentations and brief shocks were presented during these periods. The pigeons never pecked

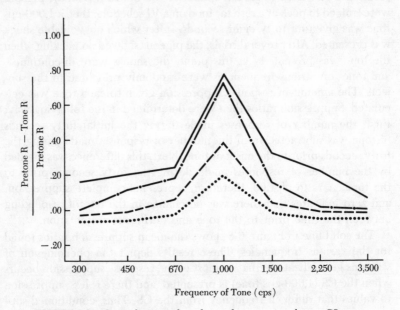

FIGURE 6-8. Generalization of conditioned suppression about a CS tone (1,000 cps) paired with inescapable shock. Solid line shows the results of the generalization test when it was given immediately following training. Dashed line indicates the results when there was an interruption of two and a half years between training and testing. Dotted line shows the gradients obtained from the previous group during the final phase of testing for generalization in extinction. Dot-dashed line indicates the gradients found when the subject received presentations of shock between tones. (Adapted from Hoffman, H. S., Fleshler, M., and Jensen, P. Stimulus aspects of aversive control: The retention of conditioned suppression. *Journal of the Experimental Analysis of Behavior*, 1963, **6**, 575–583. Copyright 1963 by the Society for the Experimental Analysis of Behavior, Inc. Reprinted by permission.)

at the disc during the dark periods, and thus no responses were punished. However, as shown by the dot-dashed line in Figure 6-8, the shocks produced a marked increase in amount of response suppression, especially to the CS value. This increase in suppression to the tones occurred even though no additional *pairings* of CS and shock were given. Apparently, the independent presentations of shock increased the general emotional state of the subjects. The increased emotionality, in turn, was responsible for the substantial increase in suppression to values resembling the CS. The notion that behavior is the result of (a) the level of a subject's emotionality prior to a trial plus (b) the fear resulting from actual presentation of the CS is also consistent with the previously described warm-up phenomenon.

The findings of Hoffman and his colleagues are important because they contribute to our understanding of the process of avoidance learning; they are also relevant to clinical problems concerned with the reduction of fear and anxiety.

NONDISCRIMINATED AVOIDANCE

The experimental paradigm for nondiscriminated or free-operant avoidance differs from discriminated avoidance in that no specific warning stimulus is presented prior to the aversive stimulus. As with the previous operant procedure, electric shocks are delivered to the subject through the grid floor of the Skinner box. Two recycling timers are used to program the shocks (see Figure 6-9). If the animal does not press the lever in the box, the first timer will control the interval between brief presentations of shock. This interval is termed the *shock-shock* (S-S) *interval.* However, if the animal should happen to press the lever, the shock will be postponed for the period of time determined by the second timer. The duration for which the shock is postponed is referred to as the *response-shock* (R-S) *interval.* The timers are never operating simultaneously, and shock presentations are determined by the S-S interval unless a response is made. After every response, the shock is postponed for the duration of the R-S interval, which overrides the operation of the S-S timer. Thus, by pressing the lever with an inter-response time of less than the S-S interval, the subject can prevent the operation of the S-S clock and continually postpone the shock. As mentioned before, there is no exteroceptive stimulus that warns the animal of the possibility of impending shock. However, the S-S and R-S intervals are fixed so that the subject can regularly avoid shock if he can learn the duration of these intervals.

The schedule described above was developed by Sidman (1953) and is often referred to as a *Sidman avoidance schedule,* or the *nondiscriminated-avoidance procedure.*

The two temporal factors that govern the Sidman avoidance schedule are the S-S and the R-S intervals. How do the durations of each of these intervals affect avoidance responding? Sidman (1953, 1966) has systematically investigated the temporal parameters of free-operant avoidance. He first trained a group of rats to press a lever in order to avoid brief shocks and then gave them training with several values

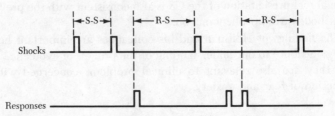

FIGURE 6-9. Schematic representation of the shock-response relationships in the free-operant avoidance procedure. S-S indicates the shockshock interval; R-S indicates the response-shock interval. (Adapted from Sidman, 1966. In: *Operant Behavior: Areas of Research and Application.* Walter Honig; Editor. Copyright ©1966 by Meredith Publishing Company. Reprinted by permission of Appleton-Century-Crofts, Educational Division, Meredith Corporation.)

of S-S and R-S intervals. Sidman then set the S-S interval at a fixed value and obtained the animals' response rate for a series of R-S intervals, given in a random order. He then changed the S-S interval and recorded rates for another series of different R-S intervals. The procedure was repeated over and over until each animal had generated a family of curves showing the relationship with the rate of avoidance responding for various S-S intervals across a number of R-S intervals. The results of this experiment for one animal are shown in Figure 6-10.

The following relationships are apparent from this figure: (1) In each S-S interval, the response rate decreases when long R-S intervals are in effect. This result obviously occurs because the longer the shock is postponed following the response, the longer the inter-response time can be without the presentation of shock. (2) In each S-S interval, the highest rate of responding occurs when the R-S interval is of the same duration as the S-S interval. (3) Responding decreases when the R-S interval is shorter than the S-S interval; when the R-S interval is approximately half as long as the S-S interval, the animal stops responding altogether. (4) As the S-S interval decreases, the peak of responding along the R-S dimension increases. Thus, the maximum rate of responding is achieved when the S-S and R-S intervals are equal and of a short duration.

In addition to enabling psychologists to study the processes of temporal conditioning in animals, the Sidman avoidance schedule is an important technique for establishing and maintaining high rates of responding. If subjects are trained on this schedule during time-in periods

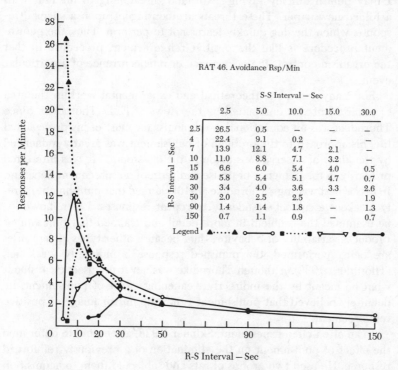

RAT 46. Avoidance Rsp/Min

	S-S Interval — Sec				
	2.5	5.0	10.0	15.0	30.0
2.5	26.5	0.5	–	–	–
4	22.4	9.1	0.2	–	–
7	13.9	12.1	4.7	2.1	–
10	11.0	8.8	7.1	3.2	–
15	6.6	6.0	5.4	4.0	0.5
20	5.8	5.4	5.1	4.7	0.7
30	3.4	4.0	3.6	3.3	2.6
50	2.0	2.5	2.5	–	1.9
90	1.4	1.4	1.8	–	1.3
150	0.7	1.1	0.9	–	0.7

FIGURE 6-10.   Table presents the average response rates for a single subject at a combination of shock-shock (S-S) and response-shock (R-S) intervals. Response rates are partially plotted in the curves. (Adapted from Sidman, 1966, by permission.)

and given rests during time-out periods, they typically show high, sustained response rates during hundreds of accumulated hours and perhaps receive only one or two shocks.

PUNISHMENT

Punishment occurs when some aversive stimulus, or the threat of such a stimulus, is made contingent upon the performance of a specific response. One of the primary effects of punishment, of course, is the suppression or elimination of the behavior responsible for the aversive stimulus. For example, if my dog jumps on a chair in the living room,

I may punish him by saying "No" and threatening to hit him with a folded newspaper. These threats are contingent upon a specific response, which the dog quickly learns not to perform. Thus, the punishment procedure is like the positive-reinforcement procedure in that the organism controls the occurrence or nonoccurrence of a particular event.

For many years, the theoretical and experimental work in the area of punishment was dominated by the views of E. L. Thorndike. Since Thorndike was an educational psychologist for most of his professional life, his approach to the problem of punishment was greatly influenced by the kinds of observations made in the classroom. He was interested primarily in the influence of praise and reproof on subsequent behavior. In his earliest writings, Thorndike (1913) claimed that punishment merely weakens a subject's tendency to repeat responses. Later, however, he examined the problem in more detail and claimed that punishment produces variability of behavior; thus, because other types of responses are being performed, the punished response is indirectly weakened (Thorndike, 1932). Although Thorndike was never precisely clear about what he meant by the indirectly weakening effect of punishment, he definitely believed that punishment is not the mirror image of positive reinforcement.

In an often-cited experiment, Skinner (1938) attempted to determine the effect of punishment on the elimination of a previously reinforced response. He used two groups of rats and subjected them to acquisition training for three days in a Skinner box. He began withholding the reward for both groups during extinction sessions. One group, the control, was given ordinary extinction experience. The experimental rats were given a different treatment. They were placed in a Skinner box with a bar that would snap back and strike their paws whenever they pressed it. These slaps did not injure the animals, but they were nevertheless harsh enough to be aversive. (This type of bar slapping is rarely used in current studies of punishment because—compared with electric shock, which can be quite accurately specified—it is a very uncontrolled aversive stimulus.) Punishment was continued throughout the first ten minutes of extinction. Figure 6-11 shows the effects of this procedure in comparison with the ordinary extinction procedure given to the control group.

Clearly, punishment did suppress the number of responses made during the first day, for the cumulative record of the subjects who were slapped by the lever is far below that of the subjects who received ordinary extinction. However, during the second day of extinction,

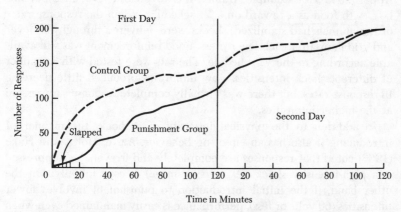

FIGURE 6-11. Cumulative number of responses of two groups of rats that underwent the same acquisition training and then were given two successive extinction sessions. Rats in the punishment group were slapped during the first ten minutes of extinction on the first day. (Adapted from *The Behavior of Organisms: An Experimental Analysis*, by B. F. Skinner. Copyright 1938 by D. Appleton-Century-Crofts, Educational Division, Meredith Corporation.)

when punishment was no longer administered, the previously punished animals responded at a faster rate than the unpunished animals. In fact, by the end of the second day of extinction, there was no significant difference between the total number of responses made by the two groups. Skinner concluded from these results that punishment may reduce the rate of responding but that this suppression is only temporary. This finding was for a long time misinterpreted by psychologists to mean that punishment is a relatively ineffective way of controlling behavior. That is clearly not true. Data to be presented later indicate that punishment can completely suppress behavior if the punishment is either of a high intensity or presented for a long duration at a low intensity. In other words, to have an enduring effect, punishment normally must be quite harsh. Unfortunately, if it were applied in everyday life, harsh punishment could produce such undesirable side effects as neurotic behavior or psychosomatic disorders.

PARAMETERS OF PUNISHMENT

How does the intensity of punishment influence its effectiveness? A large number of experiments have been concerned with this topic.

Appel (1963), for example, trained rats to press a lever in a Skinner box, with food as a reward on a VI schedule. When the response rates of the animals had stabilized, shocks were delivered through the lever and grid floor after each lever press. Food reinforcement was still available according to the VI schedule. The rats were tested with a number of different shock intensities. Low intensities produced little decrease in response rates, but there was virtually complete response suppression at the higher intensities.

In addition to the physical intensity of a shock, the manner of introducing it also has an effect on behavior. Azrin, Holtz, and Hake (1963) noted that responses are completely and irreversibly suppressed if a high-intensity shock (80 volts or more) is used initially. On the other hand, if the initial introduction to punishment involves lower intensities (60 volts or less), performance is easily maintained even when the punishment is later increased to intensities as great as 130 volts. Apparently, the absolute intensity of shock that the subject receives is not as critical as the relative change in intensity between prior shocks and those presently given.

Another important variable is the rate at which the intensity of the punishing stimulus changes. For example, Masserman (1946) found that the sudden introduction of an intense shock produces a much greater reduction of the punished response than when the intensity is gradually increased. One explanation of this finding is that the sudden onset of the punishing stimulus is both aversive and novel.

The effectiveness of punishment also depends on the length of the delay between punishing stimulus and incorrect response (the delay-of-punishment variable). Azrin (1956) found that enduring response reduction can be obtained only if the delivery of shock immediately follows the response.

Finally, the schedule for which the punishing stimulus is programmed to occur is an important parameter of punishment. Azrin, Holtz, and Hake (1963), on the basis of a series of extensive experiments, concluded that the greater the proportion of punished responses, the greater the response reduction. Thus, continuous punishment produces greater suppression than does intermittent punishment for as long as the punishment contingency is maintained. However, if the punishment contingency is discontinued, continuous punishment results in a more rapid recovery in responding—possibly because the absence of punishment can be more readily discriminated. Thus, the results of partial punishment are very much like the results of partial positive reinforcement.

The parameters of punishment discussed so far—intensity, manner of introduction, and schedule of punishment—are all variables concerned with the properties of the punishing stimulus. Other variables that influence the effect of punishment are concerned with the administration of positive reward.

> In order that a person may learn to make a certain response in the first place, some type of reinforcement is presumably necessary. If the reinforcement follows as a simple physical consequence of the act, there seems to be no reason to assume that reinforcement should cease whenever punishment begins. Indeed, if the reinforcement is long withheld, extinction sets in, and there may no longer be a response to be punished [Dinsmoor, 1952, p. 27].

Thus, in order for the effects of punishment to be permanent, the response must be reinforced as well as punished during training. Let us now examine some variables of positive reward that influence the effectiveness of punishment.

The schedule of positive reinforcement is one such variable. The choice of a particular reinforcement schedule for maintaining the punished response will determine the temporal patterning of the response during punishment. The following results for different schedules have been reported; in all instances, punishment was delivered for every response. During FR (fixed-ratio) reinforcement, the postreinforcement pause is lengthened, but the high response rate is reduced only slightly (Azrin, 1959). With FI (fixed-interval) reinforcement, the number of FI responses may be reduced considerably, but the degree of temporal discrimination remains virtually the same (Azrin & Holtz, 1961). Finally, with VI (variable-interval) reinforcement, the rate of responding is reduced, but the basic stability and uniformity in responding persist (Azrin, 1960).

A second reinforcement variable that is pertinent to the effect of punishment is the reinforcement frequency. Punishment typically leads, indirectly, to a decrease in the reinforcement frequency because of the reduction in the rate of responding. But under certain schedules, such as DRL (differential reinforcement for low rates of responding), reduction in response rate due to punishment may actually increase the frequency of positive reinforcement.

A third variable is the motivational state of the organism. The degree to which a food-reinforced response resists the effects of punishment depends on the degree of food deprivation. If this deprivation is increased, and if the intensity of the punishment is kept constant, the amount of response suppression usually is reduced. In one study (Azrin, Holtz, & Hake, 1963), punishment was rendered completely ineffective when the degree of motivation for emitting the response was increased. On the basis of such data, psychologists have assumed that a subject responding under the punishment procedure is experiencing a great deal of approach-avoidance conflict—conflict arising from the simultaneous operation of two drives, fear and hunger; the stronger of these two drives will determine whether or not the response will be performed.

The final variable that we will examine has to do with the number of responses available to the subject in the punishment situation. In most experiments dealing with punishment, there is only one response for the subject to perform, and it is the only response that the experimenter carefully studies. This is clearly a very artificial and contrived situation, because an individual punished in real life for making a particular response can usually perform a number of alternative responses. In fact, the observed suppression of the punished response may occur because the person has adopted alternative behavior that is incompatible with the punished response.

In the laboratory, Holtz, Azrin, and Ayllon (1963) have found that there is greater suppression of the punished response when an alternative response is available—and when this response produces reinforcement—than in a single-response (no-alternative) situation. This result implies that punishment will be more effective if nonpunished behavior, which will result in the same advantages as the punished behavior, is also permissible.

CONDITIONS FOR MAXIMUM
EFFECTIVENESS OF PUNISHMENT

Now that we have examined most of the important variables related to the punishment procedure, let us assume that we are interested in arranging the conditions of punishment so that they will be maximally effective. The following is a list of rules that should be adhered to in order to achieve this goal. The list will also serve to summarize the findings concerning the parameters of punishment.

1. The punishing stimulus should be arranged in such a manner that no unauthorized escape responses are possible. (For this purpose, an electrode for delivering shock directly to the animal is the most ideal punishing stimulus.)

2. The punishing stimulus should be intense and should be delivered abruptly and immediately after the occurrence of the "incorrect" response.

3. The frequency of the punishing stimulus should be as high as possible; ideally, it should be given after every response.

4. The level of motivation for making the punished response should be low. Thus, a low level of deprivation and a relatively small amount of reward should be used to reinforce the response. Likewise, the frequency of the positive reward should be reduced.

5. An alternative response should be available for the subject to perform. The suppression of the punished response will be greatest under conditions where the alternative response is never punished but instead produces greater reinforcement than the punished response.

6. Care should be taken to ensure that a punishing stimulus is not inadvertently followed by a positive reward. Otherwise, the punishing stimulus may acquire conditioned reinforcing properties. In fact, an effective way to suppress a punished response is to have the aversive stimulus consistently followed by a period of extinction. Under this condition, the aversive stimulus is not only punishing but also a cue for the withdrawal of reward. Thus, the discriminative properties of the aversive stimulus can further influence the usual suppressive effects of the punishment.

THEORETICAL INTERPRETATIONS OF PUNISHMENT

Since Thorndike's (1913) statement of the Law of Effect, numerous theories have been proposed to account for the mechanism through which punishment exerts its influence on behavior. In this section, we will categorize the various theories around two major issues. The first of these deals with the question of whether or not there is any difference between response-contingent and response-noncontingent punishment. That is, does the specific response that intervenes between a discriminative stimulus and punishment have any effect on behavior modification? The second issue concerns the role of fear as a possible mediating response that influences behavior. Although all theorists acknowledge that fear occurs with the punishment procedure, some view it as a cause for changes in behavior and others as simply a concomitant of the punishment procedure.

Depending on the positions taken with regard to these two issues, the various theories of punishment can be grouped into four classes: (1) response-contingent punishment—fear as a concomitant response,

(2) response-noncontingent punishment—fear as a concomitant response, (3) response-contingent punishment—fear as a mediating response, and (4) response-noncontingent punishment—fear as a mediating response. Within these four general categories, Table 6-1 lists six traditional interpretations of punishment. The seventh interpretation, the compound-stimulus interpretation, was only recently reported (Williams, 1969). In the remainder of this section, these theories will be discussed—first, according to the importance that each of them places on the response contingency; second, according to the assumptions each makes concerning the effects of fear on behavior.

Contingent vs. Noncontingent Theories of Punishment.   Whenever the effect of response-contingent punishment differs from that of response-independent punishment, recourse must be made to either of the two interpretations to account for the suppression of responding. Both of these interpretations assume that the response contingency is important in determining punished behavior.

Response-inhibition interpretation. Thorndike's (1913) original statement of the Law of Effect assumed a significant contingency between response and punishment and postulated some form of response inhibition in the punishment situation:

> When a modifiable connection between a situation and response is made and is accompanied by an annoying state of affairs, its strength is decreased. . . . By the strength of a connection is meant roughly the probability that the response will be made when the situation recurs. Furthermore, the weakening effect of annoyingness upon a bond varies with the closeness between it and the bond [p. 4].

The punishment aspect of the Law of Effect is almost certainly valid at a descriptive level: Other things being equal, an act is less likely to recur if its prior occurrence has led to aversive stimulation. At an interpretive level, however, this position encounters difficulty; for punishment clearly is not a simple matter of obliterating or stamping out stimulus-response bonds. In 1932, Thorndike completely revised his original conception and attributed the effect of punishment not to the weakening of the punished response but rather to the strengthening of some alternative behavior. Thus, from his revisions of the Law of Effect, Thorndike set the stage for the development of the avoidance interpretation of punishment.

Avoidance interpretation. Instead of postulating some sort of inhibition of the punished response, several theorists (Mowrer, 1947, 1960; Dollard & Miller, 1950; Skinner, 1953; Dinsmoor, 1954) have suggested that some process of reinforcement occurs for nonresponding in the punishment situation.

> The performance of any given act normally produces kinesthetic (and often visual, auditory, and tactual) stimuli which are perceptible to the performer of the act. If these stimuli are followed a few times by a noxious stimulus, they will soon acquire the capacity to produce the emotion of fear. When, therefore, on subsequent occasions the subject starts to perform the previously punished act, the result will arouse fear; and the most effective way of eliminating this fear is for the subject to stop the activity which is producing the fear-producing stimuli [Mowrer, 1947, p. 136].

Thus, the avoidance interpretation involves two critical processes for explaining the suppression of responses under punishment. First, it postulates that, through classical conditioning, the experimenter-controlled and subject-produced stimuli begin to elicit the fear response originally produced by the aversive stimulus. Second, it assumes that some form of reinforcement leads to the acquisition of an alternative response (other than the one punished) by the process of instrumental learning.

Both the inhibition and the avoidance hypotheses assume that the contingent relationship between the response and the aversive stimulus is a critical factor in the punishment procedure. But whereas the inhibition interpretation assumes that some sort of inhibition accumulates on trials in which the punished response is made, the avoidance interpretation assumes that some form of reinforcement is responsible for the learning of an alternative response. Are there any differential consequences predicted by each of these theories that can be tested empirically? A possible approach to this problem would be to observe carefully the behavior of subjects during periods when response-contingent punishment is administered. The gradual appearance of stereotyped responses during these periods would suggest that some form of reinforcement is responsible for the decrease in rate of the punished response. Such stereotyped responding would be predicted by the avoidance interpretation but not necessarily by the inhibition interpretation. Although there has been no empirical attempt of this kind to test these two interpretations, several theorists (for instance, Dinsmoor, 1954; Mowrer, 1960) have expressed a preference for the avoidance interpretation on the grounds that it does not involve any new assumptions

from those already made to explain the learning of the avoidance response. Nevertheless, in accounting for the various effects of punishment
on behavior, both explanations fail to specify the conditions under
which response facilitation, as opposed to response suppression, should
be observed. Some experiments that have demonstrated an increase
in responding as a result of the administration of punishment will be
discussed later in this chapter.

In instances where response-contingent and response-independent
aversive stimulation are shown to produce virtually identical performance, four possible interpretations have been proposed to explain the
effects of punishment. All four of these interpretations, in contrast to
the two theories described previously, can account for either response
facilitation or response suppression produced as a result of punishment.

Competing-response interpretation. Several theorists have stressed the
importance of the unconditioned skeletal response elicited by the aversive stimulus in mediating the effects of punishment. Presumably, by
the process of classical conditioning, these skeletal responses may be
elicited by discriminative or response-produced stimuli preceding the
noxious stimulus. "Punishment achieves its effects not by taking away
strength from the physiological basis of the connection, but by forcing
the animal or child to do something different" (Guthrie, 1935, p. 158).
Response suppression should occur if the unconditioned skeletal response elicited by the aversive stimulus is incompatible with the punished act, whereas response facilitation should be observed under conditions where the unconditioned response is compatible with the punished
act.

Fowler's (1959) observation probably provides some of the best evidence available in support of the competing-response interpretation
of punishment. In an extensive parametric study, Fowler trained rats
to run down a straight alley to a food compartment in which they
received a mild shock prior to eating. The intensity of the shock was
adjusted so that it reliably elicited withdrawal movements and yet did
not prevent the rats from eating soon after it was terminated. For
half of the subjects, shock was delivered to the forepaws; for the other
half, to the hindpaws. The results of this study indicated that subjects
receiving forepaw shock, which elicited a response incompatible with
the instrumental running response, ran slower with increased trials. In
contrast, the subjects given hindpaw shock, which elicited a response
compatible with running, showed a striking increase in their running
speed over trials.

TABLE 6-1

Interpretations of Punishment

	Response-Contingent Punishment	Response-Noncontingent Punishment
Fear as Concomitant Response	Response-Inhibition Interpretation (Compound-Stimulus Interpretation)	Competing-Response Interpretation Escape-Response Interpretation Discrimination Interpretation
Fear as Mediating Response	Avoidance Interpretation	Fear Interpretation

Fear interpretation. A classic experiment, reported by Estes and Skinner (1941), demonstrated that if a tone is presented to an animal prior to the delivery of shock for a number of trials, the presentation of the tone alone will be sufficient to produce a suppression of the rate of ongoing reinforced behavior. This phenomenon, described earlier, is referred to as *conditional suppression.* According to Estes (1944), the unconditioned fear response elicited by an aversive stimulus may, by the process of classical conditioning, occur to a warning or discriminative stimulus.

It is clear that a disturbing or traumatic stimulus arouses a changed state of the organism of the sort commonly termed "emotional" and that any stimulus present simultaneously with the disturbing stimulus becomes a conditioned stimulus capable of itself arousing the state on subsequent occasions [p. 36].

According to this interpretation, the emotional response (fear) is responsible for the suppression of responding.

Contrary to this position, several studies have indicated that fear may increase, rather than decrease, the rate of responding. For example, the rate of avoidance responding may be increased by the presentation of a stimulus previously associated with a noxious event (Sidman, Herrnstein, & Conrad, 1957). Likewise, if punishment is paired with positive reward during training, the punishing stimulus presented at low intensity during subsequent extinction will increase responding (Azrin & Holtz, 1961, 1966). Even as early as 1944, Estes—aware that punishment sometimes appears to facilitate behavior—emphasized the significance of possible competing responses in addition to the fear response.

As mentioned previously, neither the competing-response nor the fear interpretation of punishment requires that a contingent relationship exist between response and punishment. According to some proponents of these theories, however, conditioning of withdrawal or fear responses to the subject's own response-produced stimuli (for instance, introceptive cues of anticipatory responding) may occur. In such instances (where appeal is made to response-produced stimuli, as opposed to the experimenter-controlled cues of the subject's environment), the effect of punishment is assumed to be critically affected by the response contingency. As mentioned, however, the competing-response and fear interpretations do not *necessarily* require response-contingent punishment to account for the suppression of responding.

Escape-response interpretation.   Several theorists have emphasized the importance of the escape response as a possible mechanism mediating the effects of punishment. According to this position, a response associated with the termination of punishment may be conditioned to occur to the discriminative stimulus.

> According to drive-reduction theories of learning, punishment does not necessarily have any inhibitory effects. The only learning resulting from punishment is the learning of the responses, especially escape responses, evoked by the punishing stimulus and conditioned to cues of the punished act [Gwinn, 1949, p. 260].

This interpretation assumes that suppression of the punished response can occur only after some escape response from the aversive stimulus has been acquired. Contrary to this assumption, several experiments (Sidman, Herrnstein, & Conrad, 1957; Hoffman & Fleshler, 1962) have demonstrated effective response suppression even when the punishing stimulus of electric shock was made virtually inescapable (for instance, when the punishment was less than 100 milliseconds in duration). The animals in these studies could scarcely have learned to escape from shocks of such a brief duration, although certain forms of stereotyped, superstitious behavior could have developed.

Discrimination interpretation. The discrimination interpretation of the effects of punishment assumes that the punishing stimulus may acquire discriminative properties in addition to its aversive or emotional properties. "Whenever punishment is differentially associated with reinforcement, a discriminative property will probably influence the effectiveness of punishment" (Holtz and Azrin, 1962). If punishment is correlated with positive reinforcement during training, presentation of the same punishment during extinction may increase response rate; however, if punishment is correlated with nonreinforcement, its presentation may drastically decrease response rate during extinction. Thus, the discrimination interpretation of punishment stresses the similarity between the conditions of punishment during training and subsequent testing.

Probably the best evidence in support of the discrimination interpretation has been reported by Holtz and Azrin (1961). In this experiment, periods of intermittent food reinforcement were alternated with periods of nonreinforcement. Since no external stimulus was correlated with these conditions, the subjects had no way of discriminating the reinforcement from the extinction periods except by the consequences of their responses. The procedure was then arranged so that all responses produced a mild punishment (electric shock) during the nonreinforcement periods but not during the partial-reinforcement periods. This differential punishment procedure provided the subject with a discriminative stimulus for the presence and absence of possible reinforcement. As a result of this selective pairing of punishment with nonreinforcement, the punishing stimulus produced a drastic reduction in responding. The magnitude of this reduction, according to Holtz and Azrin, could not be attributed to the aversive property of the shock, because shock at this same level of intensity had previously been shown to result in little or no response suppression.

In a second portion of this experiment, other subjects were given similar training except that all responses during periods of reinforcement produced a fairly intense shock. This procedure also allowed the subject to use the occurrence of the punishing stimulus as a means of detecting whether or not reinforcement was available. The result of this procedure was to reverse completely the usual effects of punishment. The rate of responding actually increased during the periods in which shock was programmed and decreased during the nonpunished periods. The increased level of responding during punishment existed with an intensity of shock previously found to produce response suppression when the shock was not a discriminative stimulus. Therefore, the discriminative property of punishment apparently exerted an even greater effect on response rate than did its aversive property.

The discriminative aspect of punishment may explain some of the anomalous effects of punishment reported by several investigators. For example, Muenzinger (1934) found that rats learn a correct response in a T-maze more rapidly if the response is followed by shock and then rewarded. The punishment in this case was explicitly paired with the correct response; therefore, according to the view of Holtz and Azrin, it should also become a discriminative stimulus (and also a secondary reinforcer), since it informed the subject of the arrival of reward. Several experiments have indicated that reinforcement—if presented during the interval between completion of correct response and presentation of reward—will facilitate learning because it reduces the delay of reward. (For a detailed discussion of the mediation of gaps of time by secondary reinforcement, see Miller, 1959.)

Another paradoxical effect of punishment is found in the results of a study reported by Estes (1944). In this study, rats were trained to press a lever for food pellets on an intermittent schedule of reinforcement and then were given an extinction session. During the first five minutes of the extinction session, all responses were punished as well as nonreinforced. The subjects showed complete suppression of responding during this period; however, when punishment was later discontinued during extinction, many of the subjects showed an increase in response rate. According to Estes' interpretation of these results, punishment has only a transitory effect on behavior and is less effective than positive reinforcement in controlling behavior. According to the discrimination interpretation, however, the punishing stimulus in this experiment was effective in controlling behavior, since its termination during extinction reinstated the conditions of original training and thus brought about increased responding. The discrimination interpretation, therefore, clearly specifies the conditions under which response suppression and response facilitation should be observed. Unfortunately, however, it fails to provide a simple explanation of the reduction in response rate observed with the conditioned-suppression procedure. The proponents of this interpretation presumably would have to appeal to the aversive or emotional property of the punishing stimulus, as opposed to its discriminative property, to account for this phenomenon.

Fear as Concomitant or Mediating Response.   Of the six interpretations of punishment discussed, two (the fear interpretation and the avoidance interpretation) assume that the conditioning of emotional responses must occur if punishment is to have an effect on behavior (see Table 6-1). Estes' (1944) fear interpretation claims that an aversive stimulus may be given independently of the subjects' responses and still produce a suppression in response rate. The mere presence of a conditioned aversive stimulus is considered sufficient to produce an emotional reaction, which in turn may lead to a disruption of ongoing reinforced behavior. Thus, Estes' position predicts that response-contingent and noncontingent punishment procedures should yield similar changes in emotional responses as well as in skeletal or overt behavior. Mowrer's (1947, 1960) avoidance hypothesis emphasizes the contingent relationship between delivery of punishment and response. After several pairings of a particular response and punishment have been given during the CS, the initiation of the response during the CS is assumed to arouse an emotional or fear response. The subject can most effectively reduce this fear, according to Mowrer, either by ceasing to perform the response that produces the fear-inducing stimuli or by performing some nonpunished response instead.

Both the fear and the avoidance interpretations assume that emotional responses rapidly become conditioned under procedures involving punishment and that these responses serve to mediate the effects of punishment in controlling overt skeletal behavior. Proponents of the four remaining theories of punishment acknowledge that an emotional or fear reaction occurs in punishment situations, but they do not consider these responses as the major determinants of behavior.

Evaluation of Punishment Theories. The problem of determining the significance of the response contingency in the discriminated punishment procedure can be stated as follows: Does response suppression occur because the aversive stimulus is presented contingent to the occurrence of an operant (instrumental conditioning) or because there is contiguity between some set of neutral stimuli and the aversive event (classical conditioning)? There have been two experimental approaches to this problem. The first is concerned with whether the instrumental response is *necessary* for the response suppression. In experiments studying this question, the response or its feedback is usually blocked by pharmacological or surgical techniques during training and the block removed during subsequent testing. The findings of such experiments indicate that the muscular response is not necessary for response suppression (Black, 1965).

The second approach is concerned with whether the instrumental response in any way affects the amount of suppression. In experiments

studying this question, the decrement in performance between a response-contingent (instrumental) group of subjects and a noncontingent
(classical) group is usually compared. Estes (1944), the first investigator
to make such a comparison, found that both groups showed similar
performance. He therefore concluded that the response contingency
is not a significant factor in the punishment paradigm. However, the
noncontingent subjects in this study *never* were punished during or
immediately after a response. As previously noted, this schedule of
aversive stimulation typically produces a high rate of operant responding (Sidman, 1953). Thus, Estes' comparison is not a valid one, since
the responses of his noncontingent subjects were not completely independent of the occurrence of punishment.

In a subsequent study, Hunt and Brady (1955) also reported no difference in response suppression among contingent and noncontingent
subjects. In other respects, however, they did find differences between
the groups. The response-contingent subjects, as compared with the noncontingent subjects, showed (1) less generalized response suppression
during periods when the CS was not present, (2) less emotional dis-
turbance as measured by their frequency of defecation and crouching,
and (3) more rapid recovery in response rate when punishment was
discontinued during the extinction sessions. However, definite conclusions cannot be made on the basis of these results because the contingent
group in this study received less than half as many shocks as the noncontingent group.

In the two previously cited experiments, the investigators failed to
equate the number and the temporal distribution of shocks for the
contingent and noncontingent groups. Both of these variables are known
to be important determinants of behavior for both classical and instrumental conditioning procedures. Hoffman and Fleshler (1965) attempted to control for the effects of these two variables by using a
yoked design with paired groups of subjects. In this experiment, when
the response-contingent animals emitted a response during the CS, they
programmed shock for themselves as well as for their noncontingent
partners. The investigators found no differences in amount of response
suppression between the two groups during conditioning. During extinction sessions, in which the shocks were not presented, the response-contingent subjects showed much faster recovery from response suppression
than the yoked subjects. However, these findings must be considered
with some caution, since the intensity of the shock was changed during
the course of training and only two pairs of subjects were tested.

In a more recent experiment (Williams, 1969), the role of the instrumental response in suppressing behavior was also examined by

means of a yoked procedure. Although the difficulties in the Hoffman-Fleshler (1965) study were corrected in this experiment, the use of the yoked design nevertheless has some inherent problems. For example, Church (1963) has indicated that results obtained with this procedure are greatly affected when the partners from each group differ considerably in their reaction to the shock. Thus, the methodology employed in Williams' study should be considered as one way of investigating a theoretical issue that probably cannot be tested without the occurrence of some confounding variable.

In addition to assessing the behavioral effects of the response contingency, Williams recorded heart rate and electrical skin resistance. Although both of these autonomic responses have been used frequently as indices of fear and arousal, previous investigators had never recorded these measures during operant aversive conditioning. This experiment is therefore of particular interest because, in addition to examining the effects of response contingency, it attempts to resolve the issue of whether autonomic responses, as measures of emotionality, are causally related to changes in behavior.

In the Williams experiment, eleven pairs of rats were trained to press a lever for food reward in a Skinner type of operant chamber. This chamber was very small, restricting the degree to which the subjects could move about. By means of two stainless-steel strips on the floor of the chamber, it was possible to deliver a shock to the subjects and at the same time record changes in their skin resistance to a sub-threshold current. Furthermore, each rat in the chamber wore an elastic belt equipped with a series of cardiac electrodes. In an adjacent room, the experimenter recorded simultaneously each subject's lever presses, heart rate, and skin resistance.

The food reward for lever pressing was reinforced on a VI thirty-second schedule. After stable response rates had been achieved, high-frequency (6,000-cps) and low-frequency (2,000-cps) tones were randomly presented to the subjects for brief periods of time. The subjects were given three daily tone-habituation or adaptation sessions, with a total of three presentations of each of the tones per day.

Following the habituation phase, discrimination training was begun. For half of the subjects, the high-pitched tone served as a CS for shock and the low tone as a neutral or differential stimulus (DS), which was never associated with shock. The subjects were run in pairs, with the presentations of tone and shock occurring in each of their separate chambers at the same time. The partners were matched on the basis of the number of responses they made during the final tone-habituation session.

During the discrimination-training phase, one of each pair of subjects was assigned to a response-contingent condition and the other to a yoked condition. At the beginning of a discrimination session, each subject had the cardiac electrodes fastened about his midsection and was placed into the box with the VI schedule in effect. After ten minutes, the first tone presentation was given. After it had been on for one minute, (assuming that it was the CS value), a contingency period was in effect for an additional minute, with the tone still being heard. During this contingency period, *both* the response-contingent and the yoked rats received a brief presentation of shock when, and *only* when, the contingent animal pressed the lever. The offset of the shock was accompanied by the termination of the CS; thus, no more than one shock was given per CS presentation. If the contingent subject did not press the lever during the contingency period, the CS remained on for a total of two minutes, and neither subject received shock. Thus, the same number and temporal distribution of shocks were given to each member of a pair of subjects. Again, the presentations of shock occurred as a result of the performance of a specific response (lever pressing) for the response-contingent subjects and were independent of any specific response made by the yoked subjects.

Discrimination sessions were given to each pair of subjects until all the contingent animals had learned to "passively avoid" the shock by not responding during the three CS contingency periods of a given session. The subjects then received extinction sessions in which the presentations of tone and food were scheduled exactly as they had been during the discrimination sessions, but the subjects were not shocked. These sessions were continued until both groups failed to show significant changes in their rate of lever pressing to the high and low tones.

Difference scores were calculated in order to examine the changes in lever-pressing rate, heart rate, and skin resistance during the presentations of tones. The number of lever responses, heart beats per minute, and lowest deflections (the most valid reading) in basal skin resistance were determined for the one-minute period prior to the stimulus and for the initial minute of the stimulus. The mean response values for the prestimulus period were then subtracted from the mean for the stimulus periods. Thus, a negative difference score reflects response suppression to the stimulus. The difference scores, for each of the response measures, are shown in Figure 6-12. Each point in this figure represents the mean response reading for the three CS and DS trials received by a group on a given session. In addition, the total number of shocks received by the eleven pairs of subjects during each of the discrimination sessions is entered below the horizontal axis.

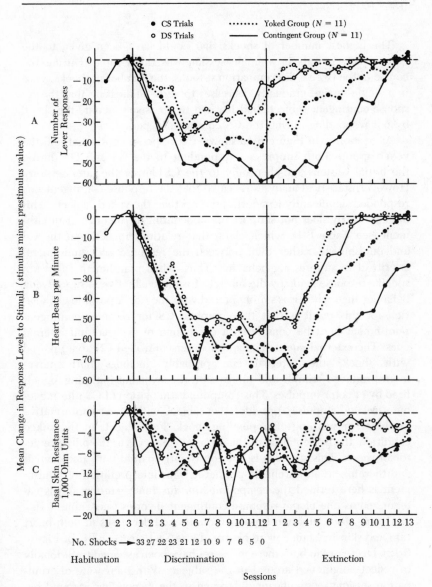

FIGURE 6-12. Mean changes in response levels to stimuli (stimulus minus prestimulus values) for the response-contingent and yoked groups during habituation-discrimination and extinction sessions. Sections A, B, and C show changes in lever responding, heart rate, and basal skin resistance, respectively. (Adapted from Williams, J., "Response contingency and the effects of punishment: Changes in autonomic and skeletal responses," *Journal of Comparative and Physiological Psychology,* 1969, **68,** 118–125. Copyright 1969 by the American Psychological Association, and reproduced by permission.)

The highest number of shocks that could have been given to the eleven pairs of rats in a single session was thirty-three. During the course of the twelve discrimination sessions, the number of shocks given in a single session gradually decreases to zero—indicating that the response-contingent subjects had learned to "passively avoid" the shock by not responding during the CS contingency period.

As Section A in Figure 6-12 shows, the response-contingent and the yoked groups both suppressed responding to the CS and DS during the initial sessions and then only to the CS during the later sessions. However, statistical analyses revealed that the response-contingent rats responded significantly less during the CS than the yoked subjects. This finding clearly does not support the noncontingent theories of punishment (see Table 6-1), which claim that relationship between the CS and punishment, rather than between the response and punishment, is critical in suppressing behavior. Thus, when punishment follows a specific response made by the subject, it is more effective in suppressing behavior than when it is simply paired with the CS. A possible explanation for this result is that the complete CS for response-contingent punishment must be considered a compound of external and internal cues. The external cue is the experimenter-controlled CS (tone) paired with shock; the internal cue probably includes both movement-produced stimuli and more central movement-initiating signals fired by effector impulses. This compound stimulation of CS plus movement-related impulses provides the subject with a very informative predictor or warning of impending shock. For subjects in the yoked condition, the presentation of the external CS serves as the only predictor of shock. This stimulus is not consistently paired with punishment and therefore is an unreliable predictor. This interpretation of punishment is here termed the *compound-stimulus interpretation* and is categorized as one of the response-contingent theories (see Table 6-1).

During discrimination training, conditioned decreases in both heart rate and skin resistance were observed (see Sections B and C of Figure 6-12). Decreases in both these measures have been assumed traditionally to reflect heightened arousal in the subject. With increasing discrimination sessions, a significant difference in the responding is found between the CS and DS. However, response differentiation to the CS and DS occurred first for lever responding (Section A) and several sessions later for heart rate (Section B). Although the conditioning of skin resistance was observed by the second discrimination session, differentiation did not appear until the extinction phase (Section C). The fact that the discrimination was learned, in effect, by the skeletal response (lever pressing) prior to changes in the autonomic responses suggests that there is no causal relationship between these two response systems.

The notion that these responses are partially dissociated is further supported by the finding that the contingent and the yoked groups differed significantly in skeletal responding but did not differ in autonomic responses. Furthermore, the extinction data shown in Figure 6-12 indicate that autonomic changes follow, rather than precede, the changes in lever pressing.

Both of the latter findings clearly contradict the avoidance and fear interpretations of punishment, which assume that autonomic responses, as indices of fear, serve as mediators of overt behavior. (Since fear appears to be a concomitant rather than a mediating response of the punishment procedure, the compound-stimulus interpretation is placed in the upper-left section of the matrix shown in Table 6-1.)

In summary, response contingency plays an important role in suppressing punished behavior. The response-related cues provide the subject with a great deal of information about the possible occurrence of punishment in the response-contingent situation. Such informative predictors of punishment are not available to subjects in the noncontingent or response-independent situation. Second, although autonomic responses show significant changes during punishment training, they are not the causes of changes in overt behavior. Perhaps these responses can best be interpreted as symptoms of a cognitive state of fear, which involves central or cortical processes.

USE OF PUNISHMENT IN CONTROLLING BEHAVIOR

The punishment procedure, primarily because of its known effectiveness, is the method most frequently used to suppress behavior. Azrin and Holtz (1966) have found that severe punishment may completely and irreversibly suppress a particular response. Unfortunately, however, aversive stimulation may be an unsatisfactory means of controlling behavior for several reasons. First, the results of punishment may have undesirable side effects, such as emotional behavior and psychosomatic disturbances. Second, the behavioral consequences of punishment are far less predictable than those of positive reinforcement. For example, punishment may indicate to a child what he should not do, but it does *not* suggest what response he *should* perform. Third, the most undesirable aspect of punishment is perhaps that it often results in social disruption. That is, the organism being punished may learn to dislike or to be aggressive toward the parent, teacher, or employer associated with the delivery of punishment.

The above cautions about the use of punishment are not meant to imply that punishment should never be employed as a method of behavioral control. Certain punishing contingencies arranged by the physical world are impossible to eliminate. For example, a young child inevitably will experience punishment in learning to stand up, walk, or run. Similarly, *time-out punishment* probably will never be eliminated. In this type of punishment, positive reinforcement is withdrawn upon the performance of some undesirable response. Such a withdrawal of positive reward affects behavior in much the same way as the administration of a physically abusive stimulus such as electric shock (see Leitenberg, 1965). To eliminate time-out punishment, we would have to do away with fines, imprisonment, dismissal from a job, and withdrawal of privileges. Thus, it appears that the various forms of aversive procedures, including time-out punishment, will continue to be used in the future by parents, teachers, employers, and institutions to control human behavior.

VII

APPLICATIONS OF OPERANT
LEARNING: BEHAVIOR
THERAPY

Operant techniques have been applied in a variety of fields—for instance, in the study of drugs, physiological pathology, space technology, child development, verbal behavior, and programmed environments for the experimental analysis of human behavior. Three of B. F. Skinner's books—*Walden Two* (1948), *Science and Human Behavior* (1953), and *Beyond Freedom and Dignity* (1971)—probably best reflect the zeal with which behaviorism has been ingeniously applied to human affairs. In this and the following chapter, we will review only two of these areas: Behavior Therapy and Programmed Instruction.

Behavior therapy—or, as it is sometimes called, behavior modification—differs in many respects from the more traditional approaches to clinical problems. Behavior therapists concentrate on the analysis of specific symptoms or behaviors, termed *targets*. The goal of the therapist is to modify or change these target symptoms by means of operant techniques and to monitor the patient's progress continuously and quantitatively. Far less attention is given by behavior therapists, as compared with other clinicians, to the early life history of the patient. Thus, subjective experiences, attitudes, dreams, and insights are for the most part ignored.

In line with the operant approach, the behavior therapist is concerned *only* with modifying the overt, observable aspects of behavior. He is therefore uninterested in internal hypothetical constructs such as the unconscious, the ego, and the superego. He focuses on the behavioral problem and does not try to get at the more elusive underlying dynamics of the illness. He admits that, because of his inattention to underlying causes, "symptom substitution" may occur and realizes that he must examine the complete response repertoire of the patient for a long time after the completion of therapy. However, when the proper experimental controls are employed during therapy, symptom substitution rarely does take place (Sherman & Baer, 1969).

Another striking difference between behavior therapy and the other clinical approaches has to do with the tools or methodologies employed. Whereas the traditional clinician relies to a great extent on empathy and transference, the behaviorist does not regard a personal relationship between therapist and patient as essential for the patient's recovery. Instead, the behavioral therapist often uses electronic programming equipment and precise recording devices in attacking the target symptoms, and he employs procedures developed mainly in the laboratory.

Some of the most important differences in assumptions and methods between the psychoanalytic approach and behavioral therapy are summarized in Table 7-1. From the superior vantage point of the 1970s, some of the points listed in this table (compiled in 1959) may appear oversimplified and biased, but they nevertheless illustrate very effectively the positions of most behavior therapists. Detailed discussions of the assumptions and contributions of the behaviorist approach appear in a number of recent textbooks (Bandura, 1969; Franks, 1969; Ullman & Krasner, 1969; Kanfer & Phillips, 1970).

The operant approach to behavior therapy involves the deliberate manipulation of reinforcers as a consequence of the occurrence of target behaviors. Thus, when the therapist is attempting to increase the strength of a particular response, such as verbal communication, its occurrence is followed by *positive reinforcement*. Or the therapist may require the patient to make the desired response in order to terminate (escape) or postpone (avoid) *negative reinforcement*. Thus, both positive

TABLE 7-1

Differences between Freudian Psychotherapy and Behavior Therapy

Freudian Psychotherapy	Behavior Therapy
1. Based on inconsistent theory never properly formulated in postulate form.	1. Based on consistent, properly formulated theory leading to testable deductions.
2. Derived from clinical observations made without necessary control, observation, or experiments.	2. Derived from experimental studies specifically designed to test basic theory and deductions made therefrom.
3. Considers symptoms the visible upshot of unconscious causes ("complexes").	3. Considers symptoms unadaptive CRs.
4. Regards symptoms as evidence of repression.	4. Regards symptoms as evidence of faulty learning.
5. Believes that symptomatology is determined by defense mechanism.	5. Believes that symptomatology is determined by individual differences in conditionability and autonomic lability, as well as accidental environmental circumstances.
6. All treatment of neurotic disorders must be historically based.	6. All treatment of neurotic disorders is concerned with habits existing at present; historical development is largely irrelevant.
7. Cures are achieved by handling the underlying (unconscious) dynamics, not by treating the symptom itself.	7. Cures are achieved by treating the symptom itself (i.e., by extinguishing unadaptive CRs and establishing desirable CRs).
8. Interpretation of symptoms, dreams, acts, etc., is an important element of treatment.	8. Interpretation, even if not completely subjective and erroneous, is irrelevant.
9. Symptomatic treatment leads to the elaboration of new symptoms.	9. Symptomatic treatment leads to permanent recovery, provided autonomic as well as skeletal surplus CRs are extinguished.
10. Transference relations are essential for cures of neurotic disorders.	10. Personal relations are not essential for cures of neurotic disorder, although they may be useful in certain circumstances.

(From Eysenck, H. I., "Learning theory and behavior therapy, *Journal of Mental Science*, 1959, 105, 67. Copyright 1959 by the Royal Medico-Psychological Association, and reproduced by permission.)

and negative reinforcement contingencies may be employed to increase the rate of performance of desirable behavior.

Obviously, the therapist is not always interested in strengthening the behavior of the subject. In fact, his goal is frequently to suppress certain target behaviors, which for some reason are not socially acceptable. The most widely used procedure for eliminating responses is *punishment*—presenting the subject with an aversive stimulus (such as an electric shock) every time the target symptom occurs. Frequently, punishment of a particular response is employed simultaneously with the positive reinforcement of alternative behaviors. As will be shown later, this combination of procedures has been found to be one of the most effective techniques for behavior modification. A second procedure for reducing the strength of certain responses is *time-out training*. With this procedure, each time the undesirable behavior occurs, positive reinforcement is denied for a given period of time. A third procedure for reducing the rate of a particular response is *experimental extinction*—a noncontingent, or response-independent, procedure. In extinction, positive reinforcement is discontinued altogether until the rate of the target behavior becomes virtually zero.

TECHNIQUES USED TO STRENGTHEN BEHAVIOR

POSITIVE-REINFORCEMENT PROCEDURES

Positive reinforcement is by far the most commonly employed procedure in behavior modification. When positive reinforcement is used to strengthen a particular response, it is usually combined with the process of extinction to weaken the response strength of alternative, undesirable responses. Two specific techniques involving positive reinforcement are *shaping* (Skinner, 1953) and *fading* (Terrace, 1963).

Shaping. As defined in Chapter 1, shaping is the selective reinforcement of successive approximations to the desired response until eventually the subject emits the response at a high operant rate. A good illustration of the use of shaping of patients in an institutional setting is seen in a study reported by Isaacs, Thomas, and Goldiamond (1960). The goal of this experiment was to reinstate verbal behavior in two schizophrenic patients who had been mute for over fourteen years. The method of successive approximations was used to shape the verbal behavior. The therapists began by reinforcing eye movements, lip movements, and grunts; then they progressed to more intelligible speech. Both patients showed a dramatic improvement in verbal behavior following the completion of therapy. One patient, who was urged to say "gum" and given a piece of chewing gum as a reinforcer for any spontaneous vocalizations, displayed no learning for several sessions and then suddenly said "Gum, please"; from this point on, he acquired many other verbal behaviors. The initial response seemed to reinstate other verbal responses. Furthermore, these subjects were able to generalize their verbal behavior from the therapists to the ward personnel, who were instructed not to respond to the patients' nonverbal requests.

Risley and Wolf (1967) shaped imitation behavior as the initial step in developing verbal skills in autistic children. In the first phase of this study, the children were trained to make reliable and correct imitations, so that the utterance of a new word in an appropriate context could be controlled eventually by the therapist's verbalizations. The therapist said a word to the child every five or six seconds and reinforced any sound that the child emitted. This type of imitation procedure, where the child is reinforced for repeating the word said by the therapist, is called *prompting*. Next, sounds that more closely approximated the therapist's speech were reinforced; finally, reward was presented only when the child rapidly emitted the correct sound. The therapist at first varied the tone, intensity, and pitch of the stimulus word in order to maintain the child's attention; as accurate imitation occurred, however, these variations were omitted or faded out.

After the child was reliably responding, the second phase was begun. During this phase, two words were presented alternately; additional words then were interspersed with the original pair until general imitative behavior was well established. Imitations to the new words were consistently reinforced, while nonimitative or irrelevant responses were extinguished. The stimulus words were presented only when the child was quiet and attentive. Thus, the word the therapist used to prompt the child served as a conditioned reinforcer for sitting still as well as a discriminative stimulus for imitating.

Figure 7-1 shows the rapid acquisition curve of appropriate imitations by an autistic child. Before therapy, this child was very withdrawn and rarely related or attended to other persons. In shaping this child to speak, the therapist used a primary reward (food) and deprived the child of one meal. When the child had increased his rate of acquisition so that only one trial was required to imitate a new word, the severity of the food deprivation was reduced. In addition, the therapist gave

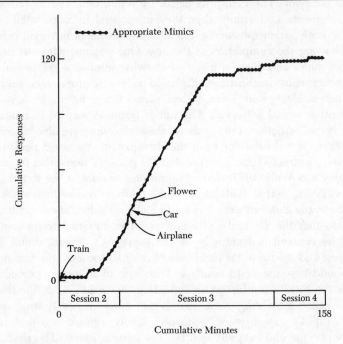

FIGURE 7-1. Cumulative record of the imitation responses made during acquisition by an autistic child. Each point represents two minutes of session time. (Reprinted with permission from Risley and Wolf, "Establishing functional speech in echolalic children," *Behavior Research and Therapy.* 1967, **5**, 73–80. Copyright 1967, Pergamon Press.)

further reinforcement by saying "Good" or "That's right" when the food was given after each correct response. The praise, then, became a *conditioned social reinforcer.* The parents also were trained to capitalize on these children's newly developed imitative repertoire. By omitting or fading out the use of verbal promptings, the parents were eventually able to establish functional phrases in their children.

In a similar study (Lovaas, Berberich, Perdoff, & Schaeffer, 1966), imitative verbal behavior was established in two autistic children who initially did not display any such behavior. In this experiment, the vocalizations made by the children were reinforced with food until a high rate of nonprompted vocalization occurred. The experimenter then began prompting the subjects and reinforcing closer and closer approximations to the words he said. In this manner, several verbal responses were reliably established and brought under the stimulus control of the therapist's speech.

In both of the above studies, the necessary condition for the acquisition of verbal behavior was the contingency relationship between the reinforcement and the correct imitative response made by the subject. When this contingency was removed by noncontingent or free presentations of food for behavior other than verbalization, the rate of correct verbalizations declined. However, verbalizations increased again when the contingency was reinstated. Thus, response-contingent reward originally established and maintained the behavior; noncontingent reward led to a reduction in responding; and subsequent training, with the reinforcement contingency in operation, resulted in the recovery of the behavior. This technique—going from reinforcement contingency to noncontingency and back to contingency—is frequently used by behavior therapists to demonstrate the influence of reinforcement in establishing behavioral control. Notice that this is exactly the same procedure employed by operant researchers when they use individual animals as their own controls. This experimental design is efficient and can demonstrate the effectiveness of reinforcement in a *single* subject.

Shaping imitative behavior can also be used to develop repertoires of nonverbal behavior. For example, Lovaas, Freitas, Nelson, and Whalen (1967) initially established a series of nonverbal responses that were easily imitated by autistic children. Then they used these responses in conjunction with other procedures to develop new behaviors, such as washing hands, brushing hair, playing games, making beds, drawing pictures. The investigators claimed that the initially imitated responses facilitated the training of these new behaviors, which otherwise probably could not have been established.

Although imitation is not a necessary condition for the shaping of an operant response, the studies cited illustrate how much more efficient it is to train complex behavior if imitative responses are first shaped and then the prompting is gradually omitted. Numerous other investigators (Rickard, Dignam, & Horner, 1960; Hewett, 1965; Kerr, Myerson, & Michael, 1965) have established verbal behavior in mentally disturbed and retarded subjects by means of shaping imitative vocalizations.

Fading.   The fading procedure, often used in conjunction with shaping, is a means of developing new discriminations that would otherwise be difficult to learn. Initially, the subject is trained to make a relatively easy discrimination; the stimulus situation is then changed at a rate gradual enough so that it does not disrupt the subject's performance.

Eventually, the behavior will come under the control of new discriminative stimuli, which are sometimes totally different from the original stimuli.

The most comprehensive laboratory research on the topic of fading has been conducted by Terrace (1963b). In Chapter 5, in connection with stimulus control, Terrace's research on errorless discrimination learning and fading was discussed. A good example of how the fading procedure can readily be applied to the therapy situation is seen in the work that Lovaas (1967) and his colleagues have done in building vocabularies in autistic children. These children were first trained through shaping with positive reinforcement to repeat a word immediately after they had heard it stated by the therapist. For example, the child would learn to say the word *shirt* upon the therapist's uttering of this word. In the next phase, the discriminative stimulus no longer was the sound of the word but the actual object itself or a picture of the object. Typically, the therapist would point to the specific stimulus (his own shirt) and say "What is this?" If the child did not respond immediately, the therapist would say "This is my shirt." The prompting was then gradually faded out; the therapist might, for instance, say the word more and more softly or not pronounce the entire word.

When the fading procedure is carried out successfully, an autistic child can eventually develop independent speech cued by the object or picture itself. Figure 7-2 presents the data of one subject's acquisition of a labeling vocabulary. The results indicate that the child gradually acquired a *learning set,* or learned about learning; as the fading procedure continued, only one prompting or labeling of the object was required in order for the child to make the correct response.

Using a procedure like the one described above, Hewett (1965) developed independent verbalization in an autistic boy. He first established imitative vocalization in the child by reinforcing successive approximations to the prompted words with food. Then he paired questions and answers and reinforced the child for imitating the word used as an answer. The answer was then gradually faded out by means of the same procedure used by Lovaas. Finally, the child was required to respond verbally in phrases outside the experimental situation in order to receive other kinds of reinforcers, such as juice, candy, and crackers.

Fading, like other discrimination procedures, often involves temporary side effects (unless the errorless-discrimination technique is used) because of the process of extinction. Risley and Wolf (1967) noted that temper tantrums and other emotional outbursts initially occurred when the S^Δ was presented in their speech training of autistic children. These

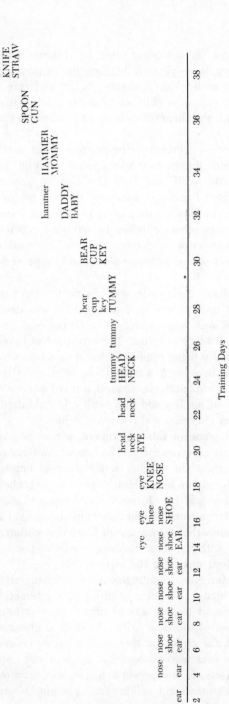

FIGURE 7-2. Acquisition of a labeling vocabulary by an autistic boy. The words are printed in lower case on the days they were presented and in upper case on days they were mastered. (Adapted from Lovaas, O. I., chapter in *Minnesota Symposium on Child Psychology, Volume I,* edited by John P. Hill, University of Minnesota Press, Minneapolis. Copyright 1967, University of Minnesota.)

outbursts, however, did not occur after the children had mastered the discrimination problem—possibly because the responses emitted later in training were emitted only during the S^D and thus were always reinforced, and because the children probably learned that they would get attention from the therapist only if they were quiet and attentive.

Social Reinforcement.   Probably the reinforcement most widely employed by behavior therapists is social reinforcement. An experiment reported by Harris, Wolf, and Baer (1964) is an impressive demonstration of how social consequences may be used to control problem behaviors. More specifically, they attempted to alter certain deviant behaviors in nursery school children by having the teacher systematically vary the number of times when she would pay attention to each child. Each subject served as his own control in a procedure involving four phases.

In the first phase, each child was observed for a period of time, and the operant level of the deviant behavior was determined. One of the subjects, it was found, spent up to 80 per cent of the observed time engaging in solitary activities. The investigators hypothesized that this boy was actually being reinforced for always being by himself and appearing lonely, because it was on these occasions that the teacher paid attention to him and encouraged him to play with his peers. Furthermore, when the boy did play with other children, the teacher no longer showed attention and concern for him.

In the second phase of this experiment, a new program was used to schedule the occurrence of reinforcement and nonreinforcement periods. For instance, the teacher was instructed not to reward the withdrawn boy by giving him attention and support when he engaged in solitary play. Instead, these forms of social reinforcement were given only when he independently sought the companionship of another child.

Figure 7-3 shows the percentage of time this withdrawn child interacted socially with the other children in either play or conversation throughout the four phases of the experiment.

After the reinforcement contingencies were changed, the child was spending approximately 60 per cent of his time interacting with other children. By the end of this second phase, he was interacting with others 80 per cent of the time. After the desired changes in behavior were established, the child was then reinforced, as before, for solitary play. This phase was used to demonstrate that the improvement in social behavior, seen in the previous phase, was definitely under the control of the reinforcement conditions. As might be expected, when

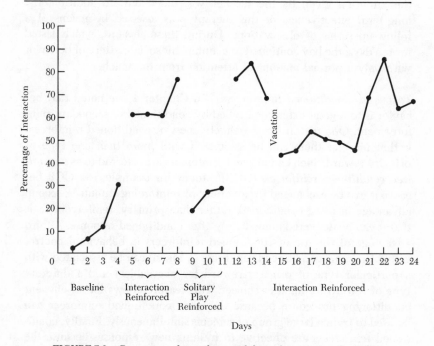

FIGURE 7-3. Percentage of time that a withdrawn boy interacted socially
in sessions before treatment (baseline), during sessions of reinforcement
(teacher's attention) for engaging in social behavior with peers, and during
sessions of reinforcement for playing alone. (Adapted from Harris, F. R.,
Wolf, M. M., and Baer, D. M., "Effects of adult social reinforcement on
child behavior," *Young Children*, 1964, **20**, 8–17. Copyright 1964 by the
National Association for the Education of Young Children, and reproduced
by permission.)

the child was consoled and given attention during periods of solitary
play, the percentage of time spent in social interaction showed a marked
decrease and was virtually the same as it had been during the baseline
phase of the experiment (see Figure 7-3). In the final phase of the
study, the therapeutic reinforcement contingencies were again introduced. Thus, the teacher again paid attention to the child whenever
he played with other children and ignored him completely when he
was by himself. The result of this final conditioning phase was successful
in that the amount of time spent in social interaction increased from
about 20 per cent to 70 per cent. Gradually, the boy appeared to
derive more and more enjoyment from playing with his peers, and

the attention given by the teacher was faded out. In addition, the long-term effectiveness of this therapy was assessed by means of a follow-up series of observations. During these sessions, which lasted for ten days, the boy continued to maintain his social pattern of behavior with only a normal amount of attention from the teacher.

Tokens as Conditioned Reinforcers.   In Chapter 4, we noted that behavior is to a great extent controlled by conditioned or secondary reinforcement. One reason for the effectiveness of conditioned reinforcers is that most of them can be associated with more than one type of primary reward. Such conditioned reinforcers are referred to as *generalized conditioned reinforcers* (GCR). Money for example, is a GCR because it can be exchanged for a variety of reinforcing stimuli. A second advantage in using conditioned, rather than primary, reinforcement is that it can be delivered immediately after conditioned response. A third advantage of the use of conditioned reinforcers in behavioral control is that the same conditioned reinforcer (a token) can be associated with a particular type of primary reward for one subject and a different type of reward for another subject. This feature allows for an efficient conditioning procedure because the same conditioned reinforcer can be used to train a large group of subjects simultaneously. Finally, conditioned reinforcers are effective in training new responses because the subject does not become satiated when receiving them in a large quantity; therefore, high-frequency reinforcement schedules can be used for long treatment sessions without the problem of satiation.

Because of the above advantages of conditioned reinforcers, a number of institutional settings are currently using them to establish desired responses in patients. For instance, conditioned reinforcers such as poker chips, tokens, gold stars, check marks, and actual money can eventually be exchanged by patients for such primary reinforcers as food, candy, or cigarettes, or an opportunity to be first in line in the cafeteria or to have special talks with the social worker or psychologist on the ward. To earn the conditioned reinforcers, patients are trained to perform services that are useful in the administration of the ward—serving meals, cleaning floors, sorting laundry. Such services produce fairly permanent, easily identifiable changes in the environment and often are brought under stimulus control in that they are to be performed at a specified time and location. Therefore, the psychologist can keep accurate records of the performance of the subjects, and the patients can learn behaviors appropriate for a given situation.

When conditioned reinforcers are used as incentives on a large, systematic scale, the system is called a *token economy* (Ayllon & Azrin, 1965). In a token economy, as in a money economy, patients earn tokens by performing desired behaviors and can spend the tokens for food, services, or privileges that they select. The powerful control that conditioned reinforcers or token economies have on behavior is probably best exemplified in a series of experiments conducted by Ayllon and Azrin (1965). In all of these studies, patients could earn tokens for serving meals, doing kitchen chores, working in the commissary, cleaning the wards, helping in the laundry room, and so forth. The tokens could later be exchanged for individual privacy, social interaction with the staff, recreation activities, or an opportunity to leave the ward or to purchase commissary items.

In one of these experiments, female patients, most of them chronic schizophrenics, were given token reinforcements for performing certain jobs previously done by paid members of the staff. In the first phase of this study, each patient selected her most preferred work assignment and was paid seventy tokens for working six hours a day at this job. When assigned to these preferred jobs, the subjects worked during the entire six-hour period (see Figure 7-4). In the second phase of the experiment, designed to determine whether job selection was influenced by extrinsic incentives (other than the tokens) or by social and intrinsic rewards, the subjects were no longer given tokens for working on the preferred assignment but were told that they could now earn tokens by working on a nonpreferred job:

> We want you to know that the people you are working for are very pleased with your job and would like you to continue working there. We have a problem, though. Other patients want to work there also, but we can't pay them because we have a limited number of tokens for the job in the laundry [lab., dietary, office]. So to be fair to everyone, we're going to give you a choice: you can continue working in the laundry but you won't get any tokens for it, or you can volunteer for another job where we have tokens available for work. One job that is still open is the dietary [lab., office]. Anyone working there gets seventy tokens daily. Now remember, the choice is all yours [Ayllon & Azrin, 1965, p. 369].

The amount of time that each patient worked on the preferred or the nonpreferred assignment was recorded each day. Figure 7-4 presents the results of both phases of the experiment.

As Figure 7-4 shows, when the token reinforcement was shifted from the preferred assignment to the nonpreferred assignment, the shift in performance from the preferred to the nonpreferred job was immediate

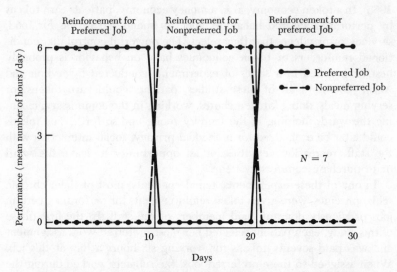

FIGURE 7-4. Mean number of hours patients worked per day when positive reinforcement was varied between preferred and nonpreferred jobs. (Adapted from Ayllon, T., and Azrin, N. H. The measurement and reinforcement of behavior of psychotics. *Journal of Experimental Analysis of Behavior*, 1965, 8, 357–383. Copyright 1965 by the Society for the Experimental Analysis of Behavior, Inc. Reprinted by permission. Additional information and related research can be found in *The Token Economy: A Motivational System for Therapy and Rehabilitation* by T. Ayllon and N. H. Azrin, published by Appleton-Century-Crofts, 1968.)

and complete and endured throughout the ten-day period of the second phase of the experiment. One of the comments made by a patient reveals the reasons why this change occurred: "No, honey, I can't work at the laundry for nothing, I'll work at the lab. I just couldn't make it to pay my rent, if I didn't get paid." Another commented, "You mean if I work at the lab, I won't get paid? I need tokens to buy cigarettes for my boy friend and to buy new clothes so I'll look nice like the other girls." Other comments also indicated that the token reinforcement was responsible for controlling the behavior of the patients.

In the third phase of this experiment, each patient was told by the ward attendant that her present (nonpreferred) job no longer paid tokens but that she could earn tokens by participating in her previously preferred job. As seen from the results presented in Figure 7-4, the subjects again participated in their preferred assignment, for which they now received tokens.

The performance of these subjects may have been influenced by the fact that the work itself was intrinsically reinforcing to them; the reinforcement, then, may have affected only job selection and not working behavior. Support for this interpretation comes from the statements of some of the workers: "It's not good to be doing nothing" and "Working six hours a day helps you to keep active."

In a subsequent experiment, involving the same patients, the importance of the response contingency for token reinforcement was examined. During the first phase of this second experiment, the subjects were presented with seventy token rewards by an attendant when each day's job was completed satisfactorily. In the next phase, the noncontingent reinforcement procedure was introduced to the patient with the following instructions:

This week you are going to receive the usual seventy tokens *before* you go to work. In a sense, you will be getting a vacation with pay. You'll get your tokens daily even if you don't work. Of course, we're pleased with your work and would like you to continue working [p. 373].

As Figure 7–5 shows, when the reinforcement was contingent upon performance (Days 1-20), the patients worked a total of about forty-five hours per day. But when reinforcement was no longer contingent upon performance (Days 21-40), the patients gradually stopped working. Some of the patients commented during the noncontingent phase, "You think I'm crazy to work without extra pay, I'll take the vacation"; "I can rest and get paid too. How nice"; "Now I can go out on my ground pass every day." Such comments suggest that the instructional statement "In a sense, you will be getting a vacation with pay" may have led the patients to believe that perhaps they should not work during this phase. In other words, the instructions here could have been misleading and therefore may have affected the results.

During the last phase of this study (Days 41-60), the patients were told that the vacation was over and that from now on they would receive their tokens after each working day. When the reward was made contingent upon responding, the patients immediately began working again for about 45 total hours per day. Thus—in spite of the statements about working to keep active or because of enjoyable social relations or personal satisfaction—the Ayllon-Azrin data indicate that

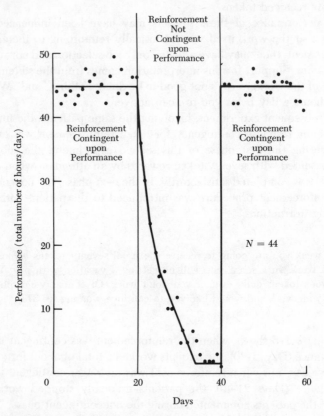

FIGURE 7-5.   Total number of hours per day a group of forty-four schizophrenic patients participated in rehabilitative activities. (Adapted from Ayllon and Azrin, 1965, by permission.)

the critical motivational factor in maintaining performance was the response-contingent token reinforcement.

In another experiment by these same investigators, the token incentives were completely discontinued, but the same privileges and institutional rewards were made available to the subjects on a "free" basis. As shown in Figure 7–6, when no reinforcement was given for working on any assignments, the performance of the subjects showed a marked decrease.

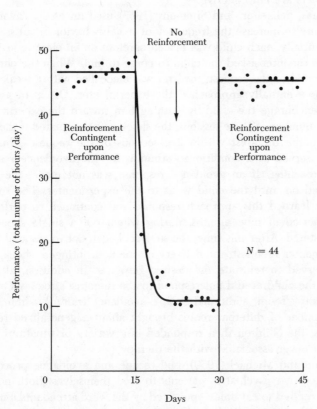

FIGURE 7-6.   Total number of hours spent per day by forty-four patients performing on-ward activities. (Adapted from Ayllon and Azrin, 1965, by permission.)

NEGATIVE-REINFORCEMENT PROCEDURES

In Chapter 6, we noted that negative or aversive stimulation can be used effectively to establish responses in animals. The methods used to develop such behaviors are referred to as *escape and avoidance procedures*. Because these procedures often involve intense aversive stimuli, such as a strong electric shock, psychologists are often reluctant to employ them with humans. However, these procedures have been especially successful in working with patients for whom traditional reinforcers are not effective.

Lovaas, Schaeffer, and Simmons (1965) used an escape/avoidance procedure to increase the frequency of social behavior in autistic children. Initially, each child was placed barefoot on an electric grid, and the experimenter asked the child to come to him. When the child did not respond to the request, the grid was electrified with a weak shock until he eventually approached the experimenter. Often an assistant would encourage the child by pushing him toward the experimenter. After a number of these sessions, the shock was terminated if the child came to the therapist within five seconds of the request. Thus, the request served as a conditioned stimulus for the avoidance response of approaching. If an avoidance response was not made, the shock remained on until the child went to the experimenter. The subjects quickly learned this approach response and continued to perform it for a period of nine months, during which not a single shock was administered. After this time, the subjects began not to respond to the experimenter's request; the delivery of one noncontingent shock, however, served to reinstate the desired response. In addition, although at first the children did not respond to the therapist's requests outside the therapy room, additional escape/avoidance training administered in a number of different rooms brought about a generalized responsiveness; the children then responded in a variety of situations, some of them never associated with the therapy.

Ayllon and Michael (1959) used escape and avoidance procedures to induce two psychiatric patients to feed themselves. Both patients usually refused to eat unless spoon-fed by the ward attendants. Furthermore, both were relatively indifferent to social reinforcement, although they did show concern for neatness and their personal appearance. The actual therapy involved the attendant's spilling the food when feeding the patients. This aversive event could be avoided by the patients if they fed themselves. They were also given verbal praise for self-feeding. The following instructions were given to the ward attendants:

> Continue spoon-feeding the patient; but from now on do it in such a careless way that the patient will have a few drops of food fall on her dress. Be sure not to overdo the food dropping, since what we want to convey to the patient is that it is difficult to spoon-feed a grown-up person, and not that we are mean to her. What we expect is that the patient will find it difficult to depend on your skill to feed her. You will still

be feeding her, but you will simply be less efficient in doing a good job of it. As the patient likes having her clothes clean, she will have to choose between feeding herself and keeping her clothes clean, or being fed by others and risking getting her clothes soiled. Whenever she eats on her own, be sure to stay with her for awhile (3 minutes is enough), talking to her, or simply being seated with her. We do this to reinforce her for eating on her own. In the experience of the patient, people become nicer when she eats on her own.[°]

At the beginning of treatment, one patient ate only about four or five times on her own during an eight-day observation period and weighed less than 100 pounds. The therapy sessions were given for a period of eight weeks. By the end of this time, the patient had fed herself in twenty of the last twenty-four meals and weighed 120 pounds when she was discharged from the hospital.

Walton and Black (1958) employed mild aversive stimulation to strengthen the amplitude of speech made by a patient suffering from functional aphonia. A person with this psychological disorder whispers almost all of his speech. In this experiment, the subject was required to read uninteresting material continuously for a fifteen-minute session. Any time the subject's voice dropped below a certain volume, an extra two minutes was added to the session. If, however, the subject made improvements during a given session, two-minute periods were subtracted from the session. Once the subject spoke with a normal volume, a fading procedure was used to have him read aloud in the presence of several persons.

Feldman and MacCulloch (1965) developed an avoidance-therapy procedure for the modification of homosexual behavior. The patients in this therapy were initially asked to rate the attractiveness of an extensive series of slides depicting both clothed and completely nude males and females. In the subsequent avoidance-conditioning phase of this experiment, a picture of a male was presented on the screen, and the patient was told that he could leave this presumably arousing picture on the screen as long as he wanted. He was also told that he might receive several electric shocks on his ankle during the viewing sessions but that he could always terminate the shock by pressing a button. This response also changed the slides. If the subject turned

[°]From Ayllon, T., and Michael, J. The psychiatric nurse as a behavioral engineer. *Journal of the Experimental Analysis of Behavior,* 1959, **2,** 323–334. Copyright 1959 by the Society for the Experimental Analysis of Behavior, Inc. Reprinted by permission.

off the slide within eight seconds after it was first presented, he could successfully avoid the shock; on the other hand, if he continued to look at the slide beyond this time, he was given a shock.

In addition to establishing escape/avoidance responses during the presentation of male pictures, Feldman and MacCulloch attempted to establish approach behavior to pictures of females. They did so by allowing the subject to request at any time a picture of a female. This naturally eliminated the possibility that he would receive a shock. Thus, pictures of females functioned as "safety" signals or periods of time out from the ongoing aversive therapy.

Initially, the least attractive male (according to the subject's ratings) was used as the conditioned stimulus for the avoidance behavior. In conjunction with this slide, the picture of what the subject considered to be the most sexually attractive female was used as the time-out stimulus. After the patient made the avoidance response within a second or two to a particular male slide, the next female picture down the hierarchy was presented when the patient requested such a female picture. Subsequently, the next male picture to be used as the conditioned stimulus was the next one moving up on the rating scale. This same process was repeated with succeeding pairs of male and female pictures until the subject was finally making a rapid avoidance response when receiving what he had previously rated as his most sexually arousing male slide and was requesting presentations of his lowest-rated female slide. Typically, the treatment session required thirty trials and a total of less than twenty minutes. Therapy was usually given for a period of fifteen sessions or until the patient's preferences substantially changed. Often, booster sessions were given after some time had elapsed upon the completion of therapy.

According to Feldman and MacCullough, three of the patients discontinued the therapy. Of the sixteen remaining patients, however, eleven—ten out of twelve under the age of forty, and one out of four older than forty—showed a complete change in their sexual orientations. These patients reported that their interest in men was greatly diminished and that homosexual practices were virtually eliminated. In addition, heterosexual interests, fantasies, and relationships showed a striking increase. In all but one case, interest in the opposite sex developed almost immediately after therapy and was still observed during follow-up periods ranging from two to fourteen months.

At present, this form of therapy has been done with forty-three patients; of these, twenty-five were improved at termination, eleven were unsuccessful, and seven defected from the treatment. These results are exceptionally promising when compared with traditional therapy successes.

Another study concerned with replacing sexual-deviate behavior with normal behavior has been reported by Blakemore and his associates (Blakemore, Thorpe, Barker, Conway, & Lavin, 1963). In this experiment, aversive stimulation was used to punish a man when he exhibited transvestite behavior. The patient was instructed to dress in his favorite female clothing while standing barefoot on an electric grid. As the patient dressed, he was given a series of pulsing shocks; he was then told that the shocks would be discontinued if he removed the feminine clothes. This response, therefore, functioned as an avoidance response. A later follow-up study indicated that this particular patient had engaged in transvestite behavior only once since the therapy.

Various other behavior disorders—such as sado-masochistic tendencies, fetishisms, and alcoholism—have been replaced by more acceptable behaviors by means of escape/avoidance procedures.

TECHNIQUES USED TO WEAKEN BEHAVIOR

PUNISHMENT PROCEDURE

In using response-contingent punishment (aversive stimulation delivered because a subject has performed a target response), the therapist seeks to reduce the frequency of such behavior or possibly to eliminate it completely. In one such study, Goldiamond (1965) reduced stuttering in a number of chronic stutterers by presenting them with periods of delayed feedback of their own voices, contingent upon stuttering. Most persons find delayed-feedback stimulation highly aversive. The success of this technique can be seen from the data presented in Figure 7-7, which shows the reading rate and the stuttering rate for a subject given delayed-feedback therapy for two weeks. The immediate effect was to reduce both reading and stuttering; after the tenth session, however, there was a dramatic increase in the reading rate, whereas the stuttering rate remained at a low level. More specifically, stuttering, which started at a rate of approximately eleven words a minute, was essentially eliminated; and reading rate, which was initially about 135 words per minute, increased to 255 words per minute by the end of the treatment.

In another punishment-procedure study, Liversedge and Sylvester (1955) treated subjects who complained of severe writer's cramps. Most

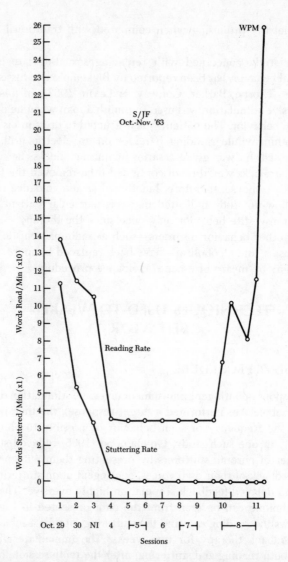

FIGURE 7-7. Elimination of the stuttering response in a chronic stutterer by means of a punishment procedure involving delayed feedback of the subject's own voice. Notice that accompanying the suppression of the stuttering response is an increase in the reading rate. (From "Stuttering and Fluency as Manipulatable Operant Response Classes" by Israel Goldiamond from *Research in Behavior Modification: New Developments and Implications* edited by Leonard Krasner and Leonard P. Ullman. Copyright © 1965 by Holt, Rinehart and Winston, Inc. Redrawn by permission of Holt, Rinehart and Winston, Inc.)

of these subjects suffered tremors and spasms of the hand muscles only when they were actually writing. Since the subjects had no common psychological characteristics, it seemed likely that specific reinforcement contingencies (rather than some "deep" psychological problem) were responsible for these cramps. Not surprisingly, the more conventional forms of psychotherapy had not proved effective in eliminating the problem. The procedure used to remove the tremors was to have each subject insert a stylus into progressively smaller holes. Whenever a subject happened to touch the side of the opening with the stylus, he received a mild electric shock. In order to treat the spasm symptoms, the subject was required to trace, with an electrified pen, certain figures (similar to letters and numbers). The subject received electric shocks from the pen when his tracings began to deviate from the figure. Over half of the subjects (24 out of 39) no longer had tremors or spasms after three to six weeks of training. These subjects were able to resume work; and follow-up studies, conducted as long as four years after therapy, indicated that the improvement was still maintained.

TIME-OUT PROCEDURE

Time-out training has not been used as extensively to reduce behavior as have the punishment and extinction procedures. In a study by Baer (1962), an effort was made to reduce persistent thumb sucking in two boys. Both boys simultaneously watched an enjoyable cartoon film, but the film was interrupted whenever the thumb-sucking behavior occurred for one of the boys. The other boy was used as a yoked, noncontingent control. Halfway through the film, the contingency roles were reversed for the subjects. Response-contingent interruption of the cartoon, as compared with the yoked condition, was found to produce a greater decrement in thumb sucking.

In another study involving time out from reinforcement, Wolf, Risley, and Mees (1964) eliminated temper tantrums and self-destructive behaviors in an autistic boy. After each of these outbursts, the boy was placed in a room alone, with the door closed. This isolation treatment removed all possibility of social reinforcement, such as attention that he would receive from the ward attendants and his peers. After the temper tantrums had stopped for ten minutes, the boy was reinforced by being allowed to leave the room and play in the ward. In a subsequent experiment involving the same child (Wolf, Risley, Johnston, Harris, & Allen, 1967), a similar time-out procedure was used;

as a result, self-slapping and the pinching of others in the nursery school were eliminated.

Ayllon (1963) has also used the withdrawal of positive reward as an effective method of eliminating stealing behavior on the part of a schizophrenic patient. The patient was a 250-pound woman who would continually steal food from the food counter and from other patients. Severe reprimands seemed to have no permanent effect in changing her behavior. For this reason, the behavior therapy finally employed consisted of removing her from the dining room whenever she was found stealing. As Figure 7-8 shows, the patient had stolen food at more than two thirds of her meals during the three-week base-line period before therapy. After this behavior was punished for one week, food stealing was virtually eliminated for a period of a year. In addition, the patient lost weight, and her general health improved.

EXPERIMENTAL EXTINCTION PROCEDURES

Extinction of Operant Responses. A number of behavior therapists have successfully been able to weaken the strength of problem behaviors

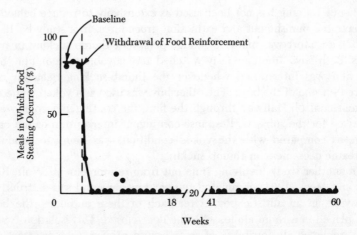

FIGURE 7-8. Elimination of food-stealing behavior by the withdrawal of food reinforcement as punishment. (Reprinted with permission from Ayllon, *Behavior Research and Therapy*, 1963, 1, 53–61. Copyright 1963, Pergamon Press.)

by discontinuing positive reinforcement, which was often inadvertently presented prior to therapy. Walton (1960), for example, noted that one of his patients had been accustomed to receiving a great deal of attention from her family and fiancé because of a skin condition she had on her neck, which she compulsively scratched. During therapy, her family was instructed by the therapist not to talk to her about the skin condition, and her fiancé was told to discontinue rubbing ointment on the affected areas. Under this form of treatment, the compulsive scratching was completely eliminated after three months.

Other investigators (Hart, Allen, Buell, Harris, & Wolf, 1964) attempted to control excessive crying behavior by the extinction procedure. The subject in their study was a four-year-old boy enrolled in the university's preschool program and reported to have as many as ten to twelve crying episodes a day. These outbursts often lasted for ten to twenty seconds, with the crying and screams heard for at least sixty feet away. The child would first make eye contact with a teacher and then begin to cry until the teacher came over and consoled him. The experiment was conducted for a period of forty days, with one therapy session given each day. Figure 7–9 presents a cumulative record of these emotional outbursts throughout the experiment. During the initial ten sessions, the baseline or operant level of these episodes was assessed. For the subsequent block of ten sessions, the teachers were instructed to ignore the child's crying (except for looking at him briefly to see that he wasn't hurt) and at the same time to reinforce all normal verbal behavior. As the cumulative record shows, the child's problem behavior was nearly extinguished after the fifth day of therapy. In order to illustrate that the crying was indeed the result of his receiving adult attention, the former reinforcement contingency was reintroduced for another ten-day period. When the teachers again showed sympathy for the crying child, the number of such outbursts increased dramatically. Finally, during the next ten sessions, this behavior was again extinguished by means of discontinuing the social reinforcement.

Another example of the use of extinction in therapy was reported by Ayllon and Michael (1959). They eliminated the disruptive visits that a psychotic patient continually made to the nurses' office. The nurses warned the patient on many occasions that she should not bother them so often, but these warnings seemed to have absolutely no effect. Actually, the patient was being reinforced by receiving attention from the nurses whenever they scolded her. Hence, the therapist instructed the nurses to withhold *all* attention when the patient entered the office without a genuine complaint. From a baseline average of sixteen entries

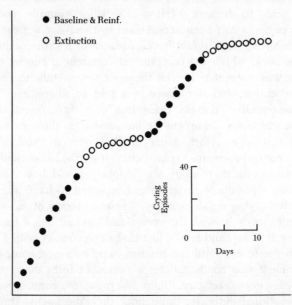

FIGURE 7-9. Conditioning and extinction record of operant crying in a preschool boy. Conditioning periods shown in the dark circles, extinction in open circles. (Adapted from Hart, Allen, Buell, Harris, and Wolf, *Journal of Experimental Child Psychology*, 1964, 1, 145–153. Copyright 1964 by Academic Press, Inc. Reprinted by permission.)

per day, the patient's visits decreased to about two entries per day after seven weeks of extinction. Similar extinction procedures have been successfully used to reduce the occurrence of delusionary speech (Rickard, Dignam, & Horner, 1960), hypochondriacal complaints (Ayllon & Haughton, 1962), extreme passivity (Johnston, Kelley, Harris, & Wolf, 1966), and hyperactivity and aggressive behavior (Allen, Henke, Harris, Baer, & Reynolds, 1967).

Extinction of Emotional Behavior: Desensitization. It has long been assumed that certain operant behaviors, which function as either escape or avoidance responses, cannot be extinguished unless the underlying emotional reaction is extinguished first. Even though the conditioning of overt skeletal behavior may occur independently of changes in autonomic responses (see Chapter 6), one of the most successful approaches in behavior therapy has been concerned with the extinction, or *desensitization,* of emotional responses.

In one of the first experiments of this type, Jones (1924) used what currently would be referred to as a *fading-in procedure* to eliminate avoidance and emotional behavior in a child. This particular child exhibited crying and withdrawal responses when shown a variety of fuzzy objects, including a rabbit, a white rat, wool, or feathers. During the therapy sessions, the child was seated in a chair and fed a meal that he liked. Simultaneously, the therapist brought a rabbit as close to the child as possible without initiating any withdrawal or crying responses. The rabbit would be brought closer and closer to the child until the child eventually began to pet the rabbit. In addition, this tolerance to a previously feared stimulus also generalized to other fuzzy stimuli, some of which the child had never seen before. Notice that the avoidance response in this experiment was not extinguished in the conventional way—that is, by having it repeatedly occur without any consequences. In fact, a deliberate attempt was made not to elicit avoidance and crying responses during the course of therapy.

Wolpe (1958), in a series of widely publicized experiments, extended Jones's procedure to eliminate phobias and other abnormal human behaviors. This therapy is often referred to as *desensitization* or *reciprocal-inhibition therapy*. The procedure used in this therapy involves three phases. First, the patient is trained to develop muscle relaxation. Second, the patient and the therapist work together to identify the specific kinds of stimuli that arouse anxiety—for instance, snakes and snakelike objects or animals. An *anxiety hierarchy* is then determined; that is, the stimuli are ranked according to the amount of anxiety they elicit. (Table 7-2 shows an anxiety hierarchy for a claustrophobic, a death, and an illness series.) Finally, the patient, who is sometimes hypnotized during this phase, is asked to imagine the least disturbing item of the hierarchy (for instance, the word *snake*) until that stimulus no longer elicits anxiety and the subject shows muscle relaxation. By progressive steps, the patient gradually works his way up the hierarchy. Since the conditioned relaxation can counteract only weak anxiety, the therapist must present each stimulus item many times before moving to the next one. Such treatment usually takes from ten to thirty sessions. Although the patient may always show some degree of emotionality when presented with the highest items on the hierarchy, he is no longer handicapped by excessive fear when confronting everyday situations.

In conclusion, behavior therapy attempts to develop and maintain behaviors necessary for effective functioning and to suppress socially undesirable behaviors. Thus, if a patient does not talk or relate to other people, the aim of the therapist is to establish verbal and social behavior.

TABLE 7-2

Anxiety Hierarchies

A. *Claustrophobic Series*

---

1. Being stuck in an elevator. (The longer the time, the more disturbing.)
2. Being locked in a room. (The smaller the room and the longer the time, the more disturbing.)
3. Passing through a tunnel in a railway train. (The longer the tunnel, the more disturbing.)
4. Traveling in an elevator alone. (The greater the distance, the more disturbing.)
5. Traveling in an elevator with an operator. (The longer the distance, the more disturbing.)
6. On a journey by train. (The longer the journey, the more disturbing.)
7. Stuck in a dress with a stuck zipper.
8. Having a tight ring on her finger.
9. Visiting and unable to leave at will (for example, if engaged in a card game).
10. Being told of somebody in jail.
11. Having polish on her fingernails and no access to remover.
12. Reading of miners trapped underground.

B. *Death Series*

---

1. Being at a burial.
2. Being at a house of mourning.
3. The word *death*.
4. Seeing a funeral procession. (The nearer, the more disturbing.)
5. The sight of a dead animal (for example, a cat).
6. Driving past a cemetery. (The nearer, the more disturbing.)

C. *Illness Series*

---

1. Hearing that an acquaintance has cancer.
2. The word *cancer*.
3. Witnessing a convulsive seizure.
4. Discussions of operations. (The more prolonged the discussion, the more disturbing.)
5. Seeing a person receive an injection.
6. Seeing someone faint.
7. The word *operation*.
8. Considerable bleeding from another person.
9. A friend points to a stranger, saying, "This man has tuberculosis."
10. The sight of a blood-stained bandage.
11. The smell of ether.
12. The sight of a friend sick in bed. (The more sick-looking, the more disturbing.)
13. The smell of methylated spirits.
14. Driving past a hospital.

If the patient's personal habits are socially unacceptable, the aim of the therapist is to develop better grooming habits. The techniques used by the therapist have been mostly developed from experimentation with animals. The major procedures include reward, escape/avoidance, punishment, time-out training, and experimental extinction. These procedures basically consist of manipulating contingencies between the patient's behavior and consequences of that behavior. The therapist's goal is to determine an effective set of procedures that will produce a beneficial and permanent change in the patient's behavior.

Behavior-modification techniques have had considerable success. As with all other therapeutic procedures, however, it appears to work well only for certain kinds of maladaptive behavior. Moreover, although it often succeeds in alleviating troublesome symptoms, behavior therapy probably never completely "cures" the patient of the "illness."

APPLICATIONS OF OPERANT
LEARNING: PROGRAMMED
LEARNING

Attention to programmed learning has occurred primarily because of the introduction of the "teaching machine" as a technological aid to education. The first of these machines was developed by Pressey (1926, 1927) as an outgrowth of the automatic test-score machines. This device required that the student read a question presented in a window of the machine, select an answer among several alternatives, and then press a button corresponding to his choice. If the student marked the correct choice, another question appeared in the window; if he made an error, the question remained, and he had to make another selection. Thus, the student received immediate feedback about the correctness of his response. Although Pressey's version of a teaching machine was effective as a teaching device, it did not become popular among educators.

In 1954, B. F. Skinner, by that time well known for his work on operant conditioning, published a paper on the automatic self-instruction method, in which he said: "Recent advances in the experimental analysis of behavior suggest that we can develop a true technology of education. Following the practice of the experimental laboratory, we will use instrumentation to equip students with large repertoires of verbal and nonverbal behavior. Even more important, the apparatus will nurture enthusiasm for continued study. The devices that will help our schools to accomplish this are called teaching machines" (p. 91). Apparently, educators were ready to investigate new methods of teaching; in a very short time, teaching machines and programmed-learning texts became a booming business.

TEACHING MACHINES

The teaching machine developed by Skinner is similar to Pressey's in many ways. However, instead of having the student select the correct answer from a number of alternatives, this machine requires him to write the answer on paper. After making a response, the student pulls a lever, which advances the paper so that his answer is now under a clear plastic window; the correct answer is seen in the aperture of the machine. Thus, the subject can see whether his answer matches the correct one; if he made an error, he puts a check mark on the answer sheet. These check marks will later be used by the author of the program to revise difficult questions, so that fewer mistakes are made by subsequent students. The student then releases the lever, which presents the next question or frame. This procedure is repeated for each successive frame.

A number of different methods have been developed beyond those of Pressey and Skinner. For example, Holland and Skinner (1961) developed a programmed workbook that can be used without an actual teaching machine. A far more complex instructional device, developed for use in the U.S. Air Force, incorporates a step-by-step movie film to teach a technician how to operate a piece of electronic equipment. A simple task is demonstrated in the film several times until it is mastered by the subject; then a more complex demonstration is given. Thus, the subject progresses at his own rate until he has mastered all aspects of the task. Even more complicated programs, which will be described later, use closed-circuit television sets in conjunction with a computer.

THE PROGRAM

Although the recent teaching machines have certainly made an important contribution to the area of education, the essence of good programming does not reside so much in the apparatus as in the way the programmed text is written and organized. Skinner (1958) was one of the first psychologists to stress the importance of good program writing. He claimed that a program of instruction should be similar in many respects to a good tutor: (1) A good tutor begins where the pupil is and does not insist on moving beyond what the pupil can comprehend. (2) A good tutor moves at a rate consistent with the pupil's ability to learn. (3) A good tutor does not permit false answers to remain uncorrected. (4) A good tutor does not lecture; instead, by his hints and questioning, he helps the pupil to find and state answers for himself.

According to Skinner, these characteristics should also be found in a good program. If a program is to be successful, it must begin with responses that the student already knows; then, through a series of promptings or hints, it introduces new information. Thus, by successive approximations, a good program shapes the student to emit the correct response. If errors should occur, it is not assumed that the student lacks ability but that the author of the program has taken too large a step between questions and has therefore confused the student. Hence, the author must be aware of the proper organization of the material to be presented, and he also must have a general idea of the number of steps or questions necessary to progress from one concept to the next. In writing the first draft of the program, the author must rely on his teaching experience and his intuition. The program is then taken by a number of students and is revised over and over again until the average student makes a minimum number of errors. Although a program can be used to test the student, its primary purpose is to allow the student to discover, on his own, the concepts and relationships pertaining to a particular body of knowledge.

At present, more than 350 different types of programs have been used to teach subjects ranging from the grade school level to graduate and professional schools. Some of the topics include *Form and Shape Discrimination, Time Telling, Steps in Reading, Spelling, Multiplication and Division, Fundamentals of Algebra, Mathematical Statistics, Beginning Electronics, Basic French, Basic Spanish, Fundamentals of Music, Introduction to the Science of Behavior, Basic Physiology, Advanced Physiology and Neuroanatomy, Appreciation of Poetry,* and *Creativity and Problem Solving.*

Regardless of the content of the material, all forms of programmed instruction have a number of features in common. First, a good program continually holds the attention of a single subject and requires that he actually participate in the operation of the machine. Second, the program requires the student to commit himself by making a response to each of the questions; thus, the student is not a passive learner, as he might be when reading a textbook or hearing a lecture. Third, the program produces immediate feedback of results after each response the student makes. In the classroom, a student often has to wait days, or even weeks, before a test paper is graded; also, many of his responses must of necessity be ignored by the teacher because of the number of students in the class. Finally, the program permits each student to progress at his own pace.

Some of the advantages of programmed instruction should be obvious from the features discussed above. For example, the student is not dependent upon the teacher and the other students in the class. This is an especially desirable feature for the exceptionally fast or the markedly slow learner. Also, the student is given immediate feedback and therefore does not perpetuate mistakes or poor learning habits. Finally, programmed learning is "self-corrective." If a program is too difficult for a student, it should be revised or completely replaced. The evaluation of classroom teaching is rarely done as objectively and critically as the evaluation of programmed material.

The methods used in designing a program rest primarily upon the principles of reinforcement. Skinner (1961b) and Gilbert (1962) elaborated on the principle of *response chaining* to develop several excellent programs. Such a method for constructing a program may be described as a linear program because the same sequence of questions (or frames) is used for all subjects. The only variable condition in the linear program is the different rate or speed with which individual students progress through the program. In contrast to the linear program, Crowder (1959) developed a *branching program*. In this type of program, questions in the initial frames are more difficult. If the student chooses the correct response, he proceeds to more difficult questions. If, however, he makes an error, he is sidetracked to a set of frames explaining his errors and then is again given the original frame, with instructions to select an answer other than the one he gave before. Thus, Crowder's program "branches" to other frames when the student makes an error, whereas Skinner's linear program ensures that the subject does not make an error because of its many small steps. Figure 8-1 compares the linear and the branching models of

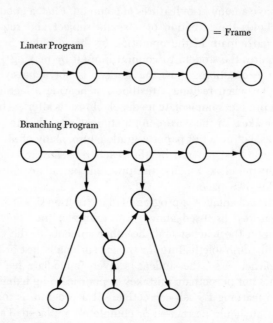

FIGURE 8-1. Diagram of the construction of Skinner's linear and Crowder's branching programs for teaching machines.

programming. Because Crowder's program can be infinitely complicated, usually a computer must be used to select the most beneficial route of questions that a particular student should take. This type of program often is best suited to the fast learner, who may become bored with the slow, deliberate pace of the linear model.

At the University of Illinois, a complex teaching machine incorporating the branching procedure is referred to as PLATO (Programmed Logic for Automatic Teaching Operations). This machine involves the use of closed-circuit television sets, located at a number of locations on campus, and a computer used for the storage and programming of thousands of frames. When the student makes a response to the item seen on television, the computer determines the correctness of the response, the latency of the response, the past history of mistakes, and finally the next optimal series of frames to be presented to the student. The amazing aspect of PLATO is that it can evaluate the input and control the sequence of frames for hundreds of students, working simultaneously in different cubicles located all over campus (Cohen, 1969).

EVALUATION OF OPERANT PRINCIPLES IN PROGRAMMED TEXTS

As mentioned before, the guidelines used in the writing of a program are based on the principles of operant behavior, which have been demonstrated and systematically studied in the laboratory. The questions that we will examine here pertain to the fundamental problem of whether operant principles really do apply to programmed learning with human subjects.

1. *How important is it for the student to emit his own response in learning programmed material?* Skinner believed that the student should emit his own response to each item, rather than selecting from a set of possible answers, because the student then actively commits himself to the process of learning. When a student reads a book, he may or may not feel that the author is writing specifically for him; when he sits in a lecture class, he may or may not be paying attention. On the other hand, when a student at his own discretion operates a teaching machine, he is likely to be more attentive and show greater concentration. Unfortunately, the empirical evidence obtained on this question is equivocal. That is, there appears to be no clear-cut difference between *response-emission* and *multiple-choice-selection* procedures (Schramm, 1964)—as long as the procedure forces the student to pause for a second just before or while he is making the response. For instance, simply underlining the correct answer apparently is as effective as writing it out completely. More research is needed to determine whether the required form of the response has differential effects upon such variables as fast versus slow learners and short-term versus long-term recall.

2. *How important is it that the student receive immediate knowledge of whether or not he made the correct response?* In all the experimental research on operant learning, probably the most important principle is the Law of Effect, which states that behavior is determined by its consequences. Thus, learning is better when reinforcement or feedback is made contingent upon responding (Williams, 1969; Ayllon & Azrin, 1965). Furthermore, even a few seconds' delay between a response and its reinforcement will greatly reduce the effectiveness of the rein-

forcement (Grice, 1948; Keesey, 1964). The findings of experiments with teaching machines suggest that a delay of knowledge of results usually, but not always, causes poorer performance.

3. *How important is it for programmed learning to progress gradually in small steps?* The linear programming model employed by Skinner moves in very small, constant steps. Skinner (1958) felt that steps should be so small that errors were rarely, if ever, committed. According to Skinner, students who find the material too difficult not only make a series of errors but also stop working and become irritable almost to the point of aggressiveness. For exceptionally fast learners, Maccoby and Sheffield (1961) found it advantageous gradually to increase the step size as the subject begins to show mastery of the material.

4. *How important is it to use a well-ordered sequence of frames in shaping the student?* When developing a complex chain of behavior with a laboratory pigeon, we might initially reinforce the response of approaching the food dispenser to the sound of the click. Soon the pigeon will learn to associate pecking on the illuminated key with the click. Next, we might teach the pigeon to press a pedal to illuminate the key, then peck the key and approach the food dispenser. This basic principle of shaping complex behavior by successive tasks is also assumed to operate for a student working on a teaching machine. The teaching-machine program moves in very finely graded steps, working from simple to an ever higher level of complexity. The ordered sequence of frame presentations is illustrated in Table 8-1. The principle of an ordered sequence of frames, according to Holland and Skinner (1961), not only helps the student perform accurately but also is the most efficient way to develop a complex pattern of responses.

Although this principle of learning appears plausible, Schramm (1964), in an excellent review of experiments concerned with programmed learning, found no clear-cut evidence that the principle applies to human learning. Of the five experiments that compared the test performance of an ordered sequence with a random sequence of frames, only one study showed significantly better learning for the ordered sequence. Furthermore, Mager (1961) found that students who order their own sequence of items do well, even though the sequences differ greatly between subjects. Perhaps this result occurred because students are more motivated by their own sequence than by a sequence constructed by an experimenter. Experimental evidence, however, does seem to indicate that students make fewer errors when the sequence of the program is ordered by the experimenter.

TABLE 8-1

Teaching-Machine Operations

Item	Correct Answer	Percentage of Students Giving the Answer
1. Performing animals are sometimes trained with "rewards." The behavior of a hungry animal can be "rewarded" with ———.	Food	96
2. A technical term for "reward" is reinforcement. To "reward" an organism with food is to ——— it with food.	Reinforce	100
3. Technically speaking, a thirsty organism can be ——— with water.	Reinforced	100
. . .		
50. A school teacher is likely, whenever possible, to dismiss a class when her students are rowdy because she has been ——— by elimination of the stimuli arising from a rowdy class.	Reinforced	92
51. The teacher who dismisses a class when it is rowdy causes the frequency of future rowdy behavior to (1) ———, since dismissal from class is probably a(n) (2) ——— for rowdy children.	(1) Increase (2) Reinforcement	86
. . .		
54. If an airplane spotter never sees the kind of plane he is to spot, his frequency of scanning the sky (1) ———. In other words, his "looking" behavior is (2) ———.	(1) Decreases (2) Extinguished (or: Not Reinforced)	94

(From *A Program for Self-Instruction* by Holland & Skinner. Copyright 1961 by McGraw-Hill, Inc. Reprinted by permission of McGraw-Hill Book Company.)

With the discovery of the technique of fading, or the gradual withdrawal of prompting stimuli, greater attention has been given to the use of ordered sequences of material in shaping new behaviors. According to Sidman and Stoddard (1967), properly ordered sequences of discrimination problems can be used to establish high levels of performance in mentally retarded children who could not otherwise learn such problems. In this study, two groups of subjects were given a discrimination-learning task. For the Program Group, a nonverbal teaching program was used; for the Test Group, the conventional reinforcement and extinction procedure was used. The task was to discriminate circles from ellipses. In the Program Group, a fading procedure was used: first, stimulus control was established on a discrimination problem of bright versus dark; then the stimulus control was transferred to form versus no form; finally, it was shifted to circle versus ellipse. The Test Group, on the other hand, began training directly on the circle-versus-ellipse problem without receiving any programmed transfer. Seven of the ten children in the Program Group learned the final task, whereas only one of the nine children in the Test Group performed well on this problem. Even more interesting is the fact that six of the nine children in the Test Group were able subsequently to learn form versus no-form discrimination when given additional training, but only three of these subjects could master the circle versus the ellipse when they were retested on this task. All seven of the children who learned the form versus no-form discrimination in the Program Group showed excellent transfer to the circle-ellipse problem. Apparently, an ordered sequence of more complex problems is not a sufficient condition for positive transfer; a gradual fading procedure must also be incorporated into the training procedure.

5. *Should the student set his own pace?* In all operant experimentation, an emphasis is placed on changing the behavior of an individual subject. Thus, it is not surprising that individualized instruction is stressed in programmed learning. One aspect of individualized instruction is to have the student proceed through the program at his own pace. This feature obviously cannot be done in the typical classroom situation as efficiently as it can be done with a teaching machine. For the most part, the experimental data seem to support the view that self-pacing is superior to group pacing. According to a study by Frye (1963), self-pacing is especially useful with heterogeneous groups of students but is not necessarily better with a homogeneous group.

EVALUATION OF PROGRAMMED LEARNING

Like any new field, programmed instruction has received both praise and criticism from psychologists as well as laymen. Perhaps the best way of beginning a review of some of these reactions is to ask: Do students learn material effectively with programmed instruction? The answer is clearly—yes, they do. Schramm (1964) reported that of the thirty-six studies comparing conventional classroom instruction with programmed instruction at all levels of education, seventeen showed programmed instruction to be superior, eighteen found no sufficient difference, and only one study showed superiority of the conventional approach.

Despite the fact that programmed instruction often is successful, many criticisms have been raised against its widespread use. Critics of programmed learning claim that it cannot attain the broad objectives of what is considered a well-rounded education. They say sarcastically: "Students taught like pigeons will act like pigeons, in that they lack spontaneity and originality of thought." Teaching-machine methods are so impersonal, these critics claim, that the student is never "caught up in the enthusiasm that a particular instructor may impart to some subject matter." Also, the student using a teaching machine does not have the experience of organizing the material for himself, and he does not learn to express complex ideas verbally because of the simple form of response that is required by the machine. Finally, according to these critics, students of programmed learning do not have an opportunity to develop proper reading skills and thus may view reading as merely a means to achieving knowledge without realizing that it can be a very enjoyable pastime that extends far beyond one's formal education.

Advocates of programmed learning, on the other hand, say that the critics are wrong in assuming that programmed learning is to serve as a replacement for all other forms of classroom teaching. It is, these supporters allege, intended only as a supplement and should not replace classroom discussion and individual student-teacher conferences. The advocates also claim that programmed instruction frees the teacher of the routine tasks of conveying facts to students and allows the good teacher to have more time for discussion and to try out new educational techniques (demonstrations, films, etc.). Finally, advocates claim that one of the major advantages of programmed instruction is for the treatment of behavior disorders. Programmed learning and teaching machines may provide relief for interpersonal anxiety that the emotional child or slow learner has continually experienced in the classroom situation.

ETHICAL PROBLEMS INVOLVING CONTROL OF HUMAN BEHAVIOR

Although there is little objection to the use of the word *control* when a laboratory animal is trained to make a particular response, many people become angry or fearful when this term is applied to human behavior. Those who become angry usually contend that man is a free agent and forever beyond the reach of operant controlling techniques. In view of the research cited earlier in this text, however, the notion that behavioral control does not exist in humans seems unsupportable. Those who become fearful undoubtedly associate control with the tyrannical rule of an evil despot or an authoritarian parent. These individuals do not realize that all people, including themselves, are constantly influencing (controlling) the behavior of others—either intentionally or unintentionally. The worker who goes on a strike and pickets a plant is attempting to control the behavior of nonunion workers and employers. The student who protests because the university is supporting defense research is trying to change the behavior of the chief administrators of the university and perhaps the general public. Likewise, a parent or teacher who praises a child for reading at an early age, playing a musical instrument, or receiving good grades in school is indirectly controlling the child's behavior. The worker, the student, the parent, and the teacher are normally not considered as behaving in an unethical or immoral manner, even though they clearly are engaged in the process of controlling the behavior of other individuals. Thus, we must acknowledge the fact that everyone controls and is controlled. That men control the behavior of one another should not be viewed as good or bad in a moral sense; rather, it should be accepted as a fact of life.

Western thought has emphasized the importance of the dignity of the individual. Democratic philosophies of government have stressed the rights of man and have asserted that all individuals are equal under the law. Likewise, Western society—in its religion, art, and literature—has emphasized the uniqueness of the individual. Finally, some of the conventional approaches to psychotherapy, such as client-centered therapy, consider that under suitable conditions man is capable of determining his own destiny. The past success of this philosophical position clearly cannot be denied. It has provided strength to individual citizens and made them energetic and productive members of society. Probably the major source of uneasiness concerning the application of control techniques is that the humanistic values of Western society would be replaced by impersonal sources of central control that would limit an individual's freedom of choice. In our own society, however, there appears to be a myth that identifies freedom with limitless individual choice. Many scientists believe that this myth, if perpetuated, will lead to the destruction of the biophysical environments and thus to a far greater loss of individual freedom.

> Ironically, the concern with safeguarding individual freedom against an alleged onrushing regimentation may have overlooked what is a very real and present danger to liberty. . . . For, in fact, the image of an intemperate state imposing its arbitrary will, in America at least, caricatures existing reality, where truly national functions go untended, or at best are administered feebly, all in the name of preserving liberty. Indeed, the time is overdue to clarify the relation of the individual to his community in an age of massive technical innovation [Schiller, 1968, p. 17].

The myth of limitless individual choice as the basis of liberty breaks down as society increases in size and complexity. The midwestern farmer, who for years had represented the true spirit of "rugged individualism," now must depend upon central agencies to control price and production quotas. Furthermore, new problems in agricultural control have resulted from the widespread use of insecticides such as DDT. In every phase of life, society must control random individual choices, which potentially produce drastic restraints on the behaviors of other individuals. If society fails to regulate the behavior of others, individual fulfillment for mankind in the future could be destroyed.

The pertinent question now becomes: Who is best qualified to exercise the control of behavior? Parents, teachers, therapists, clergymen, and politicians, who have in the past shared this privilege, will probably continue to do so. But they must realize that they will be assuming much greater responsibility. In a speech to the Royal Society, Skinner (1965) commented on the responsibility that educators must assume:

> It could well be that an effective technology of teaching will be unwisely used. It could make men all alike (and not necessarily in being equally

excellent), it could suppress the beneficial effect of accidents upon the development of the individual and upon the evolution of a culture. On the other hand, it could maximize the genetic endowment of each student, it could make him as skillful, competent, and informed as possible, it could build the greatest diversity of interests, it could lead him to make the greatest possible contribution to the survival and development of his culture.°

Because of the tremendous responsibility placed on those who will have the power of controlling behavior, it is important that the behavioral scientist pursue two objectives. First, he must continue to investigate new techniques and principles of behavioral control. His studies must encompass both basic and applied approaches to research. Second, the behavioral scientist is obligated to report his experimental findings to a number of agencies (schools, government, news media) who practice behavioral control. For only by diversity of control is it possible for us to avoid the despotism of an impersonal, central source of control.

°From Skinner, B. F., "The technology of teaching," *Proceedings of the Royal Society,* 1965, 62, 427–443. Copyright 1965 by the Royal Society, and reproduced by permission.

APPENDIX:
DESCRIPTIONS OF
COMPOUND SCHEDULES

SUCCESSIVE COMPOUND SCHEDULES

MIXED (MIX)

In this schedule, the reinforcement is programmed by two or more schedules, usually alternating at random. For example, *mix* FI 5 FR 50 represents a schedule in which a reinforcement sometimes occurs after an interval of five minutes and sometimes after a ratio of fifty responses, the possibilities occurring either at random or according to a program in any determined proportion.

INTERPOLATED (INTER)

In this schedule, a single block of reinforcements under a particular schedule is interpolated into a sustained period of responding on a different background schedule. Thus, on an FR 5 *inter* FI 10, several reinforcements on FR 5 are inserted into an experimental period in which the subject has been responding on a FI 10 schedule.

TANDEM (TAND)

In this case, a single reinforcement is programmed by two schedules acting in succession without the presentation of correlated, external stimuli. For example, in a *tand* FI 10 FR 5, reinforcement occurs when five responses are emitted after a ten-minute interval has elapsed. Most of the experiments employing tandem schedules have combined the simple schedules of FI and FR.

Ferster and Skinner (1957) found that the rate of responding of pigeons increased greatly when an FR 10 was added to an FI 45 schedule. They also reported that after the rate increase occurred on *tand* FI 45 FR 10, responding could still be maintained when the tandem FR component was increased substantially, up to FR 400. Also, the effect of introducing the tandem FR persisted in subsequent tests of performance on simple FI and FR schedules. Thus, the tandem FI-FR schedule appears to be one of the best ways of generating a high rate of responding relative to the number of reinforcements presented.

In contrast to the striking effects of tandem FI-FR schedules, the results of tandem FR-FI (and VR-FI) studies done by Ferster and Skinner (1957) are more difficult to characterize. In a tandem FR-FI, a (usually) short interval must have elapsed after the completion of a ratio before a response is reinforced. Skinner and Ferster (1957) studied the effects of a transition from CRF to a tandem FR-FI schedule with fairly large values of FR and fairly small values of FI. In one study, for example, two pigeons were exposed to a *tand* FR 240 FI 7 sec after CRF. One of the birds developed and maintained a high response rate under this schedule; the other bird did not, probably because of the very high ratio requirement. With lower ratio requirements (FR 80 and FR 140), these investigators found that subjects could sustain a high response rate. In general, however, these rates were not as high as those found with tandem FI-FR schedules.

SIMULTANEOUS COMPOUND SCHEDULES

ALTERNATIVE (ALT)

A response is reinforced on an alternative schedule depending on whichever of two schedules is completed first. For example, under *alt* FI 5 FR 50, a response is reinforced when *either* five minutes have elapsed *or* fifty responses have been performed, whichever occurs first.

INTERLOCKING (INTERLOCK)

In an interlocking schedule, the setting of one schedule is altered by the amount of the progress made in the other. For instance, in an *interlock* FI 5 FR 200, the subject is reinforced at a ratio that is slowly reduced from two hundred responses to a single response during a five-minute period. If responding is rapid, reinforcement occurs only after a large ratio has been completed; if responding is slow, reinforcement occurs at a much lower rate. If no response occurs within five minutes, then the first response made would be reinforced.

Another type of interlocking schedule is one in which the number of required responses increases (from one to two hundred responses) the longer the time since the previous reinforcement. Since the response ratio may become very large in a relatively short period of time, this insidious type of schedule may result in a decrement in responding. If the subject fails to emit a burst of responses at the beginning of the interval, clearly the possibility of his making the required number of responses later in the interval becomes doubtful.

CONJUNCTIVE (CONJ)

A conjunctive schedule demands that the requirements of two simple schedules *both* be met in order to achieve reinforcements. This schedule differs from the tandem schedule in that the sequence in which the requirements are met is not critical. In a *conj* FI 3 FR 30 schedule, for example, a response is reinforced only after the subject has emitted thirty responses *and* three minutes have elapsed since the previous reinforcement. The performance on a conjunctive FI-FR schedule usually is found to be a combination of the performances that would be generated by the two schedules if they were presented separately. During the interval between reinforcements, there is typically a pause followed by a rapid period of responding which is characteristic of FI perfromance. Then there may be the burst of responses typically found with the FR schedule. Finally, there is often another pause, which is followed by an acceleration just before the occurrence of the reinforced response. Thus, the subject manages to fulfill the requirements of both schedules by alternately performing separate response patterns.

REFERENCES

Allen, K. E., Henke, L. B., Harris, F. R., Baer, D. M., & Reynolds, N. J. Control of hyperactivity by social reinforcement of attending behavior. *Journal of Educational Psychology*, 1967, **58**, 231–237.

Amsel, A., & Roussel, J. Motivational properties of frustration: Effect on a running response of the addition of frustration to the motivational complex. *Journal of Experimental Psychology*, 1952, **43**, 363–368.

Appel, J. B. Punishment and shock intensity. *Science*, 1963, **141**, 528–529.

Armus, H. L., & Garlich, M. M. Secondary reinforcement strength as a function of schedule of primary reinforcement. *Journal of Comparative and Physiological Psychology*, 1961, **54**, 56–58.

Autor, S. M. The strength of conditioned reinforcers as a function of frequency and probability of reinforcement. Unpublished doctoral dissertation, Harvard University, 1960.

Ayllon, T. Intensive treatment of psychotic behavior by stimulus satiation and food reinforcement. *Behavior Research and Therapy*, 1963, **1**, 53–61.

Ayllon, T., & Azrin, N. H. The measurement and reinforcement of behavior of psychotics. *Journal of the Experimental Analysis of Behavior*, 1965, **8**, 357–383.

Ayllon, T., & Haughton, E. Control of the behavior of schizophrenic patients by food. *Journal of the Experimental Analysis of Behavior*, 1962, **5**, 343–352.

Ayllon, T., & Michael, J. The psychiatric nurse as a behavioral engineer. *Journal of the Experimental Analysis of Behavior*, 1959, **2**, 323–334.

Azrin, N. H. Effects of two intermittent schedules of immediate and nonimmediate punishment. *Journal of Psychology*, 1956, **42**, 3–21.

Azrin, N. H. Some effects of noise on human behavior. *Journal of the Experimental Analysis of Behavior*, 1958, **1**, 183–200.

Azrin, N. H. Punishment and recovery during fixed-ratio performance. *Journal of the Experimental Analysis of Behavior*, 1959, **2**, 301–305.

Azrin, N. H. Effects of punishment intensity on variable-interval reinforcement. *Journal of the Experimental Analysis of Behavior*, 1960, **3**, 123–142.

Azrin, N. H., & Holtz, W. C. Punishment during fixed-interval reinforcement. *Journal of the Experimental Analysis of Behavior*, 1961, **4**, 343–347.

Azrin, N. H., & Holtz, W. C. Punishment. In W. K. Honig (Ed.), *Operant behavior: Areas of research and application.* New York: Appleton-Century-Crofts, 1966. Pp. 380–447.

Azrin, N. H., Holtz, W. C., & Hake, D. Intermittent reinforcement by removal of a conditioned aversive stimulus. *Science*, 1962, **136**, 781-782.

Azrin, N. H., Holtz, W. C., & Hake, D. Fixed-ratio punishment. *Journal of the Experimental Analysis of Behavior*, 1963, **6**, 620.

Baer, D. M. Laboratory control of thumbsucking by withdrawal and representation of reinforcement. *Journal of the Experimental Analysis of Behavior*, 1962, **5**, 525–528.

Bandura, A. *Principles of behavior modification.* New York: Holt, 1969.

Bass, M. J., & Hull, C. L. The irradiation of a tactile conditioned reflex in man. *Journal of Comparative Psychology*, 1934, **17**, 47–65.

Bersh, P. J. The influence of two variables upon the establishment of a secondary reinforcer for operant responses. *Journal of Experimental Psychology*, 1951, **41**, 62–73.

Bijuo, S. W., & Baer, D. M. Operant methods in child behavior and development. In W. K. Honig (Ed.), *Operant behavior: Areas of research and application.* New York: Appleton-Century-Crofts, 1966. Pp. 718–789.

Bilodeau, J. McD. Information feedback. In E. A. Bilodeau (Ed.), *Acquisition of skill.* New York: Academic Press, 1966. Pp. 217–244.

Bitterman, M. E. Animal learning. In J. B. Sidowaski (Ed.), *Experimental methods and instrumentation in psychology.* New York: McGraw-Hill, 1966. Pp. 451–484.

Bitterman, M. E., Fedderson, W. E., & Tyler, D. W. Secondary reinforcement and the discrimination hypothesis. *American Journal of Psychology*, 1953, **46**, 393–397.

Black, A. H. Cardiac conditioning in curarized dogs: The relation between heart rate and skeletal behavior. In W. F. Prokasy (Ed.), *Classical conditioning: A symposium.* New York: Appleton-Century-Crofts, 1965. Pp. 20–47.

Blakemore, C. B., Thorpe, J. G., Barker, J. C., Conway, C. G., & Lavin, N. I. The application of faradic aversion conditioning in a case of transvestism. *Behavior Research and Therapy,* 1963, **1,** 29–34.

Blough, D. S. Dark adaptation in the pigeon. *Journal of Comparative and Physiological Psychology,* 1956, **49,** 425–430.

Blough, D. S. Spectral sensitivity in the pigeon. *Journal of the Optical Society of America,* 1957, **47,** 827–833.

Bower, G. H., Starr, R., & Lazarovitz, L. Amount of response produced change in the CS in avoidance learning. *Journal of Comparative and Physiological Psychology,* 1965, **59,** 13–17.

Brady, J. V. Ulcers in "executive monkeys." *Scientific American,* 1958, **199,** 95–103.

Brady, J. V., & Hunt, H. An experimental approach to the analysis of emotional behavior. *Journal of Psychology,* 1955, **45,** 313–325.

Brown, J. L. The effect of drive on learning with secondary reinforcement. *Journal of Comparative and Physiological Psychology,* 1956, **51,** 254–260.

Brown, J. S. *The motivation of behavior.* New York: McGraw-Hill, Inc., 1961.

Brown, J. S., Bilodeau, E. A., & Baron, M. R. Bidirectional gradients in the strength of a generalized voluntary response to stimuli on a visual-spatial dimension. *Journal of Experimental Psychology,* 1951, **41,** 52–61.

Bugelski, R. Extinction with and without sub-goal reinforcement. *Journal of Comparative Psychology,* 1938, **26,** 121–134.

Bugelski, R. *The psychology of learning.* New York: Holt, 1956.

Butter, C. M. Stimulus generalization along one and two dimensions in pigeons. *Journal of Experimental Psychology,* 1963, **65,** 339–346.

Butter, C. M., & Guttman, N. Stimulus generalization and discrimination along the dimension of angular orientation. *American Psychologist,* 1957, **12,** 449. (Abstract)

Butter, C. M., & Thomas, D. R. Secondary reinforcement as a function of the amount of primary reinforcement. *Journal of Comparative and Physiological Psychology,* 1958, **51,** 346–348.

Calvin, J. S., Bicknell, E. A., & Sperling, D. S. Establishment of a conditioned drive based on the hunger drive. *Journal of Comparative and Physiological Psychology,* 1953, **46,** 176–179.

Catania, A. C. Behavioral contrast in a multiple and concurrent schedule of reinforcement. *Journal of the Experimental Analysis of Behavior,* 1961, **4,** 335–342.

Catania, A. C. Concurrent performances: Analysis of ratio and interval schedules of reinforcement. *American Psychologist,* 1963, **18,** 241. (Abstract)

Catania, A. C. Concurrent operants. In W. K. Honig (Ed.), *Operant Behavior: Areas of research and application,* New York: Appleton-Century-Crofts, 1966. Pp. 213–270.

Church, R. M. The varied effects of punishment on behavior. *Psychological Review,* 1963, **70,** 396–402.

Clark, C. V., & Isaacson, R. L. Effect of bilateral hippocampal ablation on DRL performance. *Journal of Comparative and Physiological Psychology,* 1965, **59,** 137–140.

Cohen, J. *Operant behavior and operant conditioning.* Chicago: Rand McNally, 1969.

Collier, G., & Myers, L. The loci of reinforcement. *Journal of Experimental Psychology,* 1961, **61,** 57–66.

Crespi, L. P. Quantitative variation of incentive and performance in the white rat. *American Journal of Psychology,* 1942, **55,** 467–517.

Crowder, N. A. Automatic tutoring by means of intrinsic programming. In E. H. Galanter (Ed.), *Automatic teaching: The state of the art.* New York: Wiley, 1959. Pp. 109–116.

Crowder, W. F., Gay, B. R., Bright, M. G., & Lee, M. F. Secondary reinforcement or response facilitation? III. Reconditioning. *Journal of Psychology,* 1959, **48,** 307–310.

Crowder, W. F., Gay, B. R., Fleming, W. C., & Hurst, R. W. Secondary reinforcement or response facilitation? IV. The retention method. *Journal of Psychology,* 1959, **48,** 311–314.

Crowder, W. F., Gill, K., Jr., Hodge, C. C., & Nash, F. A., Jr. Secondary reinforcement or response facilitation? II. Response acquisition. *Journal of Psychology,* 1959, **48,** 303–306.

Crowder, W. F., Morris, J. B., & McDaniel, M. H. Secondary reinforcement or response facilitation? I. Resistance to extinction. *Journal of Psychology,* 1959, **48,** 299–302.

D'Amato, M. R. Secondary reinforcement and magnitude of primary reinforcement. *Journal of Comparative and Physiological Psychology,* 1955, **48,** 378–380.

D'Amato, M. R., Lachman, R., & Kivy, P. Secondary reinforcement as affected by reward schedule and the testing situation. *Journal of Comparative and Physiological Psychology,* 1958, **51,** 737–741.

Denny, M. R. The effect of using differential end boxes in a simple T-maze learning situation. *Journal of Experimental Psychology,* 1948, **38,** 245–249.

Dinsmoor, J. A. A quantitative comparison of the discriminative and reinforcing functions of a stimulus. *Journal of Psychology,* 1950, **40,** 458–472.

Dinsmoor, J. A. A discrimination based on punishment. *Quarterly Journal of Experimental Psychology,* 1952, **4,** 27–45.

Dinsmoor, J. A. Punishment: I. The avoidance hypothesis. *Psychological Review,* 1954, **61,** 34–46.

Dinsmoor, J. A., & Winograd, E. Shock intensity in variable-interval escape schedules. *Journal of the Experimental Analysis of Behavior*, 1958, **1**, 145–148.

Dollard, J., & Miller, N. E. *Personality and psychotherapy*. New York: McGraw-Hill, 1950.

Dyal, J. A., & Holland, T. A. Resistance to extinction as a function of the number of reinforcements. *American Journal of Psychology*, 1963, **76**, 332–333.

Easterbrook, J. A. The effect of emotion on cue utilization and the organization of behavior. *Psychological Review*, 1959, **66**, 183–210.

Eckstrand, G. A., & Wickens, D. D. Transfer of perceptual set. *Journal of Experimental Psychology*, 1954, **47**, 274–278.

Egeth, H. Selective attention. *Psychological Bulletin*, 1967, **67**, 41–57.

Egger, M. D., & Miller, N. E. Secondary reinforcement in rats as a function of information value and reliability of the stimulus. *Journal of Experimental Psychology*, 1962, **64**, 97–104.

Egger, M. D., & Miller, N. E. When is a reward reinforcing? An experimental study of the information hypothesis. *Journal of Comparative and Physiological Psychology*, 1963, **56**, 132–137.

Ehrenfreund, D. Generalization of secondary reinforcement in discrimination learning. *Journal of Comparative and Physiological Psychology*, 1954, **47**, 311–314.

Ellison, D. G. Quantitative studies of the interaction of simple habits: I. Recovery from specific and generalized effects of extinction. *Journal of Experimental Psychology*, 1938, **23**, 339–358.

Estes, W. K. An experimental study of punishment. *Psychological Monographs*, 1944, **57**, (No. 263).

Estes, W. K. Generalization of secondary reinforcement from the primary drive. *Journal of Comparative and Physiological Psychology*, 1949, **42**, 286–295.

Estes, W. K. Learning theory and the new "mental chemistry." *Psychological Review*, 1960, **67**, 207–223.

Estes, W. K., & Skinner, B. F. Some quantitative properties of anxiety. *Journal of Experimental Psychology*, 1941, **29**, 390–400.

Eysenck, H. J. Learning theory and behavior therapy. *Journal of Mental Science*, 1959, **105**, 61–75.

Feldman, M. P., & MacCulloch, M. J. The application of anticipatory avoidance learning to the treatment of homosexuality: I. Theory, technique, and preliminary results. *Behavior Research and Therapy*, 1965, **2**, 165–183.

Ferster, C. B. Sustained behavior under delayed reinforcement. *Journal of Experimental Psychology*, 1953, **45**, 218–224.

Ferster, C. B., & Skinner, B. F. *Schedules of reinforcement*. New York: Appleton-Century-Crofts, 1957.

Fitts, P. M., & Posner, M. I. *Human performance*. Monterey, Calif.: Brooks/Cole, 1967.

Fowler, H. The effects of punishment and distribution of trials on the acquisition of the runway response. Unpublished doctoral dissertation, Yale University, 1959.

Fowler, H., & Trapold, M. A. Escape performance as a function of delay of reinforcement. *Journal of Experimental Psychology*, 1962, **63**, 464–467.

Franks, C. M. *Behavior therapy: Appraisal and status*. New York: McGraw-Hill, 1969.

Frye, C. H. *Group vs. individual pacing in programmed instruction*. Portland: Oregon State System of Higher Education, 1963.

Ganz, L. Hue generalization and hue discriminability in *Macaca mulatta*. *Journal of Experimental Psychology*, 1962, **64**, 142–150.

Ganz, L., & Riesen, A. H. Stimulus generalization to hue in the dark-reared Macaque. *Journal of Comparative and Physiological Psychology*, 1962, **55**, 92–99.

Gilbert, T. F. Mathetics: The technology of education. *Journal of Mathetics*, 1962, **1**, 7-73.

Goldiamond, I. Stuttering and fluency as manipulatable operant response classes. In L. Krasner & L. P. Ullman (Eds.), *Research in behavior modification*. New York: Holt, 1965. Pp. 106–156.

Gollub, L. R. The chaining of fixed-interval schedules. Unpublished doctoral dissertation, Harvard University, 1958.

Greenspoon, J. The reinforcing effect of two spoken sounds on the frequency of two responses. *American Journal of Psychology*, 1955, **68**, 409–416.

Grice, G. R. The relation of secondary reinforcement to delayed reward in visual discrimination learning. *Journal of Experimental Psychology*, 1948, **38**, 1–16.

Grice, G. R., & Davis, J. D. Effect of irrelevant thirst motivation on a response learned with food reward. *Journal of Experimental Psychology*, 1957, **53**, 347–352.

Grosslight, J. H., Zaynor, W. C., & Lively, B. L. Speech as a stimulus for differential vocal behavior in the mynah bird (*Gracula religiosa*). *Psychonomic Science*, 1964, **1**, 7–8.

Guthrie, E. R. *The psychology of learning*. New York: Harper, 1935.

Guttman, N. Equal reinforcing values for sucrose and glucose solutions compared with equal sweetness values. *Journal of Comparative and Physiological Psychology*, 1954, **47**, 358–361.

Guttman, N., & Kalish, H. I. Discriminability and stimulus generalization. *Journal of Experimental Psychology*, 1956, **51**, 79–88.

Gwinn, G. T. The effects of punishment motivated by fear. *Journal of Experimental Psychology*, 1949, **39**, 260–269.

Hall, J. F. Studies in secondary reinforcement: I. Secondary reinforcement as a function of the frequency of primary reinforcement. *Journal of Comparative and Physiological Psychology*, 1951, **44**, 246–251. (a)

Hall, J. F. Studies in secondary reinforcement: II. Secondary reinforcement as a function of the strength of the drive during primary reinforcement.

Journal of Comparative and Physiological Psychology, 1951, **44**, 462–466. (b)

Hamilton, W. F., & Coleman, T. B. Trichromatic vision in the pigeon as illustrated by the spectral hue discrimination curve. *Journal of Comparative and Physiological Psychology,* 1933, **15**, 183–191.

Hanson, H. M. Effects of discrimination training on stimulus generalization. *Journal of Experimental Psychology,* 1959, **58**, 321–324.

Hanson, H. M. Stimulus generalization following three-stimulus discrimination training. *Journal of Comparative and Physiological Psychology,* 1961, **54**, 181–185.

Harris, P., & Nygaard, J. E. Resistance to extinction and number of reinforcements. *Psychological Reports,* 1961, **8**, 233–234.

Harris, F. R., Wolf, M. M., & Baer, D. M. Effects of adult social reinforcement on child behavior. *Young Children,* 1964, **20**, 8–17.

Hart, B. M., Allen, K. E., Buell, J. S., Harris, F. R., & Wolf, M. M. Effects of social reinforcement on operant crying. *Journal of Experimental Child Psychology,* 1964, **1**, 145–153.

Hearst, E., & Sidman, M. Some behavioral effects of a concurrently positive and negative stimulus. *Journal of the Experimental Analysis of Behavior,* 1961, **4**, 261–265.

Hefferline, R. F., Keenan, B., & Harford, R. A. Escape and avoidance conditioning in human subjects without their observation of the response. *Science,* 1959, **130**, 1338–1339.

Heinemann, E. G., & Rudolph, R. L. The effect of discriminative training on the gradient of stimulus generalization. *American Journal of Psychology,* 1963, **76**, 653–658.

Hendry, D. P. *Conditioned reinforcement.* Homewood, Ill. Dorsey Press, 1969.

Herman, R. L., & Azrin, N. H. Punishment by noise in an alternative response situation. *Journal of the Experimental Analysis of Behavior,* 1964, **7**, 185–188.

Herrick, R. M. The successful differentiation of a lever response. *Journal of the Experimental Analysis of Behavior,* 1964, **7**, 211–215.

Herrnstein, R. J. Behavioral consequences of the removal of a discriminative stimulus associated with variable-interval reinforcement. Unpublished doctoral dissertation, Harvard University, 1955.

Hewett, F. M. Teaching speech to an autistic child through operant conditioning. *American Journal of Orthopsychiatry,* 1965, **35**, 927–936.

Hodos, W., Ross, G. S., & Brady, J. V. Complex response patterns during temporally spaced responding. *Journal of the Experimental Analysis of Behavior,* 1962, **5**, 475–479.

Hoffman, H. S. The analysis of discriminated avoidance. In W. K. Honig (Ed.), *Operant behavior: Areas of research and application.* New York: Appleton-Century-Crofts, 1966. Pp. 499–530.

Hoffman, H. S., & Fleshler, M. The course of emotionality in the development of avoidance. *Journal of Experimental Psychology,* 1962, **64**, 288–294.

Hoffman, H. S., & Fleshler, M. Stimulus aspects of aversive controls: The effects of response-contingent shock. *Journal of the Experimental Analysis of Behavior*, 1965, **8**, 89–96.

Hoffman, H. S., Fleshler, M., & Jensen, P. Stimulus aspects of aversive controls: The retention of conditioned suppression. *Journal of the Experimental Analysis of Behavior*, 1963, **6**, 575–583.

Holland, J. G., & Skinner, B. F. *The analysis of behavior: A program for self-instruction*. New York: McGraw-Hill, 1961.

Holtz, W. C., & Azrin, N. H. Discriminative properties of punishment. *Journal of the Experimental Analysis of Behavior*, 1961, **4**, 225–232.

Holtz, W. C., & Azrin, N. H. Interactions between the discriminative and aversive properties of punishment. *Journal of the Experimental Analysis of Behavior*, 1962, **5**, 229–234.

Holtz, W. C., Azrin, N. H., & Ayllon, T. A comparison of several procedures for eliminating behavior. *Journal of the Experimental Analysis of Behavior*, 1963, **6**, 399–406.

Honig, W. K. Attention factors governing the slope of the generalization gradient. In R. M. Gilbert & N. S. Sutherland (Eds.), *Animal discrimination learning*. London: Academic Press, 1969. Pp. 35–62.

Honig, W. K., Thomas, D. R., & Guttman, N. Differential effects of continuous extinction and discrimination training on the generalization gradient. *Journal of Experimental Psychology*, 1959, **58**, 145–152.

Hull, C. L. *Principles of behavior*. New York: Appleton-Century-Crofts, 1943.

Humphreys, L. G. The effect of random alternation of reinforcement on acquisition and extinction of conditioned eyelid reactions. *Journal of Experimental Psychology*, 1939, **25**, 141–158.

Hunt, H. F., & Brady, J. V. Some effects of punishment and intercurrent "anxiety" on a simple operant. *Journal of Comparative and Physiological Psychology*, 1955, **48**, 305–310.

Isaacs, W., Thomas, J., & Goldiamond, I. Application of operant conditioning to reinstate verbal behavior in psychotics. *Journal of Speech and Hearing Disorders*, 1960, **25**, 8–12.

Isaacson, R. L., & Wickelgren, W. O. Hippocampal ablation and passive avoidance. *Science*, 1962, **138**, 1104–1106.

Ison, J. R. Experimental extinction as a function of the number of reinforcements. *Journal of Experimental Psychology*, 1962, **64**, 314–317.

Jenkins, H. M., & Harrison, R. H. Effect of discrimination training on auditory generalization. *Journal of Experimental Psychology*, 1960, **59**, 246–253.

Jenkins, W. O. A temporal gradient of derived reinforcement. *American Journal of Psychology*, 1950, **63**, 237–243.

Johnston, M. K., Kelley, C. S., Harris, F. R., & Wolf, M. M. An application of reinforcement principles to development of motor skills of a young child. *Child Development*, 1966, **37**, 379–387.

Jones, M. C. The elimination of children's fears. *Journal of Experimental Psychology*, 1924, **7**, 382–390.

Kalish, H. I. The relationship between discriminability and generalization: A re-evaluation. *Journal of Experimental Psychology*, 1958, **55**, 637–644.

Kanfer, F. H., & Phillips, J. S. *Learning foundations of behavior therapy*. New York: Wiley, 1970.

Keesey, R. Intracranial reward delay and the acquisition rate of a brightness discrimination. *Science*, 1964, **143**, 702.

Kerr, N., Myerson, L., & Michael, J. A procedure for shaping vocalizations in a mute child. In L. P. Ullman & L. Krasner (Eds.), *Case studies in behavior modification*. New York: Holt, 1965. Pp. 366–370.

Kimble, D. P. The effects of bilateral hippocampal lesions in rats. *Journal of Comparative and Physiological Psychology*, 1963, **56**, 273–283.

Kimble, G. A. *Hilgard and Marquis' conditioning and learning*. (2nd ed.) New York: Appleton-Century-Crofts, 1961.

Kimmel, E., & Kimmel, H. D. A replication of operant conditioning of the GSR. *Journal of Experimental Psychology*, 1963, **65**, 212–213.

Krechevsky, I. A study of the continuity of the problem-solving process. *Psychological Review*, 1938, **45**, 107–133.

Lane, H. L. Control of vocal responding in chickens. *Science*, 1960, **132**, 37–38.

Lashley, K. S. An examination of the continuity theory as applied to discriminative learning. *Journal of General Psychology*, 1942, **26**, 241–265.

Lashley, K. S., & Wade, M. The Pavlovian theory of generalization. *Psychological Review*, 1946, **53**, 72–87.

Laties, V. G., & Weiss, B. Effects of alcohol on timing behavior. *Journal of Comparative and Physiological Psychology*, 1962, **55**, 85–91.

Laties, V. G., Weiss, B., Clark, R. L., & Reynolds, M. Overt "mediating" behavior during temporally spaced responding. *Journal of the Experimental Analysis of Behavior*, 1965, **8**, 107–116.

Lawrence, D. H. Acquired distinctiveness of cues: I. Transfer between discriminations on the basis of familiarity with the stimulus. *Journal of Experimental Psychology*, 1949, **39**, 770–784.

Lawrence, D. H. The nature of a stimulus: Some relationships between learning and perception. In S. Koch (Ed.), *Psychology: A study of a science*. Vol. 5. New York: McGraw-Hill, 1963. Pp. 179–212.

Leitenberg, H. Is time-out from positive reinforcement an aversive event? A review of experimental evidence. *Psychological Bulletin*, 1965, **64**, 428–441.

Liversedge, L. A., & Sylvester, J. D. Conditioning techniques in the treatment of writer's cramp. *Lancet*, June 1955, 1147–1149.

Logan, F. A. *Incentive*. New Haven: Yale University Press, 1960.

Lovaas, O. I. A behavior therapy approach to the treatment of childhood schizophrenia. In J. P. Hill (Ed.), *Minnesota symposia on child psychology*. Vol. 1. Minneapolis: University of Minnesota Press, 1967. Pp. 108–159.

Lovaas, O. I., Berberich, J. P., Perdoff, B. F., & Schaeffer, B. Acquisition of imitative speech by schizophrenic children. *Science*, 1966, **151**, 705–706.

Lovaas, O. I., Freitas, L., Nelson, K., & Whalen, C. The establishment of imitation and its use for the development of complex behavior in schizophrenic children. *Behavior Research and Therapy*, 1967, **5**, 171–181.

Lovaas, O. I., Schaeffer, B., & Simmons, J. Experimental studies in childhood schizophrenias: Building social behaviors using electric shock. *Journal of Experimental Studies in Personality*, 1965, **1**, 99–109.

Lovejoy, E. P. An analysis of the over-learning reversal effect. *Psychological Review*, 1965, **73**, 87–103.

Maccoby, N., & Sheffield, F. D. Combining practice with demonstration in teaching complex sequences: Summary and interpretations. In A. A. Lumsdaine (Ed.), *Student response in programmed learning: A symposium.* Washington, D.C.: National Academy of Science, 1961. Pp. 77–85.

Mackintosh, N. J. The effects of overtraining on a reversal and nonreversal shift. *Journal of Comparative and Physiological Psychology*, 1962, **55**, 555–559.

Mackintosh, N. J. Selective attention in animal discrimination learning. *Psychological Bulletin*, 1965, **64**, 124–150.

Mackintosh, N. J. Further analysis of the overlearning reversal effect. *Journal of Comparative and Physiological Psychology*, 1969, **67**, No. 2.

Mager, R. F. On the sequencing of instructional content. *Psychological Reports*, 1961, **4**, 277–305.

Malott, M. K. Stimulus control in stimulus-deprived chickens. *Journal of Comparative and Physiological Psychology*, 1968, **66**, 276–282.

Marx, M. H., & Knarr, F. A. Long-term development of reinforcing properties of a stimulus as a function of temporal relationship to food reinforcement. *Journal of Comparative and Physiological Psychology*, 1963, **56**, 546–550.

Masserman, J. H. *Principles of dynamic psychiatry.* Philadelphia: Saunders, 1946.

McGuigan, F. J., & Crockett, F. Evidence that the secondary reinforcing stimulus must be discriminated. *Journal of Experimental Psychology*, 1958, **55**, 184–187.

Mechner, F. Probability relations within response sequences under ratio reinforcement. *Journal of the Experimental Analysis of Behavior*, 1958, **1**, 109–121.

Mechner, F. A notational system for the description of behavioral procedures. *Journal of the Experimental Analysis of Behavior*, 1959, **2**, 133–150.

Miles, R. C. The relative effectiveness of secondary reinforcers throughout deprivation and habit-strength parameters. *Journal of Comparative and Physiological Psychology*, 1956, **49**, 126–130.

Miller, N. E. Liberalization of basic S-R concepts: Extensions to conflict behavior, motivation, and social learning. In S. Koch (Ed.), *Psychology: A study of a science.* Vol. II. New York: McGraw-Hill, 1959. Pp. 196–292.

Miller, N. E., & Banuazizi, A. Instrumental learning by curarized rats of a specific visceral response, intestinal or cardiac. *Journal of Comparative and Physiological Psychology*, 1968, **65**, 1–7.

Miller, N. E., & Carmona, A. Modification of a visceral response: Salivation in thirsty dogs by instrumental training with water reward. *Journal of Comparative and Physiological Psychology*, 1967, 63, 1–6.

Miller, N. E., & DiCara, L. Instrumental learning of heart rate changes in curarized rats: Shaping, and specificity to discriminative stimulus. *Journal of Comparative and Physiological Psychology*, 1967, 63, 12–19.

Mowrer, O. H. On the dual nature of learning—A reinterpretation of conditioning and problem solving. *Harvard Education Review*, 1947, 17, 102–148.

Mowrer, O. H. *Learning theory and behavior.* New York: Wiley, 1960.

Mowrer, O. H., & Jones, H. M. Habit strength as a function of the pattern of reinforcement. *Journal of Experimental Psychology*, 1945, 35, 293–311.

Muenzinger, K. F. Motivation in learning: I. Electric shock for correct responses in the visual discrimination habit. *Journal of Comparative and Physiological Psychology*, 1934, 17, 437–448.

Myers, N. A., & Myers, J. L. Effects of secondary reinforcement schedules in extinction on children's responding. *Journal of Experimental Psychology*, 1962, 64, 586–588.

Newman, F. L., & Baron, M. R. Stimulus generalization along the dimension of angularity: A comparison of training procedures. *Journal of Comparative and Physiological Psychology*, 1965, 60, 59–63.

Newman, F. L., & Benefield, R. L. Stimulus control, cue utilization and attention: Effects of discrimination training. *Journal of Comparative and Physiological Psychology*, 1968, 66, 101–104.

North, A. J., & Stimmel, D. T. Extinction of an instrumental response following a large number of reinforcements. *Psychological Reports*, 1960, 6, 227–234.

Olds, J., & Milner, P. Positive reinforcement produced by electrical stimulation of septal area and other regions of rat brain. *Journal of Comparative and Physiological Psychology*, 1954, 47, 419–427.

Pavlov, I. P. *The work of the digestive glands.* Translated by W. H. Thompson. London: Charles Griffin, 1902.

Pavlov, I. P. *Conditioned reflexes.* Translated by G. V. Anrep. London: Oxford University Press, 1927.

Perin, C. T. Behavior potentiality as a joint function of the amount of training and degree of hunger in the time of extinction. *Journal of Experimental Psychology*, 1942, 30, 93–113.

Perin, C. T. A quantitative investigation of the delay-of-reinforcement gradient. *Journal of Experimental Psychology*, 1943, 32, 37–51.

Peterson, N. Effect of monochromatic rearing on the control of responding by wavelength. *Science*, 1962, 136, 774–775.

Pierrel, R., & Sherman, J. G. Train your pet the Barnabus way. *Brown Alumni Monthly*, Feb. 1963, Pp. 8-14.

Pressey, S. L. A simple apparatus which gives tests and scores and teaches. *School and Society*, 1926, 23, 373–376.

Pressey, S. L. A machine for automatic teaching of drill material. *School and Society*, 1927, **25**, 549–552.

Ratner, S. C. Reinforcing and discriminative properties of the click in a Skinner box. *Psychological Reports*, 1956, **2**, 332.

Reid, L. S., & Slivinski, A. J. A test for generalized secondary reinforcement during extinction under a different drive. *Journal of Comparative and Physiological Psychology*, 1954, **47**, 491–494.

Reynolds, G. S. Behavioral contrast. *Journal of the Experimental Analysis of Behavior*, 1961, **4**, 57–51. (a)

Reynolds, G. S. Relativity of response rate and reinforcement in a multiple schedule. *Journal of the Experimental Analysis of Behavior*, 1961, **4**, 179–184. (b)

Reynolds, G. S. Attention in the pigeon. *Journal of the Experimental Analysis of Behavior*, 1961, **4**, 203–208. (c)

Reynolds, G. S. *A primer of operant conditioning*. Glenview, Ill.: Scott, Foresman, 1968.

Rickard, H. C., Dignam, P. J., & Horner, R. F. Verbal manipulation in a psychotherapeutic relationship. *Journal of Clinical Psychology*, 1960, **16**, 364–367.

Rilling, M. Number of responses as a stimulus in fixed-interval and fixed-ratio schedules. *Journal of Comparative and Physiological Psychology*, 1967, **63**, 60–65.

Risley, T. R., & Wolf, M. Establishing functional speech in echolalic children. *Behavior Research and Therapy*, 1967, **5**, 73–88.

Rudolph, R. L., Honig, W. K., & Gerry, J. E. Effect of monochromatic rearing on the acquisition of stimulus control. *Journal of Comparative and Physiological Psychology*, 1969, **67**, 50-57.

Saltzman, I. J. Maze learning in the absence of primary reinforcement. *Journal of Comparative and Physiological Psychology*, 1949, **42**, 161–173.

Saltzman, I. J. Generalization of secondary reinforcement. *Journal of Experimental Psychology*, 1950, **40**, 189–193.

Schiller, H. I. Social control and individual freedom. *Bulletin of Atomic Scientists*, May 1968, 16–21.

Schmaltz, L. W., & Isaacson, R. L. The effects of blindness on DRL-20 performances exhibited by animals with hippocampal destruction. *Psychonomic Science*, 1968, **11**, 241–242.

Schoenfeld, W. N., Antonitis, J. J., & Bersh, P. J. A preliminary study of training conditions necessary for secondary reinforcement. *Journal of Experimental Psychology*, 1950, **40**, 40–45.

Schramm, W. *The research on programmed instruction: An annotated bibliography*. Washington, D.C.:U.S. Office of Education, 1964. (OE-34034)

Segal, E. F. Effects of di-amphetamine under concurrent VI DRL reinforcement. *Journal of the Experimental Analysis of Behavior*, 1962, 5, 105–112.

Seligman, M. E., & Maier, S. F. Failure to escape traumatic shock. *Journal of Experimental Psychology*, 1967, **74**, 1–9.

Shearn, D. Operant conditioning of the heart rate response. *Science*, 1962, **137**, 530–531.

Shepard, R. N. Approximation to uniform gradients of generalization by monotone transformations of scale. In D. Mostofsky (Ed.), *Stimulus generalization*. Stanford, Calif: Stanford University Press, 1965. Pp. 94–110.

Sherman, J. A., & Baer, D. M. Appraisal of operant therapy techniques with children and adults. In C. M. Franks (Ed.), *Behavior therapy: Appraisal and status*. New York: McGraw-Hill, 1969. Pp. 192–219.

Sidman, M. Two temporal parameters of the maintenance of avoidance behavior by the white rat. *Journal of Comparative and Physiological Psychology*, 1953, **46**, 253–261.

Sidman, M. *Tactics of scientific research*. New York: Basic Books, 1960.

Sidman, M. Avoidance behavior. In W. K. Honig (Ed.), *Operant behavior: Areas of research and applications*. New York: Appleton-Century-Crofts, 1966. Pp. 448–498.

Sidman, M., Herrnstein, R. J., & Conrad, D. G. Maintenance of avoidance behavior by unavoidable shocks. *Journal of Comparative and Physiological Psychology*, 1957, **50**, 553–557.

Sidman, M., & Stebbins, W. C. Satiation effects under fixed-ratio schedules of reinforcement. *Journal of Comparative and Physiological Psychology*, 1954, **47**, 114–116.

Sidman, M., & Stoddard, L. T. The effectiveness of fading in programming a simultaneous form discrimination for retarded children. *Journal of the Experimental Analysis of Behavior*, 1967, **10**, 3–15.

Simon, C. W., Wickens, D. D., Brown, U., & Pennock, L. Effects of secondary reinforcing agents on the primary thirst drive. *Journal of Comparative and Physiological Psychology*, 1951, **44**, 67–70.

Skinner, B. F. *The behavior of organisms: An experimental analysis*. New York: Appleton-Century-Crofts, 1938.

Skinner, B. F. *Walden two*. New York: Macmillan, 1948. Paperback edition in 1962.

Skinner, B. F. Are theories of learning necessary? *Psychological Review*, 1950, **57**, 193–216.

Skinner, B. F. *Science and human behavior*. New York: Macmillan, 1953.

Skinner, B. F. The science of learning and the art of teaching. *Harvard Education Review*, 1954, **24**, 86–97.

Skinner, B. F. A case history in scientific method. *American Psychologist*, 1956, **11**, 221–233.

Skinner, B. F. The experimental analysis of behavior. *American Scientist*, 1957, **45**, 343–371.

Skinner, B. F. Teaching machines. *Science*, 1958, **128**, 967–977.

Skinner, B. F. *Cumulative record*. (Rev. ed.) New York: Appleton-Century-Crofts, 1961. (a)

Skinner, B. F. Teaching machines. *Scientific American*, 1961, **205**, 90–106. (b)

Skinner, B. F. The technology of teaching. *Proceedings of the Royal Society*, 1965, **62**, 427–443.

Skinner, B. F. *Beyond freedom and dignity.* New York: Knopf, 1971.

Smith, M. P., & Capretta, P. J. Effects of drive level and experience on the reward value of saccharine solutions. *Journal of Comparative and Physiological Psychology*, 1956, **49**, 553–557.

Solomon, R. L., & Wynne, L. C. Traumatic avoidance learning: Acquisition in normal dogs. *Psychological Monographs*, 1953, **67**, (No. 354).

Spence, K. W. The nature of discrimination learning in animals. *Psychological Review*, 1936, **43**, 427–449.

Spence, K. W. The differential response in animals to stimuli varying within a single dimension. *Psychological Review*, 1937, **44**, 430–444.

Spence, K. W. The role of secondary reinforcement in delayed reward learning. *Psychological Review*, 1947, **54**, 1–8.

Spence, K. W. *Behavior theory and conditioning.* New Haven, Conn.: Yale University Press, 1956.

Spielberger, C. D., Levin, S. M., & Shepard, M. C. The effects of awareness and attitude toward reinforcement on the operant conditioning of verbal behavior. *Journal of Personality*, 1962, **30**, 106–121.

Stein, L. Secondary reinforcement established with subcortical stimulation. *Science*, 1958, **127**, 466–467.

Sutherland, N. S. Visual discrimination of orientation by *Octopus*. *British Journal of Psychology*, 1957, **48**, 55–71.

Sutherland, N. S. Stimulus analysing mechanisms. In *Proceedings of a symposium on the mechanization of thought processes.* Vol. 2. London: Her Majesty's Stationery Office, 1959. Pp. 575–609.

Sutherland, N. S. The learning of discriminations by animals. *Endeavour*, 1964, **23**, 148–152.

Sutherland, N. S., Mackintosh, N. J., & Mackintosh, J. Simultaneous discrimination training of *Octopus* and transfer of discrimination along a continuum. *Journal of Comparative and Physiological Psychology*, 1963, **56**, 150–156.

Sutherland, N. S., & Mackintosh, J. Discrimination learning: Nonadditivity of cues. *Nature*, 1964, **201**, 528–530.

Switalski, R. W., Lyons, J., & Thomas, D. R. Effects of interdimensional training on stimulus generalization. *Journal of Experimental Psychology*, 1966, **72**, 661–666.

Terrace, H. S. Discrimination learning with and without "errors." Unpublished doctoral dissertation, Harvard University, 1961.

Terrace, H. S. Discrimination learning with and without "errors." *Journal of the Experimental Analysis of Behavior*, 1963, **6**, 1–27. (a)

Terrace, H. S. Errorless transfer of a discrimination across two continua. *Journal of the Experimental Analysis of Behavior*, 1963, **6**, 223–232. (b)

Terrace, H. S. Errorless discrimination learning in the pigeon: Effects of chlorpromazine and imipramine. *Science,* 1963, **140,** 318–319. (c)

Terrace, H. S. Wavelength generalization after discrimination learning with and without errors. *Science,* 1964, **144,** 78–80.

Terrace, H. S. Stimulus control. In W. K. Honig (Ed.), *Operant behavior: Areas of Research and application.* New York: Appleton-Century-Crofts, 1966. Pp. 271–344.

Thomas, D. R., Freeman, F., Svinicki, J. G., Burr, D. E. S., & Lyons, J. Effects of extradimensional training on stimulus generalization. *Journal of Experimental Psychology,* 1970, **83,** 1–21. (Monograph)

Thomas, D. R., Mariner, R. W., & Sherry, G. Role of pre-experimental experience in the development of stimulus control. *Journal of Experimental Psychology,* 1969, **79,** 375–376.

Thomas, D. R., & Mitchell, K. Instructions and stimulus categorizing in a measure of stimulus generalization. *Journal of the Experimental Analysis of Behavior,* 1962, **5,** 375–381.

Thomas, D. R., Ost, J., & Thomas, D. H. Stimulus generalization as a function of the time between training and testing procedures. *Journal of the Experimental Analysis of Behavior,* 1960, **3,** 9–14.

Thomas, D. R., & Williams, J. L. Stimulus generalization of a positive conditioned reinforcer. *Science,* 1963, **142,** 172–173. (a)

Thomas, D. R., & Williams, J. L. A further study of stimulus generalization following three-stimulus discrimination training. *Journal of the Experimental Analysis of Behavior,* 1963, **6,** 171–176. (b)

Thorndike, E. L. Animal intelligence. An experimental study of associative processes in animals. *Psychological Monographs,* 1898, **2,** (No. 2).

Thorndike, E. L. *Animal intelligence.* New York: Macmillan, 1911.

Thorndike, E. L. *Educational psychology.* Vol. II. *The psychology of learning.* New York: Teachers College, Columbia University, 1913.

Thorndike, E. L. *Fundamentals of learning.* New York: Teachers College, Columbia University, 1932.

Tolman, E. C. *Purposive behavior in animals and men.* New York: Appleton-Century-Crofts, 1932.

Tombaugh, T. N., & Marx, M. H. Effects of ordered and constant sucrose concentrations on nonreinforced performance. *Journal of Experimental Psychology,* 1965, **69,** 630–636.

Trowill, J. A. Instrumental conditioning of the heart rate in the curarized rat. *Journal of Comparative and Physiological Psychology,* 1967, **63,** 7–11.

Ullman, L. P., & Krasner, L. *A psychological approach to abnormal behavior.* Englewood Cliffs, N. J.: Prentice-Hall, 1969.

Walker, E. L. Psychological complexity as the basis for a theory of motivation and choice. In D. Levine (Ed.), *Nebraska symposium of motivation.* Lincoln: University of Nebraska Press, 1964. Pp. 47–98.

Walker, E. L. *Conditioning and instrumental learning.* Monterey, Calif.: Brooks/Cole, 1967.

Walton, D. The relevance of learning theory to the treatment of an obsessive-compulsive state. In H. J. Eysenck (Ed.), *Behaviour therapy and the neuroses.* London: Pergamon Press, 1960. Pp. 153–166.

Walton, D., & Black, D. A. The application of learning theory to the treatment of stammering. *Journal of Psychosomatic Research,* 1958, **3**, 170–179.

Watson, J. B. The effect of delayed feeding upon learning. *Psychobiology,* 1917, **1**, 51–60.

Webb, W. B., & Nolan, C. Y. Cues for discrimination as secondary reinforcing agents: A confirmation. *Journal of Comparative and Physiological Psychology,* 1953, **46**, 180–181.

Weise, P., & Bitterman, M. E. Response selection in discriminative learning. *Psychological Review,* 1951, **58**, 185–195.

Wike, E. L., & Barrientos, G. Secondary reinforcement and multiple drive reduction. *Journal of Comparative and Physiological Psychology,* 1958, **51**, 640–643.

Wike, E. L., & Casey, A. The reward value of food for satiated animals. *Journal of Comparative and Physiological Psychology,* 1954, **47**, 240–243.

Wike, E. L., & McNamara, H. J. A quest for the generalized conditioned reinforcer. *Psychological Reports,* 1955, **1**, 83–91.

Williams, J. L. Stimulus generalization of a positive conditioned reinforcer. M.A. thesis, Kent State University, 1963.

Williams, J. L. Response contingency and effects of punishment: Changes in autonomic and skeletal responses. *Journal of Comparative and Physiological Psychology,* 1969, **68**, 118–125.

Williams, J. L. Effects of the duration of a secondary reinforcer on subsequent instrumental responses. *Journal of Experimental Psychology,* 1970, **83**, 348–351.

Williams, J. L., & Adkins, J. R. Operant control of human heart rate under conditions of anxiety. Paper given at the Kenyon College Lecture Series and currently in preparation for publication, 1972.

Williams, S. B. Resistance to extinction as a function of the number of reinforcements. *Journal of Experimental Psychology,* 1938, **23**, 506–522.

Wolf, M. M., Risley, T., Johnston, M., Harris, F., & Allen, E. Application of operant conditioning procedures to the behavior problems of an autistic child: A follow-up and extension. *Behavior Research and Therapy,* 1967, **5**, 103–111.

Wolf, M. M., Risley, T., & Mees, H. L. Application of operant conditioning procedures to the behavior problems of an autistic child. *Behavior Research and Therapy,* 1964, **1**, 305–312.

Wolfe, J. B. Effects of delayed reward upon learning in the white rat. *Journal of Comparative Psychology,* 1934, **17**, 1–21.

Wolpe, J. *Psychotherapy by reciprocal inhibition.* Stanford: Stanford University Press, 1958.

Wolpe, J. The systematic desensitization treatment of neuroses. *Journal of Nervous and Mental Disease,* 1961, **132**, 189–203.

Wunderlich, R. A. Strength of a generalized conditioned reinforcer as a function of variability of reward. *Journal of Experimental Psychology,* 1961, **62,** 409–415.

Wycoff, L. B., Sidowski, J., & Chambliss, D. J. An experimental study of the relationship between secondary reinforcing and cue effects of a stimulus. *Journal of Comparative and Physiological Psychology,* 1958, **51,** 103–109.

Zeaman, D. Response latency as a function of the amount of reinforcement. *Journal of Experimental Psychology,* 1949, **39,** 466–483.

Zimmerman, D. W. Durable secondary reinforcement: Method and theory. *Psychological Review,* 1957, **64,** 373–383.

Zimmerman, D. W. Sustained performance in rats based on secondary reinforcement. *Journal of Comparative and Physiological Psychology,* 1959, **52,** 353–358.

NAME INDEX

SUBJECT INDEX